# Virtual Identities and Digital Culture

*Virtual Identities and Digital Culture* investigates how our online identities and cultures are embedded within the digital practices of our lives, exploring how we form community, how we play, and how we re-imagine traditional media in a digital world.

The collection explores a wide range of digital topics – from dating apps, microcelebrity, and hackers to auditory experiences, Netflix algorithms, and live theatre online – and builds on existing work in digital culture and identity by bringing new voices, contemporary examples, and highlighting platforms that are emerging in the field. The book speaks to the modern reality of how our digital lives have been forever altered by our transnational experiences – one of those key experiences is the pandemic, but so too is systemic inequality, questions of digital privacy, and the role of joy in our online lives.

A vital contribution at a time of significant social and cultural flux, this book will be highly relevant to those studying digital culture within media, communication, cultural studies, digital humanities, and sociology departments.

**Victoria Kannen** is a Professor in the Faculty of Arts and Equity, Diversity, and Inclusion Advisor of Research at Laurentian University in Sudbury, Ontario. She is the author of *Gendered Bodies and Public Scrutiny: Women's Stories of Staring, Strangers, and Fierce Resistance* (2021). She is also the co-editor of *The Spaces and Places of Canadian Popular Culture* (2019).

**Aaron Langille** is a Professor and Coordinator of the Game Design program at Cambrian College in Sudbury, Ontario. He is a regular columnist on CBC radio where he talks about games, technology, and the impact of our digital lives. He is currently writing two textbooks, one of which is on learning to program through analogies and, the other, is on learning to program through games.

# Virtual Identities and Digital Culture

Edited by
Victoria Kannen and
Aaron Langille

NEW YORK AND LONDON

Designed cover image: Efe Kurnaz/Unsplash

First published 2023
by Routledge
605 Third Avenue, New York, NY 10158

and by Routledge
4 Park Square, Milton Park, Abingdon, Oxon, OX14 4RN

*Routledge is an imprint of the Taylor & Francis Group, an informa business*

© 2023 selection and editorial matter, Victoria Kannen and Aaron Langille; individual chapters, the contributors

The right of Victoria Kannen and Aaron Langille to be identified as the authors of the editorial material, and of the authors for their individual chapters, has been asserted in accordance with sections 77 and 78 of the Copyright, Designs and Patents Act 1988.

All rights reserved. No part of this book may be reprinted or reproduced or utilised in any form or by any electronic, mechanical, or other means, now known or hereafter invented, including photocopying and recording, or in any information storage or retrieval system, without permission in writing from the publishers.

*Trademark notice*: Product or corporate names may be trademarks or registered trademarks, and are used only for identification and explanation without intent to infringe.

ISBN: 978-1-032-31655-0 (hbk)
ISBN: 978-1-032-31508-9 (pbk)
ISBN: 978-1-003-31073-0 (ebk)

DOI: 10.4324/9781003310730

Typeset in Times New Roman
by codeMantra

This book is dedicated to everyone who has pivoted each time technologies and the world have changed.

# Contents

*List of Contributors*   xi

Introduction: Exploring Digital Lives and Cultures   1

## SECTION I
## Online Identity and Connections   19

1. "Hey Handsome": Gay Dating Apps and a Critical Digital Pedagogy of Identity   21
   SEAN MICHAEL MORRIS

2. "We're Here for You During This Pandemic, Just Not Financially or Emotionally": What TikTok Reveals about Student Life during the COVID-19 Pandemic   29
   SHARON LAURICELLA AND EMILY SMALL

3. Mediated Identities: How Facebook Intervenes in the Virtual Manifestation of Our Identities   38
   LUIS A. GRANDE BRANGER

4. Reassessing Clicktivism: A Tool of the (Pandemic) Times   48
   ADIKI PUPLAMPU AND IAIN MACPHERSON

5. "Victims of the System": Anti-Government Discourse and Political Influencers Online   57
   MICHELLE STEWART, MAXIME BÉRUBÉ, SAMUEL LAPERLE, SKLAERENN LE GALLO AND STÉPHANIE PANNETON

6. From Networks to Assemblages: An Analysis of Feminist Activism against Digital Violence in Mexico   69
   MARCELA SUÁREZ

7 Navigating Nii'kinaaganaa (All My Relations) Online 79
JOEY-LYNN WABIE AND MICHELLE KENNEDY

8 Virtually Authentic? Digital Bodies, "Blank" Squares, and Staring Online 89
VICTORIA KANNEN

9 From a Group of Friends to a Mainstream Audience: *Critical Role* and New Media Publics 97
BETSY BREY AND ELISE VIST

SECTION II
**Games & Play** 105

10 Not All Fun and Games in #mypokehood: The Politics and Pitfalls of Universal Game Design in Pokémon GO! 107
KIERA OBBARD AND ABI LEMAK

11 Lip Dubbing for Fido: Listening to the Internet through Viral Pet Video Memes 117
KATE GALLOWAY

12 'Turn Off That Friggin' Radio!': The Canadian Soldier Figure and Identity Formation in Videogames 126
JASON HAWRELIAK AND VENUS TORABI

13 Inventing with Zoom: How Play and Games Uncover Affordances in Digital Environments 136
JACOB EUTENEUER

14 Interfaces and Their Affordances: Critical Game Design, Identity, and Community in MMORPGs 144
CHRIS HUGELMANN

15 Better than the Real You? VR, Identity, Privacy, and the Metaverse 152
IAIN MACPHERSON AND ADIKI PUPLAMPU

16 Our War Game: Hacker Games as Laborious Play 161
ALEX DEAN CYBULSKI

17 Listening to and Playing Along with the Soundscapes of Videogame Environments 169
KATE GALLOWAY

## SECTION III
## Reimagining Traditional Media      179

18  Netflix as the New Television Screen: A Queer Investigation
    into Streaming, Algorithms, and *Schitt$ Creek*      181
    LAUREN McLEAN

19  The Missing *Live* Ingredient: The Search for Ephemerality
    in the Screening and Streaming of Theatre      190
    AMANDA DI PONIO

20  From Videotape Exchange Networks to On-Demand
    Streaming Platforms: The Circulation of Independent
    Canadian Film and Video in the Digital Era      201
    MARIANE BOURCHEIX-LAPORTE

21  Platforms and Poetry as a Popular Form of Engagement      211
    TANJA GRUBNIC

22  Lil Nas X, TikTok, and the Evolution of Music Engagement
    on Social Networking Sites      221
    MELISSA AVDEEFF

23  "No Friends in the Industry": The Dominance of Tech
    Companies on Digital Music      231
    KRISTOPHER R. K. OHLENDORF

24  Say Their Name: How Online News Reports the Death of
    Transgender People and Its Intersection with Transnormativity      240
    RACHEL PATTERSON

25  The 'Affinityscapes' of Young Adult Dystopian Fiction: A
    Study of *The Hunger Games* Series' Participatory Culture      248
    ZAHRA RIZVI

26  Reboot and Rebirth: Artificial Intelligence and Spiritual
    Existence in *The Good Place*      256
    LIZ W. FABER

*Index*      263

# Contributors

**Melissa Avdeeff** is a Lecturer in Digital Media in the Division of Communication, Media and Culture at the University of Stirling. As a scholar of all things popular, her research is at the intersections of technology, posthumanism, sociability, and reception. She has published works on Beyoncé and celebrity self-representation Instagram; Justin Bieber and evolution of YouTube stars; iPod culture and sociability; Kim Kardashian and postfeminism; and AI popular music.

**Maxime Bérubé** is an Assistant Professor of Forensic Science at the Université du Québec à Trois-Rivières. His research interests focus on digital data identification, processing and interpretation, specifically in regard to issues related to terrorism, extremism, propaganda, and national security. In addition to improving our understanding of criminal/delinquent behavior through the study of digital traces, his research aims to improve the effectiveness and efficiency of investigative practices when massive amounts of data are involved, as well as the management of digital data in the context of legal proceedings. Maxime is also a lead member of the Open Source Analysis, Research and Development Group (GARDESO), and a regular researcher of the International Centre for Comparative Criminology.

**Mariane Bourcheix-Laporte** is a Bombardier Doctoral Scholar and PhD candidate at Simon Fraser University's School of Communication. Her research focuses on Canadian cultural policy and artist-run organizations. In 2019, she received the Canadian Communication Association's Doctoral CRTC Prize for Excellence in Policy Research for the paper "Creative Canada: A Critical Look at a 'New' Cultural Policy Framework." She is a member of the Cultural Policy, IP and Rights Ecosystems Working Group for Archive/Counter Archive, a multi-year research project based out of York University. Mariane obtained an MFA in Interdisciplinary Arts from SFU's School for the Contemporary Arts in 2012 and has exhibited artistic and curatorial projects across Canada. She has worked as lead consultant on various sectoral research and community consultation projects commissioned by national and provincial arts service organizations.

xii  *Contributors*

**Betsy Brey** is a PhD candidate in the Department of English Language and Literature at the University of Waterloo. Her research focuses on narrative in video games. She is particularly interested in the intersections of game play and narrative structure and how game stories are perceived and constructed by communities of fans. Additionally, her work examines the social and cultural practices of the communities that play or enjoy games, including questions of collaboration, digital labor, canonicity, and the cultural economies of fans and fandoms. Her work has been published in a number of books, including *Indie Games in the Digital Age* (2020), *Narrative Tactics for Mobile and Social Games: Pocket-Sized Storytelling* (2018), *Beyond the Sea: Navigating BioShock* (2018), and *The Play Versus Story Divide in Game Studies: Critical Essays* (2015), as well as journals such as *Rhetor* and *The Journal of Contemporary Rhetoric*.

**Alex Dean Cybulski** is a PhD candidate at the University of Toronto's Faculty of Information, from Brampton, Ontario. His studies include digital games, information security, hackers, and surveillance. In the past, Alex has worked as an information security consultant and a journalist.

**Amanda Di Ponio** completed her doctoral studies at the University of St Andrews and currently holds the rank of Assistant Professor of English and Cultural Studies at Huron University College in London, Ontario, Canada. She is the author of *The Early Modern Theatre of Cruelty and Its Doubles: Artaud and Influence* (2018). Her areas of interest include drama and performance, early modern social history, and twentieth-century theory.

**Jacob Euteneuer** is an Assistant Professor of Digital Rhetoric at Hampden-Sydney College where he helps direct The Rhetoric Studio, a multimodal makerspace. He writes about how play and games can help us better understand the world around us. His work has appeared in a number of journals and publications including *Computers and Composition* and *The Journal of Virtual Worlds Research*. He can be reached at jeuteneuer@hsc.edu.

**Liz W. Faber** (PhD) is the Chair of the Arts & Sciences Division at Labouré College of Healthcare and the author of *The Computer's Voice: From Star Trek to Siri* (U Minnesota Press, 2020). Her research areas include science fiction, science communication, computer history, feminist and queer media studies, and American studies.

**Kate Galloway** is on faculty at Rensselaer Polytechnic Institute where she teaches in the Electronic Arts, Music, and Games and Simulation Arts and Sciences/Critical Game Design programs. Her research and teaching address sonic responses to environmentalism, sound studies, digital culture, sound art, and interactive media.

Contributors xiii

**Luis A. Grande Branger** was born and raised in Venezuela. He grew up in a turbulent political climate that included coups d'etat, civil unrest, the rise of socialism, and a transition from corporate-owned to state-controlled media. These experiences led Luis to dedicate himself to the study and praxis of media and communication. He has worked in this field for more than a decade as a TV producer, radio producer, journalist, videographer, film editor, film critic, instructor, and activist. In 2012, Luis obtained a BA in Media Production from the University of Puerto Rico. He later moved to Miami where he obtained a MA in Liberal Studies (2017). He then returned to Puerto Rico to complete a MA in Communication with a focus on theory and research (2020). For his Master's in Communication, Luis wrote a paper on the manifestations of identity within communication processes mediated by Facebook. Luis is currently a PhD student in Communication, Culture and Media, and a Blue Fellow at Drexel University in Philadelphia.

**Tanja Grubnic** is a PhD candidate in English at the University of Western Ontario. Her dissertation considers the transnational circulation of Canadian-based Instagram poets on social media. She is a co-founder of Instasociety.org, an open-access resource exploring social media and popular culture. Her research, supported by two Ontario Graduate Scholarships, has also appeared in *The Australasian Journal of Popular Culture*.

**Jason Hawreliak** is an Associate Professor of Game Studies and Director of the Centre for Digital Humanities at Brock University in Ontario, Canada. His research examines meaning in videogames with a focus on multimodality and persuasion. He is the author of the monograph *Multimodal Semiotics and Rhetoric in Videogames* (Routledge 2018) and a co-founder of the game studies periodical, *First Person Scholar*.

**Chris Hugelmann** (he/him) is a PhD candidate at Toronto Metropolitan University. His educational background is in cognitive and social psychology, communication theory, and user experience design. His dissertation uses a research-creation and self-microethnographic methods to discover the design of interfaces in MMORPGs for identity creation and community formation, and create best practices and improved interfaces based on academic literature. He can be contacted at https://chugelmann.com.

**Victoria Kannen** (PhD) is the author of *Gendered Bodies and Public Scrutiny: Women's Stories of Staring, Strangers, and Fierce Resistance* (Women's Press 2021). She is also the co-editor of *The Spaces and Places of Canadian Popular Culture* (Canadian Scholars 2019). Victoria is an interdisciplinary educator who teaches Sociology, Communication and Media Studies, and Gender Studies. She is also an Equity, Diversity, and Inclusion Advisor of Research at Laurentian University.

**Michelle Kennedy** (she/her) is Onyota'a:ka from Oneida of the Thames First Nation in Ontario. Currently she lives in N'Swakamok where she is a guest on Atikameksheng Anishnawbek territory (Sudbury, Ontario, Canada). Michelle is a PhD candidate in the Cultural Studies program at Queen's University. Her passion is teaching and working in community, whether it is through formal education, research, or community activism. She is a sessional instructor in the Schools of Education and Indigenous Relations at Laurentian University. Michelle is an Auntie, sister, and partner.

**Aaron Langille** (PhD) is a Professor in and the coordinator of the video game design program at Cambrian College. He is an OCUFA teaching award winner, a contributor to The Conversation Canada, and a regular columnist on CBC Morning North. He has previously been the Scientist in Residence at Science North and a former open education fellow with eCampus Ontario.

**Samuel Laperle** is currently finishing his Master's degree in Linguistics at the Université du Québec à Montréal. His Master's project examines the computational challenges of automatic irony detection. His other research projects explore discourse analysis, experimental semantics and pragmatics.

**Sharon Lauricella** is full Professor in the Communication and Digital Media Studies program at Ontario Tech University (Canada). She holds a PhD from the University of Cambridge (UK), a BA from Wheaton College (MA), and a certificate in Higher Education Teaching from Harvard University (MA).

**Sklaerenn Le Gallo** is a Postdoctoral Fellow and Lecturer at the Université du Québec à Montréal. Her research interests focus on critical epistemologies in intercultural communication and on how specific political identities are constructed, maintained, and confronted in Quebec's "conspiverse." Her focus on far right and populist discourses in France and Quebec sheds light on the complex phenomenon of the normalization and acceptance of discourse that used to be left on the fringe of the public sphere.

**Abi Lemak** is a PhD candidate in Literary Studies, having returned to the University of Guelph after completing her MA in Book History and Print Culture at the University of Toronto. She's an unabashed tech-nerd working across the cultural-digital divide, deeply interested in how humans communicate and connect with one another both on and offline. Her SSHRC-funded project, "Recasting (e)Bibliographies," examines how humans are shaped by communication technologies, from social media to books, and looks at how politics and aesthetics come together in print culture. At the core of her study lies the argument that book design shapes the socio-political world of both printers ("you are what you make") and imagined readers ("you are what you read") alike. Abi is a member of The Orlando Project, Canadian Writing and Research Collaboratory (CWRC), and The Humanities Interdisciplinary Collaboration (THINC) Lab at the University of Guelph.

**Iain Macpherson** (PhD) is an Associate Professor in the Department of Communication Studies, Faculty of Fine Arts and Communications at MacEwan University in Edmonton, Alberta, Canada. His teaching and research interests are eclectic, but they mostly center in the fields and overlaps of Organizational Communication, Intercultural Communication, and Japan Studies. He welcomes emails at macphersoni3@macewan.ca.

**Lauren McLean** (she/her/hers) is a PhD student in Literary Studies and Theatre Studies at the University of Guelph. She completed her MA at McMaster University in Gender Studies and Feminist Research. Her current research interests include gender, sexuality, homonormativity, algorithmic culture, and trauma. Lauren is a self-declared feminist killjoy hoping for change.

**Sean Michael Morris** is currently a Senior Instructor of Learning Design and Technology in the School of Education and Human Development at the University of Colorado Denver. He is also the Director of Digital Pedagogy Lab, an international professional development gathering for educators committed to issues of diversity, equity, inclusion, critical digital pedagogy, and imagining a new future for education. His work has been featured on National Public Radio, in *The Guardian*, *Times Higher Ed*, Inside Higher Ed, *The Chronicle of Higher Education*, *Izvestia*, and numerous other publications and podcasts.

**Kiera Obbard** is a PhD student in Literary Studies in the School of English and Theatre Studies at the University of Guelph in Ontario, Canada. Her current project, The Instagram Effect: Contemporary Canadian Poetry Online examines the complex social, cultural, technological, and economic conditions that have enabled the success of social media poetry in Canadian publishing, how the technological affordances of social media platforms mediate reading and writing, and the relationship between social media poetry and data mining practices. She completed her MA in Cultural Studies and Critical Theory at McMaster University and her Honors B.A. with a joint major in English and Communication at the University of Ottawa. She is currently a fellow at The Humanities Interdisciplinary Collaboration (THINC) Lab, an editorial board member of the Centre for Media and Celebrity Studies and WaterHill Publishing.

**Kristopher R. K. Ohlendorf** is an emerging scholar and professor of Interactive Media at Humber College in Toronto, Ontario. His research on the relationship between popular music and the Internet has been presented across Canada and cited internationally.

**Stéphanie Panneton** is a PhD student at the Université du Québec à Montréal (UQAM). Her research interests focus on the impact of the textile and clothing industry in the context of the environmental crisis. More specifically, Stéphanie is interested in the authentic experience of coproducing sustainable fashion, through emotional capitalism ("emodity") reflected in consumption practices.

**Rachel Patterson** got her MA in Media Research in 2021 from The University of Memphis. She will continue her education this fall at Pennsylvania State University with plans to get a PhD in Mass Communications. Throughout her time as a researcher, she has studied social media, crisis, eating disorders, message effectiveness, and LGBTQ+ studies. Her research interests also include health communication and online activism.

**Adiki Puplampu** is a Master's student in the Department of Communication Media and Film at the University of Calgary. Her research interests are centered around race-related media effects, organizational culture, and political communication. Email: puplampua@mymacewan.ca.

**Zahra Rizvi** is a PhD scholar and Senior Research Fellow in the Department of English, Jamia Millia Islamia, India, and founder member of Game Studies India. She was recently MHRD-SPARC Fellow (2020) in the Department of Linguistics and Germanic, Slavic, African and Asian Language Studies, Michigan State University, and works in the fields of cultural studies, utopia/dystopia studies, and video game studies. She has delivered lectures at Michigan State University, Jamia Millia Islamia, and Zakir Husain Delhi College, University of Delhi. She also writes creative fiction and poetry in English and Urdu.

**Emily Small** holds a BA in Communication and Digital Media Studies from Ontario Tech University, Canada.

**Michelle Stewart** is a Professor in the Department of Social and Public Communication at the University of Quebec at Montreal and Adjunct Director of the Cultural Action major. She is the co-editor of *Global Indigenous Media* (with Pam Wilson, Duke UP, 2008). Her latest research addresses digital heritage and digital cinema, in particular the ways in which Internet art and culture complicate our expectations and standards for self and cultural representation. She is the principal investigator of "Viral Populism: The Amplification of Right-Wing Extremism Online," recipient of Social Science and Humanities Research Council and Digital Citizen Research Initiative of Heritage Canada funding (2021–2024). Her publications have appeared in various film and media journals, including Jump Cut, TOPIA, and *Film Quarterly*. She has been a Fulbright Scholar,

Kempner Distinguished Professor at Purchase College (SUNY), and a fellow at the Institute for Advanced Studies in Marseille.

**Marcela Suárez** is a Professor of Political Science at the Lateinamerika-Institut, Freie Universität Berlin. She also holds a PhD in Political Science from the Freie Universität. Marcela Suárez is specialized in the interdisciplinary field of Science and Technology Studies and Political Science on topics of digital culture, feminist politics, asymmetries of knowledge and digital methods, and qualitative research. Her current research project is entitled "Feminist Politics and the fight against violence in the era of digitalization."

**Venus Torabi** is a PhD candidate in the Interdisciplinary Humanities program at Brock University, Ontario, Canada. Her research examines how the extremist group, ISIS, uses videogames for recruitment and propaganda dissemination. She is the author of the novella, *P.S. OperaTor*, which is set against the back drop of the downing of Ukraine Airlines Flight 752 in 2020.

**Elise Vist** is a PhD candidate in the Department of English Language and Literature at the University of Waterloo. There, they study queer fans and our relationships to each other in our intimate fandoms. Their research is grounded in contemporary feminisms, queer theory, and queer phenomenology, as well as fan studies and literary theory. Their dissertation titled "Longing for Queerness in the NHL: Intimate Fandoms and Real Hockey Person Fanfiction" argues that some fandoms operate like intimate publics online, especially when their needs and desires are unwelcome in public fandom spaces. They have also written about queer games, queerbaiting, and immersion while also supporting graduate student writers in the University of Waterloo's Writing and Communication Center.

**Joey-Lynn Wabie** is an Algonquin Anicinabe ikwe from Mahingan Sagahigan (Wolf Lake) First Nation in Quebec. She is an Assistant Professor in Indigenous Social Work and the Director of the School of Indigenous Relations at Laurentian University located on Atikameksheng Anishnawbek territory (Sudbury, Ontario). Joey-Lynn works in community at the grassroots level focusing on wellness, culture, and bringing people together. Her research interests are Indigenous youth's perspectives on Truth and Reconciliation, spiritual wellness/healing, and land-based teaching/learning. Joey-Lynn takes the role of sister, auntie, cousin seriously and is dedicated to ensuring her culture and traditions are passed on through storytelling, ceremony, and the occasional latte.

# Introduction
Exploring Digital Lives and Cultures

Living online is not a new concept – many of us feel like we have been living online for "decades" at this point. But, there is something new in the digital air. The COVID-19 pandemic impacted everyone and, for many of us, our relationship with technologies had no choice but to intensify and change. Those of us who are educators pivoted to unexpected synchronous, asynchronous, or hybrid online teaching modes. Our students made similar pivots with their learning. Outside of academia, relationships with many of our loved ones were relegated to the realm of social media, texts, and Facetime calls. We stopped going to the movies. Instead, we streamed everything that we could; sometimes out of interest, sometimes out of "stay-at-home" boredom. We played old games on old consoles, bought and played new games on new consoles, and immersed ourselves in different worlds than the one we were living in. All of these elements – online teaching and learning, virtual visits, and digital play – were certainly a part of our pre-pandemic lives, but they were not our primary and, in some cases, only sources of living and connecting. For us, there is no doubt that we could have created *Virtual Identities and Digital Culture* a few years ago, but perhaps it wouldn't have been as relevant as it is now. The intensification of our relationships with technology, both positive and negative have ebbed and flowed prior to 2020, but it feels like there are some new elements that will stay with us forever: Zoom meetings, remote learning, skipping the movie theatre to stream new releases, to name a few. As we said, there is something new in the digital air and this collection will explore it.

Before we dive into the significance and structure of the book, we want to define some basic terms and clarify how these concepts are functioning here. As this is primarily a book about online experience, it is important to understand what we mean by concepts such as "technology," "the Internet," "digital," "virtual," and what it might mean to "live online."

The first concept – **technology** – often seems synonymous with something electronic, digital, or mechanical, but the actual definition of technology is far broader. The word technology is from the Greek "techne," which means art, craft, or skill. Technology is complex; it is interwoven into the circumstances and rhythms of social life and it is fundamental to our understanding of what culture is and how it is transmitted (Kannen and Shyminsky, 2019). In his seminal text, *The Nature of Technology: What It Is and How It Evolves*, W. Brian Arthur explained three mainstays of technology:

1. The first and most basic one is a technology is a means to fulfill a human purpose. …As a means, a technology may be a method or process or device… Or it may be complicated… Or it may be material… Or it may be nonmaterial. Whichever it is, it is always a means to carry out a human purpose.
2. The second definition is a plural one: technology as an assemblage of practices and components.
3. I will also allow a third meaning. This is technology as the entire collection of devices and engineering practices available to a culture. (2011, 28)

When we begin to consider all of the materials, artefacts, skill sets, and media that can fall under the category of "technology," then the concept and our relationship to it are dynamic and ongoing.

The second – **the Internet** – in simplest terms, is a global system of computer networks that communicate with each other to transmit information. Perhaps more important for our purposes is considering the role that the Internet plays within the function of social existence. Think to yourself: How many times a day do you access the Internet? What would your day look like without it? What would learning, work, or entertainment be like without the Internet? The role of the Internet in our functioning as a modern society cannot be understated.

The third – **digital** – comes from Latin meaning digitus, or finger, and refers to one of the oldest tools for counting. When information is stored or transmitted in digital format, it is converted into numbers – at the most basic machine-level as "zeroes and ones." We will use the term digital to represent technology that relies on the use of microprocessors: this includes computers and any applications or devices that are dependent on the Internet and digitization such as smartphones, other mobile devices, and gaming systems. While digital media, as a concept, did not come into everyday usage until the late twentieth century, the conceptual understandings that we have of digital media can be credited to Vannevar Bush (1945) in his essay "As We May Think," published in *The Atlantic Monthly*. In it, he states, "[c]onsider a future device… in which an individual stores all [their] books, records, and communications, and which is mechanized so that it may be consulted with exceeding speed and flexibility. It is an enlarged intimate supplement to [their] memory" (Bush 1945, n.p.). In 1945, this likely seemed impossible, but to us, it is embedded within the rhythm of our daily lives.

The fourth concept – **virtual** – can seem a bit more abstract. For our purposes, in order for something to be virtual, it implies that it does not physically exist, but that it is created by technology, or software to be specific, and to appear as though it does physically exist. It is some*thing* carried out, accessed, or stored by means of technology, but it has no materiality to it. Here, we can think of YouTube Live graduation ceremonies as virtual convocations, chasing ghosts in the virtual world of Pac-Man, and swiping left or right in the virtual "speed-dating" of Tinder. Taking the concept of virtual to its logical extreme, virtual reality (VR) represents the state-of-the-art limitations of what current technology can render, but does not physically exist. Modern head-mounted VR displays have existed since 1965, though the term virtual reality wasn't coined until 1984 (Bown et al. 2017). It is only in the past decade that VR hardware has increased in power and decreased in cost, to make it accessible to mass markets. In that time, its uses in industry, medicine, education and training, and videogames have increased exponentially. The ability to create truly immersive spaces for exploration, education, and entertainment represents an important milestone in our digital culture.

This brings us to our final concept – to **live online**. Life (as we know it) is inherently biological, while the online realm is manufactured, artificial, and more or less virtual. When thinking about what it means to live online, the concept of liminality is useful. To refer to a space as **liminal**, is to claim that it is an in-between space. Victor Turner defines liminal spaces and identities as "neither here nor there; they are betwixt and between the positions assigned and arrayed by law, custom, convention, and ceremony" (1969, 95). The online world is intangible in the way that we cannot touch it; rather, the online world is liminal because it occupies a position that is essentially a boundary or a threshold between a space where we are and one we can also not be physically within. There is something inherently abstract about liminal spaces. We often use examples such as purgatory, being at a crossroads, or standing on a geographical border line because it is in those moments where one could ask: Where exactly am I? The Internet is a similar space – familiar to many of us, yet hard to define, imagine, and even talk about. In fact, you will see throughout this collection that words, ideas, and concepts regarding virtual identities and digital cultures are defined in a variety of ways. This is intentional. These concepts are interpretable, contextual, and fluid, which is also why they are so compelling.

## We Live Online: Virtual Identities and Digital Cultures

Before we discuss the virtual elements of identity, let's take a look at how we can understand the concept of **identity** itself. Identity is a word that many people commonly use, but how we use it might vary. An identity is some element of who we are that we understand in relation to someone or something else. Identity can be defined as, "...a relational process through which we understand ourselves/others/groups at any given time in any given place" (Kannen 2013, 179). This means that identity is not a neutral or absolute fact, but identities are actually variable and context-dependent. Our age, for example, changes over the course of our lives and we have certain expectations for how to behave and dress when we are teenagers, which is quite different from the expectations that we have for someone in their 60s. You might be wondering: what does this have to do with living online? Well, our identities are in no way separate from who we are in virtual spaces, even when we may take on differing forms and use varying presentations of self. This might sound complicated, but stay with us.

In this book, when we are referring to identities, we are discussing those elements of ourselves that are often politicized such as gender, race, sexuality, class, disability, and so on. Using a social constructionist perspective, we understand that the meanings attached to these identities are created and constructed.

> If we look at the things in our lives, they themselves do not have meaning, but we construct meaning for these things using systems of representation, such as language. We name things. The name and the thing are not connected in any natural way, but it is through language that the way we represent things comes to be seen as natural. The key idea in this is "construct"; to construct something means to build or create it. The constructionist approach does not prioritize "things" as having natural qualities, rather it explores how these qualities are taught, learned, and reproduced through social interactions and relations.
>
> (Kannen 2021, 5)

For example, gender is not a scientific fact. **Gender** refers to the socially constructed roles, behaviours, processes, activities, and attributes that relate to understandings of masculinities, femininities, and non-binary representations in every society. Often, gender is presumed to be something inherent, rather than something we learn, but we know it is learned because gendered behaviours, understandings, and performances vary across communities, cultures, and throughout history. Here, we could also discuss the ways in which people can identify as cisgender, transgender, agender, genderless, gender fluid, and so on. We assume that when we learn about gender through our interactions with each other that it has come to us naturally, but it is, in fact, learned social behaviour. When we consider online representations of gender, it becomes even more obviously constructed. Liz W. Faber (2020) notes that even in online spaces, non-living bodies and objects are often inscribed with gendered markers in order to reinforce rigid gendered understandings. In these moments, we can understand that our gender offline is still relevant online because the effects of gender are still working in both realities.

In many societies, gender has historically been organized hierarchically. Quite often, one gender is associated with holding privilege and power in most domains of life, such as the ability to lead a country as an elected official, while the other only takes up these privileges as an exception rather than the rule. In Western societies at least, gender is also frequently understood as a binary; if one is masculine one cannot by definition also take on the attributes of femininity. In other words, value and status may accrue to one gender more than the other, and these advantages are sometimes gained at the expense of the other. It has been the work of many different groups of people to recognize the limitations these hierarchies and binaries impose. Despite the existence of rules about gender, most of us can think of multiple examples where those rules are contradicted, including within our own experiences. In what follows, we focus on how masculinities and femininities are produced. Instead of saying masculinity or femininity, it is important to pluralize them (as they are in the previous sentence). As a social product, gender is manifested in the ways that people relate to and interact with each other. Drawing from the social sciences' symbolic interactionist tradition, we can think of gender as more like a verb than a noun or an adjective – we all "do" gender, embedding it in the way we relate to other people. This perspective on gender focuses on everyday life and the ways in which people communicate and act with each other.

Defining gender strictly in terms of a singular masculinity or femininity is a problematic suggestion as it implies that only two, separate and discrete, gender categories exist. Here, we could discuss the ways in which people can identify as cisgender, transgender, agender, genderless, gender fluid, and certainly in other ways that will or already have been articulated elsewhere. One aspect of the complexity of gender talk stems from the ways in which understandings of gender are understood to be natural: "Gender difference...is largely culturally constructed, yet appears entirely natural" (DeMello 2014, 118). This is often the case in gendered representations online – it seems like the ways that people represent themselves are either entirely authentic OR clearly manufactured, but it is always more complex than this.

**Race**, like gender, is both an identity and a social institution because these are social constructions that we use to make sense of ourselves and categories through which societies are organized. The physical differences that many people think of as "race" mean really very little biologically. However, they mean a great deal culturally and socially. "Race is a social, economic, and political system of division and inequality" (DeMello 2014, 101). Inherited traits such as the colour of one's skin or the texture of one's hair have, throughout modern history, become associated with the concept of race. Skin colour and hair texture are no different from other inherited physical traits – such as height or eye colour – and they are far more difficult to distinguish with precision but throughout modern history, these traits have been given arbitrary significance, often in the service of defining membership to a ruling class versus people whose labour could be exploited. Vic Satzewich and Nikolaos Liodakis (2013) discuss the ways in which "race" (which they consistently place in quotation marks to indicate that it is a constructed term) has come to have meaning over time through pseudo-scientific classifications, which were used to foster "biologically informed racism" (14). The authors argue that while this was a historical occurrence, racially informed scientific practices continue today in order to attempt to prove that there are significant genetic differences between people of differing racial "origins." Satzewich and Liodakis (2013) heavily critique these claims in their discussion of the Human Genome Project, for example, and then speak to the process of racialization.

A better way to think about these constructions is that we, collectively, create them. As the concept of "race" is a social construction, it "is best understood in terms of social and political processes of racialization, or race-making" (Baum 2006, 10). In other words, racialization is the process by which relationships, social practices, or groups come to have racial meanings in society. The limits of language, Satzewich and Liodakis (2013) point out, mean that we use the term "race" to mean a wide variety of things and "despite the analytical problems with the concept of 'race', Canadian society still tries to measure and quantify 'race' and 'racial diversity'" (20). The relevance of "race" is further evidenced in the ways that racial identity is managed through the manipulation of laws, politics, citizenship, and the distribution of resources.

These discussions of identity lead us to a key way to understand identities as constructed, while also within relational processes. This is referred to as **intersectionality**, a term coined by Kimberlé W. Crenshaw (2004) to describe how a person cannot be reduced to just their gender or race or any other singular identity, but rather these identities impact one another and help define each other. For example, you are never just a student. At all times, you have gender, race, age, class, sexuality, ability, and so on which are always informing your experience and your relationships to others.

All of this to say: Identities are essential to our sense of self, both offline and online. However, identities don't just happen; they are something that we enact and perform within our cultures. **Culture** is an umbrella term which encompasses a wide range of practices, including behaviours, beliefs, representations, and practices. When individuals come in contact with others, they are engaged in a process of impression management (Goffman 1959) in which they strategically use their bodies, as well as the space and the things around them, to portray a desired self. When considering identities and cultures online, the role of performance is fundamental. David Kreps (2008) states that online identity performance reflects a "soup of masks...through which users present themselves differently to a variety of constituents (e.g., family, friends, professional acquaintances)" (87–88). This is saying that the ways we present ourselves online is malleable and selective in terms of the choices that we make in curating an online identity. If you consider your choice of profile picture, for example, what factors affect your decision in selection? In this way, it is clear how our online identities are constructions as well.

When online, we have profile pictures but we can also have avatars to function as representations of our identities. According to the Oxford English Dictionary (2022), an **avatar** can be "a graphical representation of a person or character in a computer-generated environment, *esp.* one which represents a user in an interactive game or other setting, and which can move about in its surroundings and interact with other characters." The key to this understanding is the intention behind the decision. When considering our performances of self online, the intentional choices that we make when selecting an avatar, a profile picture, and so on to function as the representation of our selfhood (whether this is an idealized version or otherwise), is meaningful both to ourselves and to how we foster relationships online. According to Ulrike Schultze, "...users rely on their avatars as a medium for experiencing not only the virtual world but also themselves in it" (2014, 85). When thinking about our online identities and the virtual cultures that we are within, it is these intentional elements that we want to consider, while also reflecting on how our identities are received and exist beyond our control.

## Book Structure

The concepts in the title of this collection, *Virtual Identities and Digital Culture*, unfold through the following three sections: Online Identity and Connections, Games and Play, and Reimagining Traditional Media. The theme of virtual identities and digital culture run throughout each of them and function as a thread to tie each section together. Each section reflects how digital culture is made meaningful in our lives through the communities we belong to, the play we engage in, and the media we create, consume, and resist.

This collection is created for those keen to learn about virtual experiences on a global scale. While a number of the chapters in this text prioritize a Canadian voice – as the editors are Canadian – the context of nearly every chapter is decidedly borderless. Further, the Internet is not bound to a nation or limited to understandings of citizenship, so this work is inherently transnational. A key significance in this text is also prioritizing the voices of authors whose work in the realm of digital media and technology have been historically silenced. This collection features a

8  *Introduction*

diversity of voices – including those folks who identify as women, BIPOC, 2SLGBTQIA+, and disabled, to name a few. Representation is important for all of us – to gain new perspectives, hear new voices, and listen to unique approaches to the digital realm.

As you move through the collection, you will see that each chapter contains key words, which are bolded (as you have likely noted throughout this introduction). These words are then defined at the end of each chapter (see below) and are followed by a section on Critical Thinking Questions after each individual chapter. These questions have been created in order to enable a deeper engagement with the ideas in each chapter, as well as to aid in classroom discussions and/or personal reflections following your reading.

Below, we will briefly explore each of the three main sections of *Virtual Identities and Digital Culture* in more detail so that you have an accessible framework to help prepare you for what you are about to read. Keep in mind that there is a key thread that binds them all together – virtual identities and digital culture are always already intertwined and do not exist outside of the various topics that you will be presented with.

## Online Identity and Connections

Through relationships with each other, we learn what cultural norms are and what it means to respond, replicate, or resist them. It is through culture that we form community. In its simplest form, an online or digital community is a group of people with a shared interest or purpose who then use the Internet to communicate and connect with one another. Arguably, online daters form one of the quintessential online communities. According to eHarmony Canada (2021):

- Thirty six per cent of Canadians use online dating
- Twenty per cent of current committed relations began online
- Sixty four per cent of people who use online dating sites are looking for someone with common interests
- Sixteen per cent of Canadians aged 18–34 have had a sexual encounter with someone they met online

As you can see from this example, online communities matter to how we live and interact both online and off. Further, online communities often have their own set of guidelines and needs, like online community engagement, moderation, and management. Donna Z. Davis and Karikarn Chansiri (2019) argue that virtual communities can provide safer spaces for people to create experiences that reflect a life they want to lead by selecting which information to share and how to portray themselves. Again, the role of performance is discussed here, but it adds the new layer of considering how performances lead to social connection.

Our connections online do not simply end there, of course. Here, we could discuss social media as a prime example. **Social media** are technologically mediated tools that allow people to create, share or exchange information, ideas, pictures, and videos in virtual communities and networks (Carr and Hayes 2015). Furthermore, social media is now seen to depend on mobile and web-based technologies to create highly interactive platforms through which individuals and communities share, co-create, discuss, and modify user-generated content. Facebook, Instagram, Twitter, Snapchat, and TikTok, to name some of the current most popular platforms, enable billions of users around the world to connect, create, share, re-share, and manage content in countless ways.

Connection, however, is not always positive. There are innumerable examples of how online spaces can lead to toxicity, often inspired by the anonymity of users. Internet trolls are those people (or automated programs) that attempt to disrupt some element of online life, but posting inflammatory, insincere, aggressive, or off-topic messages in an online community, with the intent of provoking other users into displaying emotional responses, or manipulating others' perception. On a macro-level, this type of disruption occurs during political elections, such as the United States Presidential campaign of 2016. On a micro-level, online harassment, defamatory comments, or mis-information can be proliferated by trolls in local/community Facebook groups and Instagram comments on accounts with tens of followers.

While these negative realities are explored in our collection, balancing this discussion with positive explorations online exposes the possibilities for self-exploration and interpersonal connection. For example, online communities, such as gaming spaces, can allow people to create their virtual bodies, select physical characteristics of their avatars, and/or completely abandon the identity of their physical selves (Davis and Chansiri 2019). These freedoms exist in the virtual world and help to foster the connections that people may not feel able to achieve offline. The ability to play with identity through avatars is particularly potent in game spaces due to the unique control players have in games that does not necessarily exist in other spaces. While we can portray ourselves differently in profile pictures and "bio" summaries, the ability to act (through play) with a different identity is powerful and important.

The chapters in this section consider how identities are made meaningful within online communities. They explore connections, such as online friend groups, gay dating apps, hashtag movements, intra-pandemic educational supports, and intimate publics via social media platforms such as Facebook, Instagram, and TikTok and streaming platforms such as Twitch and YouTube. The online connections that we have are fostered through platforms, but are intimately connected to our understandings of ourselves, our identity manifestations, our histories, our families and friends, as well as strangers. These chapters include contributors who speak to transnational feminism, Indigenous understandings, as well as clicktivism and right-wing political influencers to point to the politicization of our online connections. This section also introduces us to the idea of digital affordances – properties of apps, games, software, and other technological tools that define the ways in which we are able to successfully, and sometimes unsuccessfully, interact with those tools. While they are introduced here, affordances also feature prominently in Games and Play.

## Games and Play

Before proceeding, take a moment to think about the words "play" and "game" – could you explain these common words to someone who had never heard them before? We tend to use these words often, but formalizing our intuitive understanding of what they mean is tricky, and furthermore there is a tendency to inextricably link them together. For example, Johan Huizinga (2014, 22) defines **play** as "a free act that takes place... within a specially designated time, in a specially designated place, according to specific rules which are strictly adhered to." Despite being a definition of play, we see elements that are common to games including time constraints, location (stadium field, game board, etc.), and especially rules. In defining **games**, Hans Scheuerl describes them as "improvised or established agreement and rule structures ... in the norm of which one uses play activities to produce and give form to such [a] series of movements" (Neitzel 2011, 229). These and similar classical definitions (see Calleja 2011, 46–50; Egenfeldt-Nielsen et al. 2016, 44–48; Shell 2015, 36–46) certainly cover many of the cases we might consider – when we're engaged in baseball, *Monopoly* (Parker Brothers 1935), or *Fortnite* (Epic Games 2018), we typically play within the constraints imposed by the game.

Whether offline or online, we play games for many reasons, the most common of which are entertainment, diversion, and escapism. We can also connect with games for learning, therapy, emotional exploration, and social connection though all of these reasons for engaging can be found in other media, including books, music, television, movies, and online streaming. What is unique to games is the element of control – we are active participants with a meaningful degree of agency over the eventual outcome. This is true for all types, but since this is a collection about digital culture and online identities, we'll focus on videogames. **Videogames** also lack a formal, established definition (Arjoranta 2019), but a simple working definition is: videogames are games played on electronic or computer-driven devices.

As technology has advanced, the electronic nature of videogames has allowed them to grow into a mainstream media. Ever-increasing computing power has allowed us to explore countless virtual worlds, experience deep and compelling narratives, and has vaulted videogames into the conversation of what qualifies as art (Bourgonjon et al. 2017). The ubiquity of connected devices, from small clusters of networked friends to vast segments of the Internet, has allowed videogame players to effectively erase both geographical and congregating limitations. On December 1, 2020, the Twitter account for the popular survival/battle royale game *Fortnite* tweeted:

> We defeated him! A record 15.3 million concurrent players joined forces in our biggest event ever to fight back Galactus in today's in-game event, while more than 3.4 million cheered and watched on @YouTubeGaming and @Twitch!
>
> (@FortniteGame 2020)

While this is only one example, two important points are highlighted here. First, the popularity of video games, combined with the interconnected power of the Internet allows (potentially massive) groups of like-minded people to play together. Second, online platforms such as YouTube, Twitch, Twitter, and more foster various (again, potentially massive) communities around games and play. Outside of mass cultural experiences, games resonate in personally meaningful ways through compelling narratives, visual aesthetics, sound effects and music, avatars, and even in-game interfaces.

We feel that it is important to point out that while games rely on play, we can just as easily play outside of games. Consider the following definitions of play:

> Play is manipulation that indulges curiosity.
>
> (Schell 2015, 40)

> Play is free movement within a more rigid structure.
>
> (Salen and Zimmerman 2004, 304)

These two definitions give us more freedom and with it we can *play* outside of the typical structure and rules of games. For example, we can "play with" identity, ideas, toys, words, and more (see Kannen and Langille 2020).

The chapters in this section explore how games and play exist within online and digital spaces, but they also explore the elements of play that extend beyond these understandings. These chapters introduce us to the roles of music and sound, game communities, avatars, and videogame interfaces and their affordances. They also provide insights into the complexity of play and playfulness both within specific videogame contexts, such as *Pokémon GO!*, *Call of Duty 3*, and *Stardew Valley*, and outside of such contexts including gamified learning, virtual existences, and the role of sound in connecting our online and IRL-selves.

## Reimagining Traditional Media

When talking about media, it helps to understand the key elements by introducing the ideas of mass media and new media. The **mass media** can be understood as a vehicle through which communication to a wide audience (aka a mass audience) takes place. A single form of mass media can involve multiple media types. For example, a YouTube video of someone singing a song includes the language of the song, the sound of the singer's voice and of the instruments used, the video itself, and the Internet. Various mass media are woven into society through a legal and regulatory framework, particular types of ownership, professions, associated institutions, particular technology, available leisure time, and content. As such, **traditional mass media** is any form of mass communication available before the advent of digital media. This includes television, radio, newspapers, books, and magazines. **New media**, on the other hand, emerged in the 1990s as a set of practices, and institutions designed to facilitate broad participation in communication on a mass scale. New media are framed as extending and deepening these relationships, with social media, podcasts, blogs, and other new media offering more opportunities for people to engage with each other, create their own content, and engage with traditional media.

Communications technology has the ability to shrink space. If we start all the way back at the telegraph, and then consider the development of the telephone, radio, television, and, then, the Internet, what does it mean to shrink space? Using media to "shrink space" implies that every time we develop new technology, the world seemingly gets smaller as we are reducing the time it takes to coordinate action and communication across space (Harvey 1989). There is now no better example of our ability to shrink space than that of streaming media.

**Streaming** is a time-reducing delivery method where we can engage with media immediately and do not have to wait for the download of an entire file prior to viewing or listening to it. Currently, streaming is most popular through video-on-demand, television-on-demand, and music-on-demand services, such as Netflix, Disney+, Amazon Prime Video, CraveTV, YouTube, Spotify, and Apple Music to name but a few. You will note that "on-demand" is the element of streaming that is most desirable to our current cultural climate. While livestreaming – the real-time transmission of content while it is happening – is desirable for news and sporting events, streaming allows us to participate with our traditional media immediately from our own devices and not have to wait for the download or go to a theatre or wait for the television show to air in a specified time slot, and so on.

We are in a position to observe this reimagining in real-time, and to note the tension that exists between traditional media and other forms. For example, on July 9, 2021, Disney released its summer blockbuster, *Black Widow* (2021), simultaneously in theatres and on its streaming service Disney+. While the bulk of its $218 million "opening weekend" revenue came from traditional theatre viewing, over $60 million (27%) was a result of streaming (McClintock 2021, n.p.). While these figures are certainly impressive, *Black Widow* doesn't hold the record for opening weekend sales, nor was it the first film to be simultaneously released in theatre and on a streaming platform. What is perhaps most interesting, is that with this film Disney was the first major studio to publicly quantify the value of and interest in streaming as a parallel option to in-person viewing. Streaming, it had seemed, was simply a place-holder during peak-pandemic to satisfy the collective desire to watch new releases while staying home. *Black Widow* demonstrates that the shift to streaming is not going anywhere even though a return to the theatre is now possible. Our collective desires for options in our viewing for traditional mass media have undoubtedly expanded and will continue to evolve.

This section of the collection explores the ways that streaming technology enables a reimagining of traditional forms of media. These chapters primarily focus on the ways that film, television, music, and literature have been engaged with and reimagined via streaming services. The authors here address how these media have both reached new audiences and exceeded their traditional roots through streaming and how the *demands* of the audience continue to evolve. Specifically, analysing the role of queerness, algorithms, and Netflix, as well as streaming live theatre or albums, and participating in online book culture exposes readers to the contemporary realities of "watching television," "listening to music," "experiencing a play," and "going to book club." This re-imagining of traditional media is also evidenced in the evolution of media delivery from physical exchanges of VHS tapes, to the dissemination of journalism through online news outlets and the Instagram-ification of poetry. We close this section, and the collection, on a unique note – by considering the implications of digital spirituality in the context of *The Good Place*.

As we turn this collection over to you, we hope you will feel challenged, engaged, curious, and inspired to think about your own relationship(s) to virtual identities and digital culture. We are all at a critical juncture where our engagements with technologies have intensified and changed. We hope that you continue (or start!) to reflect on your own virtual identities and daily practices and consider yourself, your relationships, and your media interests in new or provocative ways. We would love to digitally hear from your virtual selves: connect with us on Twitter @victoriakannen and @aaron_langille.

## Key Words

**Avatar**: An avatar can be "a graphical representation of a person or character in a computer-generated environment, *esp.* one which represents a user in an interactive game or other setting, and which can move about in its surroundings and interact with other characters" (Oxford English Dictionary 2022).

**Culture**: Culture is an umbrella term which encompasses a wide range of practices, including behaviours, beliefs, representations, and practices.

**Digital**: The concept of digital can represent technology that relies on the use of microprocessors: this includes computers and any applications or devices that are dependent on the Internet and digitization such as smartphones, other mobile devices, and gaming systems.

**Games**: In defining games, Hans Scheuerl describes them as "improvised or established agreement and rule structures … in the norm of which one uses play activities to produce and give form to such [a] series of movements" (Neitzel 2005, 229).

**Gender**: Gender refers to the socially constructed roles, behaviours, processes, activities, and attributes that relate to understandings of masculinities, feminities, and non-binary representations in every society.

**Identity**: Kannen has defined identity as, "…a relational process through which we understand ourselves/others/groups at any given time in any given place" (2013, 179). This means that identity is not a neutral or absolute fact, but identities are actually variable and context-dependent.

**The Internet**: In general, the Internet is a global system of computer networks that communicate with each other to transmit information.

**Intersectionality**: Intersectionality refers to how biological, social, and cultural categories such as gender, race, class, ability, sexual orientation, size, and other axes of identity interact and intersect on multiple and often simultaneous levels.

**Liminal**: To refer to a space as liminal, is to claim that it is an in-between space. Turner defines liminal spaces and identities as "neither here nor there; they are betwixt and between the positions assigned and arrayed by law, custom, convention, and ceremony" (1969, 95).

**Mass Media**: The mass media can be understood as a vehicle through which communication to a wide audience (aka a mass audience) takes place. A single form of mass media can involve multiple media types.

**New Media**: New media are a set of practices, and institutions designed to facilitate broad participation in communication on a mass scale. New media are framed as extending and deepening these relationships, with social media, podcasts, blogs, and other new media offering more opportunities for people to engage with each other, create their own content, and engage with traditional media.

**Play**: Huizinga (2014, 22) defines play as "a free act that takes place... within a specially designated time, in a specially designated place, according to specific rules which are strictly adhered to."

**Race**: Race, like gender, is both an identity and a social institution because these are social constructions that we use to make sense of ourselves and categories through which societies are organized.

**Social Media**: Social media are technologically mediated tools that allow people to create, share, or exchange information, ideas, pictures, and videos in virtual communities and networks (Carr and Hayes 2015).

**Streaming**: Streaming is a time-reducing delivery method where we can engage with the media immediately and do not have to wait for the download of an entire file prior to viewing or listening to it.

**Technology**: Technology is derived from the Greek "techne," which means art, craft, or skill. Technology is the entities, both material and digital, created through the application of social knowledge, which then achieves cultural us and value.

**Traditional Mass Media**: Traditional mass media are any form of mass communication available before the advent of digital media. This includes television, radio, newspapers, books, and magazines.

**Videogames**: Videogames are games played on electronic or computer-driven devices.

**Virtual**: In order for something to be virtual, it implies that it does not physically exist, but that it is created by technology, or software to be specific, to appear as though it does physically exist. It is some*thing* carried out, accessed, or stored by means of technology, but it has no materiality to it.

## References

Arjoranta, Jonne. 2019. "How to Define Games and Why We Need to." *The Computer Games Journal* 8, no. 3: 109–20.

Arthur, W. Brian. 2011. *The Nature of Technology: What It Is and How It Evolves*. New York: Free Press.

"avatar, n.". OED Online. September 2022. *Oxford University Press*. https://www-oed-com.librweb.laurentian.ca/view/Entry/13624?redirectedFrom=avatar (accessed November 20, 2022).

Baum, Bruce. 2006. *The Rise and Fall of the Caucasian Race: A Political History of Racial Identity*. New York: New York University Press.

Black Widow. 2021. Directed by Cate Shortland. Marvel Studios.

Bourgonjon, Jeroen, Geert Vandermeersche, Kris Rutten, and Niels Quinten. 2017. "Perspectives on Video Games as Art." *CLCWeb: Comparative Literature and Culture* 19, no. 4: 1–10.

Bown, Johnathan, Elisa White, and Akshya Boopalan. 2017. "Looking for the Ultimate Display: A Brief History of Virtual Reality." In *Boundaries of Self and Reality Online*, 239–59. Cambridge, MA: Elsevier Press.

Bush, Vannevar. 1945. "As We May Think." *The Atlantic Monthly*. Accessed July 14, 2021. https://www.theatlantic.com/magazine/archive/1945/07/as-we-may-think/303881/

Calleja, Gordon. 2011. *In-Game: From Immersion to Incorporation*. Cambridge, MA: MIT Press.

Carr, Caleb T., and Rebecca A. Hayes. 2015. "Social Media: Defining, Developing, and Divining." *Atlantic Journal of Communication* 23, no. 1: 46–65.

Crenshaw, Kimberlé W. 2004. "Intersectionality: A Tool for Gender and Economic Justice." *Women's Rights and Economic Change* 9 (August): 1–8.

Davis, Donna Z., and Karikarn Chansiri. 2019. "Digital Identities – Overcoming Visual Bias Through Virtual Embodiment." *Information, Communication & Society* 22, no. 4: 491–505.

DeMello, Margo. 2014. *Body Studies: An Introduction*. New York: Routledge.

Egenfeldt-Nielsen, Simon, et al. 2016. *Understanding Video Games: The Essential Introduction*. Third Edition. New York: Routledge.

eHarmony Editorial Team. April 28, 2021. "10 Online Dating Statistics You Should Know." eHarmony. Accessed July 14, 2021. https://www.eharmony.ca/online-dating-statistics/

Faber, Liz W. 2020. *The Computer's Voice: From Star Trek to Siri*. Minneapolis, MN: University of Minnesota Press.

Fortnite (@FortniteGame). 2020. Twitter. Accessed July 13, 2021. https://twitter.com/FortniteGame

Goffman, Erving. 1959. *The Presentation of Self in Everyday Life*. New York: Anchor Books.

Harvey, David. 1989. *The Condition of Postmodernity*. Hoboken, NJ: Wiley Blackwell.

Huizinga, Johan. 2014. *Homo Ludens: A Study of the Play Element in Culture*. Mansfield Centre, CT: Martino Publishing.

Kannen, Victoria. 2013. "Pregnant, Privileged and PhDing: Exploring Embodiments in Qualitative Research." *Journal of Gender Studies* 22, no.2: 178–91.

Kannen, Victoria. 2021. *Gendered Bodies and Public Scrutiny: Women's Stories of Staring, Strangers, and Fierce Resistance*. Toronto: Women's Press.

Kannen, Victoria, and Aaron Langille. 2020. "Playing with Identity: Exploring the Role of Gender, Death Positivity, and Queer Representation in *A Mortician's Tale*." In *Women in Popular Culture in Canada*, edited by Laine Newman, 209-21. Toronto: Canadian Scholars Press.

Kannen, Victoria, and Neil Shyminsky. 2019. "Technology." In *The Spaces and Places of Canadian Popular Culture*, edited by Victoria Kannen and Neil Shyminsky, 222–6. Toronto: Canadian Scholars Press.

Kreps, David 2008. "My Facebook Profile: Copy, Resemblance, or Simulacrum?" *ECIS 2008 Proceedings*. 141. https://aisel.aisnet.org/ecis2008/141

McClintock, Pamela. July 12, 2021. "'*Black Widow*' Stunner: Disney's Streaming Revenue Reveal May Be Game-Changer." *The Hollywood Reporter*. Accessed July 13, 2021. https://www.hollywoodreporter.com/movies/movie-news/black-widow-disney-revenue-game-changer-1234980611/

Parker Brothers. 1935. Monopoly [Board game]. Parker Brothers.

Neitzel, Britta. 2005. "Narrativity in Computer Games." In *Handbook of Computer Game Studies*, edited by Joost Raessens and Jeffrey Goldstein, 215–45. Cambridge, MA: MIT Press.

Oxford English Dictionary. 2022 "Avatar." *OED Online.* Accessed July 12, 2021.
Satzewich, Vic, and Nikolaos Liodakis. 2013. *"Race" and Ethnicity in Canada. Third Edition.* Don Mills, ON: Oxford University Press.
Salen, Katie, and Eric Zimmerman. 2004. *Rules of Play: Game Design Fundamentals.* Cambridge, MA: MIT Press.
Schultze, Ulrike. 2014. "Performing Embodied Identity in Virtual Worlds." *European Journal of Information System*s 23: 84–95.
Schell, Jesse. 2015. *The Art of Game Design: A Book of Lenses. Second Edition.* Boca Raton, FL: Taylor & Francis.
Epic Games. Fornite: Battle Royale. Epic Games. PC/Mac. 2018.
Turner, Victor. 1969. *The Ritual Process: Structure and Anti-Structure.* Ithaca, NY: Cornell University Press.

# Section I
# Online Identity and Connections

# 1 "Hey Handsome"

## Gay Dating Apps and a Critical Digital Pedagogy of Identity

*Sean Michael Morris*

Throughout the COVID-19 pandemic, almost every human being learned to live outside of our anatomical boundaries. More so even than we had already, we adopted screens as the interfaces through which we might scratch at the embodied interactions that we had been accustomed to, needed, longed for, but which were necessarily unavailable. Bodies and screens, if you will, adhered, personalities and text bonded together; the differentiation between who we were and what we posted online blurred. In education, learning happened in boxes on a screen; in families, Facebook, Snapchat, Instagram filled in for holiday gatherings, birthday celebrations, graduations. For lovers or would-be lovers, for the lonely and the single, technology necessarily became the carriage for intimacy.

Technology, according to Sherry Turkle, is the architect of our intimacies (2017, 1). During the pandemic, technologies—and particularly social media—became the means through which intimates at a distance (families, spouses, friends) sustained their intimacy. Yet, technologies are not just the architects of intimacy between intimates, but also between strangers seeking intimacy. In particular for the gay community, dating apps have provided interfaces through which we might encounter intimacy. Mobile and geo-specific apps like Grindr and Scruff became the means for connection when sexual encounters were locked down during the pandemic.

The implications of technology architecting our intimacies can be profound. From the perspective of **critical digital pedagogy**—a field of inquiry that examines the relationship between humans and technologies, people and platforms, and the often dehumanizing results of that relationship—allowing our most intimate connections to be digitally mediated can result in a corrosion of our **digital identity**, our sense of possibility and hope, and our ability to discern human connection from mechanisms of the interface.

Because the concern at the heart of this chapter is human relationship, I feature here not only my own voice, but the (anonymous) voices of men I've met through queer dating apps like Grindr and Scruff. As I explore the way these two apps have altered how men meet (and how I have met men), how they sustain relationships, and how they think about what's

DOI: 10.4324/9781003310730-3

possible, I do so from the standpoint of both a user and critic of these apps, and from the perspective of critical digital pedagogy.

## Public Intimacy

Opening one of these apps, I'm welcomed by a seemingly endless wall of faces and bodies, displayed on a grid, each image a choice made by the user, a representation of who they hope they are that I (and others) will find attractive. These images are an artifice, a conjecturing at identity. They are like windows on a dark night. But also like cereal boxes on the grocery store shelf.

I don't hesitate, because here I can be anyone.

I'm on Grindr, messaging with a user less than half my age. He's looking for a dominant male sexual partner and is "into older guys." This is extremely common on Grindr, and sometimes leads to connections between middle-aged men and 20-somethings, both of them looking for some relief from the boundaries of their ages. This particular young man, K., asks me to describe what we would do together in a sexual situation. I oblige, writing a fantasy I think he'll enjoy, one that plays to the desires he's already expressed. My background in creative writing as well as my people-pleasing nature, allow me to assume a persona that is entirely *not* me, but one with whom this young man might feel intimate, connected; my writing is attentive, and my intention is to make K. feel desired. I know we'll never meet, that none of what I write will take place—but online, text can be as intimate and as real an experience as physical intercourse.

At the end of our intimate scene, I tell K. "I'm nothing like this in real life." And he assures me that doesn't matter, and that neither is he. "I'm shy, and you probably wouldn't even notice me in a room." What transpires between me and K. is an intimacy that is both unreal and real, digital but also embodied. This is the essence of digital identity, or the who-we-are online. I can both be anyone, so long as I construct that anyone well enough to be believed, and I cannot be anyone else but myself.

Digital identity is a complicated idea. On the one hand, as I'll talk about soon, our digital identities are made from what we construct online: our profile pictures, our biographical statements, but also how we talk there, who we interact with, what we like or don't like, what information or other media we choose to promote, the presence we create (from relative anonymity to influencer). On the other hand, our digital identity is likewise formed and informed by how platforms dictate interaction, conversation, relationships between human users.

On an app like Grindr or Scruff, identity is part advertisement, part seduction, part wishful thinking, part absolute honesty. And it's an identity that is necessarily public, even when we are having private conversations.

To understand how I'm using "public" here, consider: in a truly public place—a bar, a club, a coffee shop—we are in constant interaction with strangers, whether we intend to be or don't. How we dress, where we cast our gaze, where we sit down, how we dance, what we drink—all of these are observable. We are in conversation at all times with the room around us and the people in it.

Apps like Grindr provide spaces for texting, and these messages are private between two people. Yet there is a public nature to these apps. Even if the conversation between me and K. cannot be seen by any other user, it's taking place precisely because he found me here, and reached out to me just as any other user might. Grindr is a public space, a room where we can be seen, observed, a room in which we present ourselves in specific and particular ways.

I go there to be seen. And when I'm in conversation with someone like K., my face is still there upon the platform for anyone else to interact with. Unlike the public space of a bar or club or coffee shop, I am available to have multiple conversations at once, and this makes an app like Grindr or Scruff a *hyper-public* interface. I can be many places at once, speaking to many men at the same time, simultaneously private and public exactly because I am always visible and being visible means I am available for a variety of intimate encounters. Men who send me unsolicited pictures of their bodies can do so not only because the app makes it possible, but because here the lines between public and private, intimate and distant disintegrate.

Moreover, Grindr and Scruff allow me to present a digital identity that's both a synopsis of my complicated personality—reduced to what I like, what I'm looking for, what I do in my spare time—and a **montage**, a sequence of carefully shot and chosen photographs that, together, make a picture of my body that is also a representation of what I want men to desire about me. I am my own mannequin here, displaying the postures, clothing, scenes, expressions, body language—in still form—that are impossible to display any other way than on the app.

I produce myself for men in a much more carefully edited way than would be possible in another public space. Referring to one of her interview subjects, Turkle reports, "Technology encourages Liam to see his romantic life in terms of product placement. He is the product and he is direct marketing. You pass your photo through Photoshop and then others go photo shopping" (2015, 182). The pictures I post, but also the conversations I engage in, are the version of myself I think men might find most attractive, a digital slice of my identity—enough of my real personality to avoid catfishing, but not so much that the intimacy of discovery is obviated. This is the *me* I want men to see, the *me* I cannot express outside of the app. The *me* that can only find purchase in this hyper-public interface "Online, we do not become different selves," Turkle observes. "Our online identities are facets of ourselves that usually are harder for us to express in the physical realm." And so we enter this hyper-public space to carry on an intimacy impossible in any other space: an intimacy that is itself public and a performance, but also an intimacy that is built, constructed, and efficient.

## Cut-and-Paste Connection

After several weeks of not communicating, G., a young man with whom I enjoyed a single movie night, texts and says, "I'm sorry I've been quiet. After our date, I knew I wanted more between us, and I needed some space to sort myself out."

Another young man, L., who had come to my apartment twice to watch movies and enjoy some physical togetherness, likewise disappears from text for weeks. When he resurfaces, it's because I ask him why he's **ghosted** me. He writes back, "I'm sorry. You didn't do anything wrong. I realized I wanted more from you, and I had to give myself some space."

These two men, roughly the same age, never met one another; and yet, their reasons for leaving me in silence are so similar it's uncanny. And it strikes a familiar note: as an online English teacher, for years I watched students cut-and-paste their personalities into discussion forums. Introductions were always the same, reactions to other students' posts came as a refrain of "Good observations!" and "I agree!" and "I love what you said." As genuine as some of the sentiment might be behind those remarks, the reproduction of them class after class created a kind of glassy-eyed and fundamentally untenable community. This wasn't the students' fault at all, it was the fault of the interface, the design, which inspired the most unimaginative of connections. As if somewhere there existed a cheat sheet of common phrases to use in discussion. So, when I was rejected by both of these men in such a similar manner, I had to wonder: is there a cheat sheet for how to ghost someone?

The fact is that our technologies make our interactions more mechanical. On Twitter, we retweet and "like" relentlessly—maybe because, for the five seconds it takes for us to read the tweet, we become an advocate for the writer; but more likely, it's because the platform makes split-second interaction possible. The same goes for Facebook, Instagram, TikTok. We don't need to consider our choices to promote a given post or tweet, and in fact, the platform discourages us from taking the time to do so.

On gay dating apps, the same occurs. On Grindr, I can indicate my level of immediate interest in someone by tapping the "fire" button, which will signal that they've caught my eye; on Scruff, I "woof" men by tapping on the wee symbol of a paw. Both of these are exceedingly easy, quick ways of saying, in essence, "I like what I see." And there are users on both platforms that write disclaimers into their profiles: "I woof a lot. If I'm interested, I'll message you." Messages are a lot rarer than woofs or likes on these platforms, but when a message *is* sent, the opener is almost always one of a brief variety:

"What's up?"
"U Looking?"
"Hey handsome."

Dating apps give gay men an inadvertent facility for delivering an intimacy more public than private, making intimacy into an exchange, a production, even a *re*production. When our kindnesses and pillow talk become mechanical, our capacity to exercise intimacy becomes not only digitally inflected and performative, but also estranged from our ability to reflect upon what is meaningful human contact, discourse, connection.

G., who has now become a friend of mine, writes to me that "I'm going to be honest, I don't take the apps seriously at all. And only typically when I want a distraction or I'm bored." Similarly, J., a man I met on Scruff, tells me that he and his friends treat Tinder—an app where users swipe left or right to indicate their interest in someone—as a game, sometimes swiping people's profiles for each other, making split second choices that are twice removed from a personal connection. In this case, as with G., the apps are entertainment more than anything else, and not a place to find connection. "A person online just isn't 'real' until you meet them," G. writes to me. This explains why tapping the "woof" button or opening a conversation with "Hey handsome" makes sense. The interactions are trivial, are meant to be trivial.

And yet, amongst all the men I've spoken with, met, or with whom I've had other encounters, the desire for romance, for something sustainable, for a meaningful connection, remains.

## Platforms vs. People

From the perspective of so many gay men, apps have both enabled and utterly erased the possibility of finding a romantic partner. "You can't meet people on Grindr, for sure," M., a therapist, tells me. "Scruff is a little better, but no one is really there to make a commitment." Finding a partner, a boyfriend, even a reliable romantic friend is complicated by the sheer number of options; and the fact is, those knowable choices mean there is always the chance that another choice is better than the most recent one you've made. "Abundance of choice (and this would apply to choices in products, career paths, or people)," Turkle writes, "often leads to depression and feelings of loneliness" (2015, 183). More, in this case, is not only not better; it changes how we consider each choice we make, each person we meet on one or another app.

Consider the interface of apps like Grindr or Scruff. Opening the app, one is presented with a grid of profile pictures—usually faces or torsos, but occasionally pictures of landscapes, dogs, or other images meant to convey the user's interests. The grid is closely packed, like a crowded room of men staring back at you, waiting on you to make a choice. Here, there's no visible hierarchy in place, proxemics are forced by the interface, everyone is in high definition—the Grindr or Scruff grid puts every man on equal ground, which is to say no ground at all. There are very few ways to differentiate between the men on the grid aside from their profile picture. While I can sort and filter by distance, interests, etc., the results of even the most careful criteria present in precisely the same way: a seemingly unending grid of faces and torsos from which I can choose.

In other words, I can go photo shopping, without any or much consideration for the human being who has posted that photo, who is behind that photo, who made the series of choices to present that montage of himself that is the *him* he wants men to see, the *him* he cannot express outside of the app. The strange irony of the platform is that men post with the desire to be desired but use the app with indifference.

From the lens of critical digital pedagogy, this strange irony is telling of a profound if guileful **dehumanization**. As stated in the introduction, critical digital pedagogy is a humanizing approach concerned more with people than platforms. So, as a user and observer of these apps, I am concerned with how technology has not simply informed but shaped human interactions. Maxine Greene, an educational philosopher and pedagogist, writes, "technology will inevitably overthrow everything that stands in the way of the internal logic of its development, and human processes will in time be subordinated to technological ends" (1968, 386–7). We have seen the ways in which new technology has shaped human life: the iPhone, for example, not only introduced a hand-held Internet, but also all new relationships of texting and messaging; not to mention, the device also introduced apps, without which the way people meet might never have shifted this direction. Often, we begin using technology not because we need to, but because it's appealing, promises efficiency or connection, or simply because we don't want to fall behind.

J., my friend from Scruff, tells me that the introduction into his life of his first iPhone ended his long-term relationship. "I think if I hadn't gotten a phone, we'd still be together." The iPhone introduced him to Grindr, Scruff, and other dating apps, and the options, suddenly before him, changed the way he viewed future possibilities with his partner. But now, the message from J. is: "I've given up. Monogamy isn't possible. Finding someone isn't possible." Technology reshaped the way that J. understands the possibility of intimacy and connection—in effect by showing him all possible options and encouraging a public (or **hyper-public**) intimacy that doesn't translate beyond the screen. By entering into a digital space that permits a person to be simultaneously present and absent, public and private, in relationship or conversation with multiple individuals at once, J. lost track of the unique, individual relationship required by monogamy.

### So, What Now?

Greene observes that "[i]t has become part of conventional wisdom today to believe that the once radiant individual is in fact a powerless creature, that the freedoms he once possessed have been eroded, that he has no control over his life" (1972, 147). Apps like Grindr and Scruff appear to give the single gay male power, freedom, and control. The apps appear to enable agency, appear to give a gay man the ability to choose his future, to participate in the construction of the reality he wants (a relationship), when in fact they obfuscate that agency.

But this is not the future we need to have. We do not need to be subject to the tools that have been built for us upon the imaginations of engineers. We can decide to "affirm responsibility as full persons with respect to" technology, "if we continue to create ourselves as persons in good faith" (Greene 1968, 393).

Though my seductive conversation with K. may seem like a deception, or a surrender to the nameless anchorage of Grindr's text space, in fact my intentions with him were an attempt to move past what the technology expects—to humanize through a validation of his desires, his very presence upon the app. We do not need to surrender our behaviours to the mechanics of an interface, or to the repercussions of its conceits. If the technology wants us reduced to montages of ourselves, we must find ways to break through the limits of the grid to make contact wherever we can. Only then will we be reunited with our ability to reflect upon what is meaningful human exchange, discourse, connection.

## Key Words

**Critical Digital Pedagogy**: Critical digital pedagogy is a field of inquiry concerned with the relationships between humans and technology, and especially with the ways that technology can dehumanize people, their behaviours, relationships, and their lives.

**Digital Identity**: Digital identity is a complicated theoretical construction that consists of both the information a person posts online about themselves, the conversations and interactions they have with others that can be seen to constitute in part their personalities online, and the influence that interfaces, algorithms, and technology has on how they think about themselves and how they perform their identity in relationship with those.

**Ghost**: To ghost is a verb that expresses the act of ceasing communication with or ignoring a person with whom one has been intimate.

**Humanization/dehumanization**: Humanization/dehumanization is the fulfillment or lack of fulfillment of human potential.

**Hyper-public**: Hyper-public is a digital space that permits a person to be simultaneously present and absent, public and private, in relationship or conversation with multiple individuals at once, and one wherein all interactions are both grounded in and inform a publicly constructed digital identity.

**Montage**: A montage is the effect of producing a composite whole from fragments of pictures, text, or music.

## Critical Thinking Questions

1 Digital identity can be thought of as the way we present ourselves online. In this chapter, the author writes about his digital identity as formed by the "montage" of images that he compiles for his profile. How do you think digital identity can be affected by how that montage is perceived? Does another person's interaction with your identity online alter that identity—making it different, more, or less than, or entirely re-perceived from the one you've presented. Can the mere act of interaction between your own and another's digital "self" change how you think about yourself?
2 How do you make connections in digital spaces, apps, and/or social media? How are the connections you make there facilitated by or blocked by the design of the interface itself?
3 The author uses the iPhone as an example of how technology has fundamentally changed human life. Can you think of the introduction of another technology (since the iPhone) that has altered the way we interact, behave, or go about our lives?

## References

Greene, Maxine. 1968. "For the Record: Technology and the Human Person." *Teachers College Record* 69, no. 4: 385–93. https://maxinegreene.org/uploads/library/technology_human_person.pdf

Greene, Maxine. 1972. "Defying Determinism." *Teachers College Record* 74, no. 2: 147–54. https://maxinegreene.org/uploads/library/defying_determinism.pdf

Turkle, Sherry. 2017. *Alone Together: Why We Expect More from Technology and Less from Each Other*. 3rd Edition. New York: Basic Books.

Turkle, Sherry. 2015. *Reclaiming Conversation: The Power of Talk in a Digital Age*. New York: Penguin.

# 2 "We're Here for You During This Pandemic, Just Not Financially or Emotionally"

## What TikTok Reveals about Student Life during the COVID-19 Pandemic

*Sharon Lauricella and Emily Small*

Even before the COVID-19 pandemic swept through higher education students' academic and social lives, students had 99 problems, and **mental health** issues were more than one of them. The global pandemic added new struggles on top of the dumpster fire that was burning with overwhelm, depression, and negative anxiety amongst the student population. Challenges with social isolation, adapting to online learning, and increased concern for the health of themselves, family, and friends became added stressors to students all over the world. In a 2021 survey of undergraduate students, *all* respondents reported being negatively affected by the pandemic in some manner, and 59% reported high levels of psychological impact (Browning et al. 2021).

In the throes of nearly every facet of student life shifting online, it is not surprising that students turned to social media to address the many issues that they faced during the pandemic, and especially to express struggles with mental health. Amongst all social media channels, TikTok, as described below, was a platform where many students expressed issues associated with mental health and well-being. This chapter addresses what TikTok videos and user comments reveal about undergraduate student mental health during the COVID-19 pandemic. It highlights issues with which students struggled and what they needed – and continue to need – from their universities, faculty, administration, and friends in order to live a more vibrant student life online.

### Pre-Pandemic Student Mental Health

According to Paul Ritvo, psychology professor at York University, "Things were going downhill in mental health for students across North America before COVID" (Mastroianni 2021). In 2016, CBC News reported that Ontario campus counselors were "drowning in mental health needs" (Pfeffer 2016) and that both general and severe mental health issues were increasing. A 2016 survey of postsecondary students showed

DOI: 10.4324/9781003310730-4

that rates of depression, anxiety, and suicidality all increased in comparison to 2013 (American College Health Association 2016). Further, 46% of students reported feeling so depressed that it was difficult to function within the previous year and 65% experienced overwhelming anxiety, compared to 40% and 58%, respectively, in 2013 (American College Health Association 2016).

Mental health issues were clearly part of student life before COVID-19, though the reasons for such an increase had not yet (and still have not) been clearly identified (Chiose 2016). Part of the reason may simply be that university is a time during which many students are considered to be within the developmental stage of emerging adulthood. Jeffrey Jensen Arnett (2000) argues that young adulthood is a period of frequent change and when "various possibilities in love, work, and worldviews are explored" (469). Jennifer L. Tanner (2016) identified that emerging adults could experience distinctive mental health challenges, in part or in whole, as they navigate through this developmental period.

It is clear that some student mental health challenges are characteristic of this age group, and would have existed whether there was a global pandemic or not. However, Justin Hunt and Daniel Eisenberg (2010) noted that pre-pandemic reports of students seeking mental health services have increased not only in number but also in severity. Thus, even if the caseload of mental health issues increased, the prevalence of more severe cases will have increased as well. The increase in mental health issues may be a product of increased awareness and reduced stigma of mental health issues, though this potential explanation has not yet been quantified. And the issue remains: students were and are struggling. What do university students need, and how can universities help?

## Why TikTok?

In 2020, TikTok became a platform in which activism and change blended with humor and dance trends (Smith Galer 2020). Activists used TikTok as a way to spread their messages from home: movements such as #BlackLivesMatter reached 23 billion views combined (Smith Galer 2020). At the same time, dance trends were also a large part of TikTok activity in 2020; for example, the dance to Blinding Lights by The Weeknd took off in the early days of the pandemic, and resulted in family or "quarantine bubble" iterations. TikTok is a digital medium in which both unabashed rawness, unfiltered humor, and social activism have all coexisted in a space that is easy to interact with and allows discovery of other users.

TikTok boasts a decidedly youthful user group: about 50% of all TikTok users in the US are under age 29 (Statista 2021) and 48% of US adults between 18 and 29 use TikTok (Pew Research Centre 2021).[1] TikTok exhibits a significantly different purpose and function than other social media channels. For example, Instagram, also popular amongst the university-age demographic, functions more like a "highlight reel" in which photos are edited and polished to reflect the user's aspirations and successes. By contrast, TikTok tends to be less stylized and cultivated, but more spontaneous. It allows users to creatively share everyday life, whereas other social media apps don't encourage this kind of content (Barker 2020).

In the absence of in-person gatherings, social media channels quickly became the primary, if not only, medium through which students could communicate with one another during the pandemic; such **communication** included friends, acquaintances, audiences, and randos alike. What used to be videos of late-night study sessions, complaints about exams, parties, or campus gym workouts, morphed into students lamenting studying, stressing, or dealing with depression and anxiety... alone.

## Student Identity during COVID-19

While it's not a pretty picture, TikTok provided a clear perspective on what it means to be a student during COVID-19. We collected TikTok videos hashtagged with #mentalhealth, #university, #mentalhealthmatters, or #covid19 and were relevant to what it means to be a student during the COVID-19 pandemic. We also gathered all of the comments to the videos so that we could capture dialogue about the student struggle. All of the videos that we consulted were posted between 1 March 2020 and 30 May 2021. We created a new user profile so that we worked within a clean algorithm. We removed from our dataset all comments that were unclear or irrelevant to the project (i.e., tagging another user or one-word replies). All of the videos were made by students; we did not include videos made by a university, charity, or organization (such as a university directing students to services, or an organization presenting facts about mental health). We worked with a complete dataset of 692 videos and comments.

## What's Beefing Students during COVID?

Almost all of the videos and comments that we collected – 94% – were student expressions of frustration, exhaustion, confusion, **stress**, and overwhelm. General student life during COVID-19, according to TikTok videos and comments, was characterized by burnout and fatigue. Students described an increased workload associated with an abrupt and ongoing shift to online learning, a rise in stress relative to grades and fear of failing, regret for being in university at this time, ideations of dropping out, and even complaints about other students. Students described that the university experience was already stressful enough, and the confusion and disorganization associated with the pandemic escalated an already baseline level of depression and anxiety.

The general student angst that we observed is not to say that students were suffering silently. It is clear that many students attempted to get mental health support, but comments and videos showed that resources were increasingly inaccessible. Students expressed frustration with the inability to book appointments via their university's mental health supports, long wait times, and therapists' lack of preparation. Students also expressed that while universities attempted to help them, mental health supports such as therapy dogs are a nice idea and can be both enjoyable and helpful, but that the COVID situation prevented such assistance. Thus, students felt very much alone.

Student comments in our data showed frustration with the inability to go on vacation and/or have a break from classes. Given that most COVID-19 restrictions in North America began in March, 2020, many universities cancelled spring breaks. Thus, students who had travel plans – even if such plans were not to a rowdy beach – were forced to cancel or rearrange them. It is unclear whether students were upset with the issues associated with the inability to travel due to airlines and hotels cancelling bookings, or if they were upset that the weeklong break was cancelled by their universities. Nevertheless, some universities offered additional "Wellness Days" later in the term; these generally took the format of an extra Friday or Wednesday off classes. However, students did not feel as if these days were helpful. Our data showed that students perceived occasional weekdays off as performative and superficial. Overall, students expressed that the lack of extended periods of time away from coursework was negatively affecting their mental health, rest, and workload.

Students also expressed objections to communication and expectations of both their universities and faculty members. The primary beef with such communique was that there were "too many emails," and that such messages didn't accomplish anything or communicate anything of note. Faculty were the brunt of student complaints as well; students expressed frustration with instructors who assigned more work, had unclear expectations, neglected students, or disregarded mental health issues. One TikTok user commented that their university implied that, "We're here for you during this pandemic, just not financially or emotionally." In other words, the student felt that the university provided shallow communication and lacked genuine, meaningful support.

## TikTok Meets Pandemic Student Life

The COVID-19 pandemic highlighted the myriad mental health issues that already were characteristic of the undergraduate student identity. Generally speaking, a pandemic will increase stressors such as infection fears, frustration, boredom, inadequate information, financial loss, and stigma (Brooks et al. 2020). This phenomenon has been observed amongst students: according to Browning et al. (2021), issues such as quarantine, isolation, shelter-in-place, and social distancing amplified "the burden on the mental health of this vulnerable population." Similarly, a study of students in the UK showed that over half (57%) of students reported that their mental health became worse throughout the pandemic (Higher Education Policy Institute and YouthSight 2020).

Despite the flavor of complaint and dismay that we observed on TikTok, colleges and universities have indeed responded to students' mental health crises. Perhaps most notably, many offered counseling and **therapy** appointments via online channels such as Zoom, Microsoft Teams, or GoogleMeet. Most impressive was that the shift to online provision of mental health supports was nearly immediate; for example, in 2019, only 5% of Canadian postsecondary institutions offered online therapy sessions, but within three weeks of campus shutdowns due to COVID-19, 90% of postsecondary institutions in Canada pivoted to offer remote mental health services (Rashid and DiGenova 2020). This sudden shift to online sessions was equated to "building a plane while flying" (Nath 2021) given the delivery challenges associated with technology, confidentiality, and funding.

Part of what fueled student complaints about mental health supports is funding. Financial allocation to such services is a barrier for many postsecondary institutions. Online platforms to schedule and deliver counseling and therapy in secure formats are quite simply too costly for some colleges and universities. Thus, an increase in both cases and urgency due to COVID-19 stressors put additional strain on resources that, at many colleges and universities, were already stretched.

Ironically, one of the challenges associated with student access to mental health services is that there are so many options. For example, in addition to a college or university's own localized services, Canadian students can access CAMH's COVID-19 discussion forum, Saskatchewan's UniWellbeing, BC's Here2Talk, Alberta's text-based Text4Hope, Nova Scotia's HealthMindsNS and Good2Talk, a phone service for students in Ontario and Nova Scotia. In the US, Active Minds is a national organization dedicated to mental health advocacy, and hosts over 450 chapters on campuses across the country. Private organizations in the US such as Project Semicolon, She Writes Love on Her Arms, Mental Health America, and other specific mental health assistance for LGBTQ students (such as The Trevor Project LGBT Lifeline and LGBT National Youth Talkline) are available for talk, text, or information. A similar variety of services are available in Australia and the UK. Patrice Cammarano of St. Thomas University's mental health society says that "the overlapping resources make it hard to know who to contact" (Nath 2021). When a student is anxious, depressed, or in crisis, wading through online resources, phone numbers, and an assortment of options to contact is not only inefficient but can also add to the sense of overwhelm.

One of the most significant issues with access to student mental health is associated with the expected role of colleges and universities in supporting student mental health. Are universities and colleges obligated or expected to manage mental health issues, and should they allocate funds to serve students in terms of counseling and therapy? Or is mental health care beyond the scope of educational institutions?

According to some higher education administrators, mental health services should have limited purpose on college and university campuses. For example, Ted Mitchell and Suzanne Ortega (2019) argue that student mental health and well-being "is a serious and complex problem and should not be the sole purview of our campuses' counseling centers." Similarly, Sandy Welsh, vice-provost, students, at the University of Toronto, suggests that, "Mental health, and especially providing the treatment needed in complex cases, is primarily the responsibility of the Ontario public healthcare system" (Treleaven 2020). In the US, such mental health care is often channeled through private health insurance. Many colleges and universities, citing underfunding and lack of a centralized system, argue that they are not equipped to address mental health problems, and need the support of public or private healthcare and/or community organizations.

By contrast, others argue that colleges and universities ought to create and sustain initiatives that consider and improve student mental health. For example, Ed Mantler, vice president of programs and priorities at the Mental Health Commission of Canada argues that "post-secondary institutions can be change agents on mental health" (Treleaven 2020). In their study of psychological impacts of COVID-19 in the US, Browning et al. (2021) recommend that "university administrators take aggressive, proactive steps to support the mental health and educational success of their students at all times, but particularly during times of uncertainty and crisis – notably, the COVID-19 pandemic." Students also believe that universities are obligated to address student mental health. In an article in her university newspaper, Aiken (2018) argued that universities have a responsibility to provide timely, professional, and accessible mental health care to students – but she was unsatisfied with her own university's ability to provide such care and attention.

Our study of students' TikTok posts about mental health indicates that students are searching for meaningful solutions to their challenges. However, they are frustrated with systemic issues in both higher education and healthcare that prevent productive solutions to crises and student-centric problems. Many of the issues that students experienced in this study are inherent in modern higher education experiences. But does it have to be that way? Does university and college have to be characterized by misery and stress? Students in this study are seeking postsecondary studies that are less stressful, healthier, and more productive. We suggest that systemic issues in education must be critically examined so that students can enjoy good health, and thus experience a more effective and meaningful education.

## Conclusion

We know that students at greatest risk of mental health crises during the pandemic are those who know someone who is or was infected with COVID-19, women, younger students, students with pre-existing health concerns, and those spending at least one-third of their day on screens (Browning et al. 2021). However, most of the information about student mental health during the pandemic has come from university-sanctioned surveys and reflect self-reported data. Our study of student life during the COVID-19 pandemic using TikTok videos and comments provides a less filtered and arguably more realistic perspective of how and why students have struggled during this "unprecedented time" (another catchphrase that students on TikTok loathe). Our data suggest that while depression, anxiety, and burnout were already evident in the identity of a university student, the pandemic both escalated these issues and created new challenges such as adjusting to online learning and social isolation. If the TikTok student struggle were to be heard, universities would increase access – or at least streamline the process toward – mental health supports, offer more extended breaks, communicate clearly and genuinely, and offer flexibility around grades and assessments when students need them. While colleges, universities, public and private healthcare systems, and community organizations have in their own ways responded to student needs, our data from social media indicates that students seek a clear and accessible route toward mental health supports – even after the crisis phase of the pandemic has passed.

## Key Words

**Communication**: Communication is a process by which information is exchanged between individuals through a common system of symbols, signs, or behaviour.
**Mental Health**: Mental health refers to a person's condition with regard to their psychological and emotional well-being.
**Stress**: Stress is a state of mental or emotional strain or tension resulting from adverse or very demanding circumstances.
**Therapy**: Therapy is the treatment of mental or psychological disorders by psychological means.

## Critical Thinking Questions

1. Reflect upon how social media channels reflect users' identities. Do you have the same identity on TikTok, Instagram, and Snapchat? Why or why not?
2. What are the benefits and challenges of examining the issue of student mental health via social media vs. via university-sanctioned surveys?

3 Consider the construction of mental health access points in your institution, city, or province/state. Where do students turn? Why? What avenue is most effective? Should such access points be streamlined?

## Note

1 Worldwide demographic profiles of TikTok users are nearly impossible to estimate given that TikTok is banned in some countries (i.e., Pakistan) due to "immoral" and "indecent" content (Koul 2021).

## References

Aiken, Rachel. 2018. "Universities Have a Responsibility to Care for Students' Mental Health." *Queen's University Journal*, October 24. https://www.queensjournal.ca/story/2018-10-24/editorials/universities-have-a-responsibility-to-care-for-students-mental-health/

American College Health Association. 2016. "Ontario Canada Reference Group Executive Summary." http://oucha.ca/pdf/2016_NCHA-II_WEB_SPRING_2016_ONTARIO_CANADA_REFERENCE_GROUP_EXECUTIVE_SUMMARY.pdf

Arnett, Jeffrey Jensen. 2000. "Emerging Adulthood: A Theory of Development from the Late Teens through the Twenties." *American Psychologist* 55: 469–80.

Barker, Bryony. 2020. "TikTok Reality vs Instagram Aesthetic: Where Should You Spend?" *Talking Influence* (August 21). https://talkinginfluence.com/2020/08/21/tiktok-reality-vs-instagram-aesthetic-where-should-you-spend/

Brooks, Samantha K., Rebecca K. Webster, Louise E. Smith, Lisa Woodland, Simon Wessely, Neil Greenberg, and Gideon James Rubin. 2020. "The Psychological Impact of Quarantine and How to Reduce It: Rapid Review of the Evidence." *Lancet* 14, no. 395: 912–20. https://doi.org/10.1016/S0140-6736(20)30460-8

Browning, Matthew H. E. M., Lincoln Larson L., Iryina Sharaievska, Alessandro Rigolon, Olivia McAnirlin, Lauren Mullenbach, Scott Cloutier, et al. 2021. "Psychological Impacts from COVID-19 among University Students: Risk Factors across Seven States in the United States." *PLoS One* 16, no. 1: e0245327. https://doi.org/10.1371/journal.pone.0245327

Chiose, Simona. 2016 September. "Reports of Mental Health Issues Rising Among Postsecondary Students: Study." *The Globe and Mail*, September 8. https://www.theglobeandmail.com/news/national/education/reports-of-mental-health-issues-rising-among-postsecondary-students-study/article31782301/

Higher Education Policy Institute and YouthSight. 2020. "Students' Views on the Impact of Coronavirus on Their Higher Education Experience in 2020/2021." HIPI Policy Note 27, *December*. https://www.hepi.ac.uk/wp-content/uploads/2020/12/HEPI-Policy-Note-27-Students-views-on-the-impact-of-Coronavirus-on-their-higher-education-experience-in-2020-21-FINAL.pdf

Hunt, Justin and Daniel Eisenberg. 2010. "Mental Health Problems and Help-Seeking Behaviour among College Students." *Journal of Adolescent Health* 46, no.1. https://doi.org/10.1016/j.jadohealth.2009.08.008

Koul, Antra. 2021. "5 Countries That Have Banned TikTok." *Viebly*, May 5. https://viebly.com/countries-that-have-banned-tiktok/

Mastroianni, Julia. 2021. "The Pandemic Has Made Post-Secondary Students' Mental Health Even Worse." *NOW Toronto*, January 25. https://nowtoronto.com/covid-19-pandemic-post-secondary-students-mental-health

Mitchell, Ted and Suzanne Ortega. 2019. "Mental Health Challenges Require Urgent Response." *Inside Higher Ed*, October 29. https://www.insidehighered.com/views/2019/10/29/students-mental-health-shouldnt-be-responsibility-campus-counseling-centers-alone

Nath, Ishani. 2021. "How Mental Health Services for Students Pivoted During COVID-19." *University Affairs*, April 20. https://www.universityaffairs.ca/features/feature-article/how-mental-health-services-for-students-pivoted-during-covid-19/

Pew Research Centre: https://www.pewresearch.org/internet/2021/04/07/social-media-use-in-2021/

Pfeffer, Amanda. 2016. "Ontario Campus Counsellors Say They're Drowning in Mental Health Needs." *Canadian Broadcasting Corporation (CBC) News*, September 26. https://www.cbc.ca/news/canada/ottawa/mental-health-ontario-campus-crisis-1.3771682

Rashid, Tayyab and Lisa DiGenova. 2020. "Campus Mental Health in Times of COVID-19 Pandemic: Data-informed Challenges and Opportunities." In *Campus Mental Health: Community of Practice (CoP)*. Toronto, ON: Canadian Association of Colleges and University Student Services. Retrieved from https://campusmentalhealth.ca/wp-content/uploads/2020/11/Campus-MH-in-Times-of-COVID-19_Rashid_Di-Genova_Final.pdf

Smith Galer, Sophia. 2020. "How TikTok Changed the World in 2020." *BBC Culture*, December 16. https://www.bbc.com/culture/article/20201216-how-tiktok-changed-the-world-in-2020

Statista Research Department. 2021. "TikTok User Ratio in the U.S. by Age Group." April 15. https://www.statista.com/statistics/1095186/tiktok-us-users-age/

Tanner, Jennifer L. 2016. "Mental Health in Emerging Adulthood." In *The Oxford Handbook of Emerging Adulthood*, edited by J.J. Arnett, 499–520. New York: Oxford University Press.

Treleaven, Sarah. 2020. "Inside the Mental Health Crisis at Canadian Universities." *Macleans*, October 8. https://www.macleans.ca/education/inside-the-mental-health-crisis-at-canadian-universities/

# 3 Mediated Identities

## How Facebook Intervenes in the Virtual Manifestation of Our Identities

*Luis A. Grande Branger*

Every day, more than 2.5 billion people interact through Facebook acting as producers, curators, and consumers of content, and in doing this, they share information, opinions, expressions, and emotions. Through these interactions, users also build media representations of themselves. After all, Facebook, like many other social platforms, is a form of media, therefore, all representations found within it respond to editing processes – that is, selection, omission, and emphasis on information (Cartwright and Sturken 2001). So, we need to keep in mind that when we interact with someone on Facebook, we are not interacting with them, but with a representation of that person. Which does not mean they are not real, just that what we see is not necessarily the whole story.

These online representations of ourselves involve a variety of elements, such as:

- A visual representation of the physical appearance of each user that is built through photos and videos posted on the social network (aka avatars).
- A representation of how the individual expresses themselves verbally, either through videos and/or written words.
- A representation of their interests built through fan pages liked by the user.
- A representation of their character, behaviour, and personality through their social interaction with the content and representations of other users.

Together, all these elements build an identity manifestation of the user. I will illustrate with a personal anecdote: Recently, I shared on Facebook: "If I were to present a Ted Talk, on what subject would you automatically assume that I would present?" Personally, the topic that I would talk about in a Ted Talk would probably be related to the connection between media and culture. However, none of my Facebook contacts suggested that. Instead, they said things like veganism, political activism, or videogames. Even though I am doing a Ph.D. in Communication, Culture, and Media, and I have been a film critic for years, the representation of

DOI: 10.4324/9781003310730-5

my identity created by my latest posts – in which I emphasized certain themes and didn't include many details of my daily life – offered a version of my identity to the friends who answered my question. Reviewing my Facebook posts in the months leading up to this incident, most dealt precisely with the suggested topics and only a few had to do with communication.

But, what factors are involved in the process of sharing these posts? Beyond the individual, internal motivations of each user, driven by personal interests, uses, and gratifications, it is necessary to ask ourselves what external factors, inherent to the platform, intervene when we post content on Facebook. This is an important question because, since our identity is manifested through every interaction we have on the social network, every element that influences our behaviour ends up shaping that manifestation of identity as well. To answer this question, I will review which elements of Facebook allow its users to virtually manifest their identities and the mechanisms that influence the way we use those elements.

## How Do We Manifest Our Identity?

Richard Jenkins explains that "identity is the human capacity – rooted in language – to know 'who's who' (and hence 'what's what'). This involves knowing who we are, knowing who others are, them knowing who we are, us knowing who they think we are, and so on" (2014, 5). **Identity** is a social construct determined by a series of meanings attributed to an individual. Sociologist and social psychologist Erving Goffman stated that this construction contains a series of consciously manifested signs and another group of signs that are unconsciously presented (Van Dijck 2013). Among the first group, we have all the things over which we have control when manifesting our identity, while in the second group are involuntary expressions – body language, facial expressions, biochemical processes of the body, etc. – and the assumptions others may have about us based on their biases and their interpretation of those expressions.

Identities are not rigid and static. Our manifestation of identity shifts and adapts to the people we interact with and the social and emotional context we face in each situation. To understand how this process of adaptation works, Susan R. Jones and Marylu K. McEwen suggest a multidimensional model of identity (2000). It presents that people have various manifestations of identity that revolve around a core identity formed by personal attributes, characteristics, and sense of identity (see Figure 3.1). These multiple manifestations are constructed and adopted concerning the social environment in which the person is, taking elements of the nucleus and the identities of other people present in the environment. Thus, if an individual is in an academic environment, they will manifest an identity according to this context, while, if the person is with their friends and family, will manifest a more casual identity.

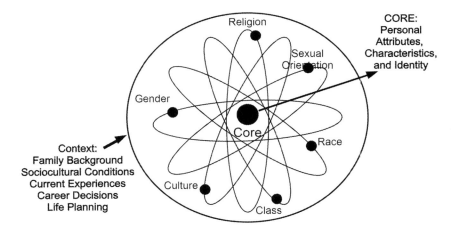

*Figure 3.1* Jones and McEwen's model of multiple dimensions of identity.

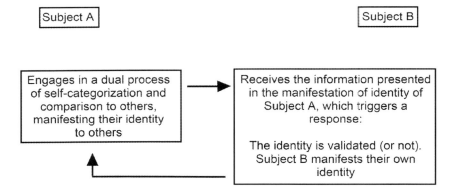

*Figure 3.2* Identity construction and manifestation.

This process happens also on Facebook. On this social medium, users adapt their manifestation of identity to the environment created both by the characteristics of the social medium and their followers or "friends."

Furthermore, identities are a collective social construction since they involve the total sum of every manifestation of identity carried out by an individual and an acceptance of those around him who receive said manifestations (Zhao et al. 2008). This means that in manifesting our identity, we engage in a dual process of self-actualization and comparison (Figure 3.2).

Hence, the construction of our identities is a social experience that is done through communication, since "the semiotic exchange in the processes of communication is the basic requirement for the formation and transformation of personal identity as a coherent entity" (Figueroa 2017, 61). This social experience is replicated when it is lived through Facebook posts. However, this technological mediation of the communicational exchange is altered by the intervention of the social media platform characteristics, as we will see later in this chapter.

## Producing and Consuming Content on Social Media

Clay Shirkey says that "in the age of the internet, no one is a passive consumer anymore because everyone is a media outlet" ("The Moral Economy of Web 2.0 (Part Two) — Henry Jenkins" n.d.). On social media, we become media content producers and curators, offering other users in our network a flow of publications, while receiving the same thing in return. This is why Internet users are known today as **prosumers** – a mix of producers and consumers – or **produsers** – producers and users – ("The Moral Economy of Web 2.0 (Part Two) — Henry Jenkins" n.d.).

During this exchange, our manifestations of identity are built through the sum of all these posts. Each user "consciously and deliberately constructs how [they want] to present themself to the rest" (Figueroa, 2017). In this process, we have major control over the elements that make up the construction of our identities, since the software of social media platforms allows us to minimize the amount of involuntary and unconscious elements present in the manifestation of identity. This is the process of selection, omission, and emphasis on information that end up building a representation of us or what is known as an avatar.

## How Does Social Media Influence Our Posts?

When we interact with each other through computer-mediated communication, "senders engage in selective self-presentation. Senders can be more deliberative about choosing the message elements that convey their most desired impression online than in spontaneous speech" (Walther and Whitty 2021, 122). That is, they can present themselves in a nicer or more aggressive version of themselves, compared to their non-mediated personas. This is what is known as **hyperpersonal communication**.

All digital interactions are limited by the programming of the software and the interface built for the exchange (Manovich 2013). As our interactions are increasingly mediated through computer programs, operating systems, and applications, the design features of different interfaces and operational rules of the programming with which these media work, define in many instances the behaviour we have when communicating. The way we create and edit content is modified, not only by the fact that these materials are digital in themselves, but because the processes of media generation are subject to the software that governs the environment in which we are operating.

The content we post on social media is also influenced by elements of design present on each platform interface that inform us of how we can use the elements of the platform and persuade us, without being deterministic, to use them in specific ways. This is what is known as **affordances** (Evans et al. 2016). Affordances not only guide the user, so they know how to operate technology but at the same time, these elements of design limit the user's options, making it more difficult for them to use the technology in other ways. This is particularly influential on Facebook since the way in which its website is designed – that is, its elements, what the design allows the user to do or not – influences how we socialize on this social medium (Fox and Moreland 2015).

Finally, there is one more intrinsic set of elements of social media that affect both the content found in them and our behaviour. This is what is known as **social media logic** (Van Dijck and Poell 2013). The four main elements of social media logic are:

- *Programmability:* This is "the ability of a central agency to manipulate content in order to define the audience's watching experience as a continuous flow" and "the ability of a social media platform to trigger and steer users' creative or communicative contributions, while users, through their interaction with these coded environments, may in turn influence the flow of communication and information activated by such a platform" (Van Dijck and Poell 2013, 5). It is relevant to notice that this logic involves both technical and social characteristics. The technical features include algorithms, software, and affordances that persuade users to post and engage in a constant flow of content. The social features include user participation and human agency over trends, as well as the existence of forum human moderators that decide what content is allowed or not.
- *Popularity:* This dimension refers to how social media gives priority and importance to content and users. Each social network has its specific ways of counting popularity and, in the case of Facebook, you see it reflected in the number of "friends" a user has and the number of reactions – likes or other emoticons, and/or comments – in a post, along with the number of times the content is shared by others. Because of this, these reactions become a kind of currency or reward craved by the users of the platform, which, in turn, motivates them to make more similar posts so they can earn more reactions.
- *Connectivity:* Social media has always been promoted as a way to connect human beings, and this is written in Facebook's corporate mission, which is to "give people the power to build a community and bring the world closer together. People use Facebook to stay connected with friends and family" ("Facebook - Resources" n.d.). Connectivity also "refers to the socio-technical affordance of networked platforms to connect content to user activities and advertisers" (Van Dijck and Poell 2013, 8), as well as to brands and corporations.

Social networks and Facebook, in particular, connect their thousands of millions of users with millions of content generated by advertisers, brands, artists, film and television producers, etc. YouTube and Facebook videos, digital newspaper news, and countless other cultural products are made not only by the users of the network but also by companies that, in turn, also influence the content of users who participate in these communicational exchanges.
- *Datafication:* This is "the ability of networked platforms to render into data many aspects of the world that have never been quantified before: not just demographic or profiling data yielded by customers in (online) surveys" (Van Dijck and Poell 2013, 9). Every content, behaviour, and relationship is traduced in quantitative data that can be used to study and analyze users and markets, and more importantly, to predict their behaviour. "All three elements heretofore explored—programmability, popularity, connectivity—are grounded in the condition of datafication" (Van Dijck and Poell 2013, 9). In terms of Facebook, there are different elements within the design and the software of the platform that works in the programmability and popularity of users and content, the connectivity between users and companies and other users, and finally, these elements persuade users to participate in exchanges within the social medium, allowing for the datafication of this behaviour.

In response to the social media logic, Facebook users are continually motivated to generate content on their profiles, react to the content of others, and seek the social reward from the approval of their "friends." "Users, for their part, have become increasingly skilled at playing the game of self-promotion, while advertisers and other interested parties, such as (prospective) employers, are getting leverage out of these tools for their own purposes" (Van Dijck 2013, 210).

There are eight main sections in a Facebook profile: name, bio, info, the three sections designed specifically for photos – profile photo, cover photo, and featured photos – the friend list, and the wall. After analyzing each one in regard to how these sections allow for manifesting our identity – that is, how they let users go through the dual process of self-categorization and comparison – and how the content on these sections is influenced by social media logic, we can trace a relationship between the logic and the content we share in these sections, and therefore, how the logic influences the identity that we manifest on Facebook.

## How Does Facebook Transform Our Identity Into a Brand?

When we communicate with others, we manifest our identity. As illustrated in Figure 3.3, when we interact with each other on Facebook, the platform mediates and modifies this manifestation of identity. The affordances present in the design make us translate that identity manifestation

44  *Luis A. Grande Branger*

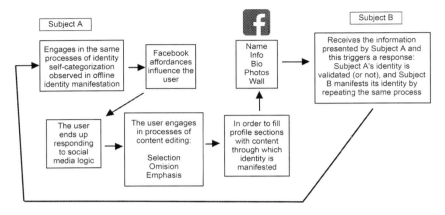

*Figure 3.3* Construction of identity mediated by Facebook.

into a media representation through editing processes, to respond to the logic of the social media environment. Finally, another user receives this information and, similar to what happens offline, the identity gets validated or not, through a response. This response is another identity manifestation mediated by the Facebook platform.

Under the pressure of responding to the logic of social media and the affordances of Facebook, the Name, Info, Bio, and Photo sections of a user's profile work together to build a mediated identity or an avatar. This identity gives value, meaning, credibility, authority, and familiarity to the posts that the user publishes on their wall and comments made in other users' content. At the same time, these posts are also manifestations of identity that reinforce the user's identity. In this process, we become media content producers and curators, and in the same way companies and corporations that produce and curate content on traditional media need to be consistent with their brand, our identity also becomes a brand, shaping the content we share so it resonates with our brand/identity.

A corporative brand is the identity of a corporation, which differentiates the entity from others, associates it with the products or services generated by it, and builds a reciprocal connection of value between the entity and these services and products in the mind of the consumer. In other words, the brand of a company is that connection in the mind of the consumers between the entity and the product or the service that they provide (Maurya and Mishra 2012, 125). In this sense, our brand/identity is that connection between us and our content that our "consumers," that is, our "friends" – and other users who might end up receiving our posts – end up creating (Figure 3.4).

This is the reason why people tend to post about a limited number of themes. Even those who might think that they post about a wide variety of topics on their pages, most of the time still have a finite number of themes

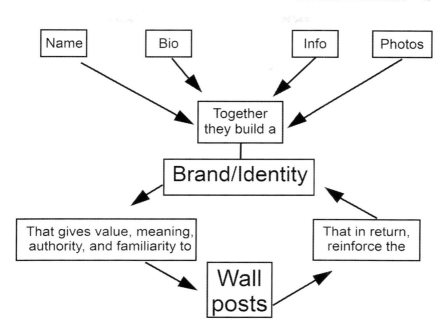

*Figure 3.4* Relationship between the Facebook profile sections and our identity.

represented in their posts. Their curation might encompass a greater array of subjects and is less specific than the curation of others, but that diverse curation is precisely their brand/identity. Responding to social media logic, we end up behaving in ways that promote and reinforce our brand/identity, and this has "become a normalized, accepted phenomenon in ordinary people's lives. Following the examples of celebrities' self-promotion, many users (especially young adults and teenagers) shape their online identities in order to gain popularity and hopefully reach a comfortable level of recognition and connectedness" (Van Dijck 2013, 203).

We all behave according to our personality. This is true both offline and online. The brand or identity generated on Facebook differs from our face-to-face identity, as it is built under the influence of the platform's affordances and responds to the logic of social media that operates on all content shared by the user. This content reinforces our brand or identity by generating a reciprocal relationship that motivates the user to continue participating in the communicational exchange through the social media platform.

**Key Words**

**Affordances**: Elements of design and cultural frameworks that work as non-deterministic guidelines on how to use a tool or technology, dissuading the individual to use them in other ways.

**Brand/Identity**: The result of the mediated manifestation of our identity on social media. It is how the identity is built and reinforced by the continuous flow of content that we continuously post on our social media profiles.

**Hyperpersonal Communication**: The result of interpersonal communication being mediated by technology that offers fewer nonverbal codes than face-to-face communication.

**Identity**: Identity is a social construction determined by a series of meanings attributed to an individual.

**Identity Manifestation**: How we present our identity to others, through social interaction by a dual process of self-categorization and comparison that in return reinforces that identity.

**Media Logic**: According to David Altheide (2016), media logic is a series of normalized and socially accepted principles, strategies, and performative tactics through which the content of that particular medium is created, distributed and consumed. Television logic, for example, involves ratings, short format, and fast pace, among other elements.

**Produsers**: Produsers are a mix of producers and users. Like prosumers, individuals who consume and create content on the Internet and social media.

**Prosumers**: Prosumers are a mix of producers and consumers. Individuals who consume and also create content on the Internet and social media.

**Social Media Logic**: The "processes, principles, and practices through which these platforms process information, news, and communication, and more generally, how they channel social traffic" are known as social media logic (Van Dijck and Poell 2013, 5).

## Critical Thinking Questions

1. What are the themes associated with the brand/identity that you manifest on Facebook (or other social media)?
2. How do you feel about your online identity being influenced by the corporate decisions of social media tech giants?
3. What assumptions do you make about a person's identity when you meet them offline? What assumptions do you make about a person's identity when you meet them online? Compare the two.

## References

Altheide, David. 2016. "Media Logic." In *The International Encyclopedia of Political Communication*, edited by Gianpietro Mazzoleni. The Wiley Blackwell-ICA International Encyclopedias of Communication. Chichester: John Wiley & Sons. https://books.google.com/books?id=qdPMjwEACAAJ

Cartwright, Lisa, and Marita Sturken. 2001. *Practices of Looking*. Oxford: Oxford University Press.

Evans, Sandra K., Katy E. Pearce, Jessica Vitak, and Jeffrey W. Treem. 2016. "Explicating Affordances: A Conceptual Framework for Understanding Affordances in Communication Research." *Journal of Computer-Mediated Communication* 22, no. 1: 35–52.

"Facebook - Resources." n.d. Accessed November 19, 2021. https://investor.fb.com/resources/default.aspx.

Figueroa, Heidi. 2017. *Imaginarios de Sujeto en la era digital: Post(identidades) contemporáneas*. Ediciones CIESPAL.

Fox, Jesse, and Jennifer J. Moreland. 2015. "The Dark Side of Social Networking Sites: An Exploration of the Relational and Psychological Stressors Associated with Facebook Use and Affordances." *Computers in Human Behaviour* 45: 168–76. https://doi.org/doi.org/10.1016/j.chb.2014.11.083

Jenkins, Richard. 2014. *Social Identity*. New York: Routledge.

Jones, Susan, and Marylu McEwen. 2000. "A Conceptual Model of Multiple Dimensions of Identity." *Journal of College Student Development* 41, no. 4: 405–14.

Manovich, Lev. 2013. "Media after Software." *Journal of Visual Culture* 12, no. 1: 30–7. https://doi.org/10.1177/1470412912470237

Maurya, Upendra Kumar and P. Mishra. 2012. "What is a Brand? A Perspective on Brand Meaning." *European Journal of Business and Management* 4, no. 3: 122–33.

"The Moral Economy of Web 2.0 (Part Two) — Henry Jenkins." n.d. Accessed November 20, 2021. http://henryjenkins.org/blog/2008/03/the_moral_economy_of_web_20_pa_1.html

Van Dijck, José. 2013. "'You Have One Identity': Performing the Self on Facebook and LinkedIn." *Media, Culture & Society* 35, no. 2: 199–215. https://doi.org/10.1177/0163443712468605

Van Dijck, José, and Thomas Poell. 2013. "Understanding Social Media Logic." *Media and Communication* 1, no. 1: 2–14. https://doi.org/10.12924/mac2013.01010002

Walther, Joseph B., and Monica T. Whitty. 2021. "Language, Psychology, and New New Media: The Hyperpersonal Model of Mediated Communication at Twenty-Five Years." *Journal of Language and Social Psychology* 40, no. 1: 120–35.

Zhao, Shanyang, Sherri Grasmuck, and Jason Martin. 2008. "Identity Construction on Facebook: Digital Empowerment in Anchored Relationships." *Computers in Human Behavior* 24, no. 5: 1816–36. https://doi.org/10.1016/j.chb.2008.02.012

# 4 Reassessing Clicktivism
## A Tool of the (Pandemic) Times

*Adiki Puplampu and Iain Macpherson*

Activism has long taken place in digital spaces, from the 1990s hacktivism of the Zapatistas to Edward Snowden's digital leaks and modern-day online petitions (Karatzogianni 2015). In contemporary digital culture, online activism is often characterized as **clicktivism**, or dismissed as **slacktivism**, and defined as "low-risk, low-cost activity via social media whose purpose is to raise awareness, produce change, or grant satisfaction to the person engaged in the activity" (Rotman et al. 2011, 821). Less generously, it can be defined as "acts of participating in effortless activities as an expedient alternative to expending effort to support a social cause" (Hu 2014, 354). Despite its unfavourable reputation in both academic and non-academic writing, clicktivism became an undeniably powerful tool at the height of the COVID-19 pandemic. Lockdowns forced people around the globe to stay home for extended periods of time, resulting in increased exposure, via various media, to local and global social issues. This intensified social consciousness, in combination with public health orders prohibiting large gatherings, fostered clicktivism as a primary method of social activism, shedding new light on its qualities, both positive and negative.

Criticisms of clicktivism fall into two main themes. First, many consider it inferior and counterproductive to "real world" activism which is characterized by actions such as street demonstrations (Halupka 2014, 116). Second, critics argue that motivations for clicktivism are murky because of the slippery slope between genuine activism and mediated **virtue-signalling**. In more theoretical terms, there is a concern that **impression management**, efforts to influence others' perception of us, is the motivation for clicktivist action, not a desire for social change.

In response to criticisms of clicktivism we contend that these arguments hinge on misconceptions around online activism and identity construction. In the case of online activism, critics often assume it always involves what psychologists call **moral balancing**: reliance on previous moral action, such as "liking" a political social-media post, to excuse future (in)action such as not demonstrating or donating. In fact, people are at least equally motivated to maintain consistency between past, present, and future behaviour (Lee and Hsieh 2013). As for impression management, critics associate it with deception, diametrically contrasting it with

DOI: 10.4324/9781003310730-6

authenticity. This perception fails to recognize that everyone regularly impression manages in their face-to-face and technologically mediated interactions with others, and typically not from vanity or insecurity (Goffman 1959).

## Criticisms of Clicktivism

From the commodification accusations of Micah White (2010) to the narcissism condemnations of Evgeny Morozov (2009), criticisms of clicktivism are scathing and diverse. While much literature is careful to frame negative analysis around "slacktivism" rather than "clicktivism," the close relationship between the terms makes this distinction rather superfluous. A key objection to online activism is that functionally, it is pointless (Morozov 2009). In the same way that offline slacktivism in the form of emblems like bumper stickers fails to engender change, critics argue that online activism is performative, primarily functioning to demonstrate endorsement for a cause (Skoric 2012, 79). The #blackouttuesday initiative, a component of the online activism around the Black Lives Matter (BLM) movement in 2020, is illustrative of these performativity criticisms.

In the summer of 2020, a protest movement for Black Lives spread across the world. While the offline world saw over 15 million people participating in demonstrations, online solidarity was demonstrated through the #blackouttuesday movement (Buchanan 2020). The brainchild of two Black female music executives, this initiative was originally a campaign titled #TheShowMustBePaused that called for a day of rest and reflection for African American communities in light of widespread racial violence (Romano 2020; Willingham 2020). The campaign then spread beyond the music industry, shifting to a call for a general social media blackout (Romano 2020).

While the hashtag was created with good intention, the cascade of black squares and BLM hashtags exemplified slacktivism in its largely performative nature. The deluge of black squares across social media was ironic, considering the goal of the campaign was to create a noise-free platform for unheard voices. Instead, the platform was coopted by people who had no desire to contribute substantively to the movement and took up space from those who did. Additionally, the campaign inadvertently damaged integral information channels for protesters because the BLM hashtag overwhelmed search feeds (Willingham 2020). This campaign is a textbook example of the type of performative clicktivism that critics like Morozov (2009) refer to when disparaging clicktivism. Participation in this campaign was, for many, an opportunity to align their idealized personas with their online activity in a superficial and labour-free way, which did more to soothe the consciousnesses of white allies and create a venue for collective performativity than support protesters, community organizers, or victims and their families.

Because of the low participation threshold, online activism is more accessible than on-the-ground activism, and though it is unmatched in its ability to generate awareness, the argument is that awareness does not equate to action, especially considering "social loafing" (Morozov 2009; Skoric 2012). **Social loafing** posits that when a collective participates in an action, individuals within the group are more likely to contribute less to the group effort (Morozov 2009; Skoric 2012). In the case of the BLM movement, its magnitude allowed individuals to "contribute" with slacktivist actions such as posting black squares on social media.

Related to the argument of social loafing is the idea that online activism's low threshold of entry is a magnet for individuals looking to enhance their self-perceptions (Morozov 2009; Skoric 2012). As Jorgensen says, "just like we need stuff to furnish our homes to show who we are, on Facebook we need cultural objects that put together a version of me that I would like to present to the public" (as cited in Morozov 2009, para. 3). This idea of activism as commodity is also raised by White (2010), who calls clicktivism the Wal-Mart of activism, saying that movements reliant on clicktivism "colonize emergent political identities and silence underfunded radical voices" (para. 6). A final major argument against online activism is that it often marks the height of an individual's activism because it diminishes their desire to act, creating a sense of complacency (Lee and Hsieh 2013; Skoric 2012).

Much of the critical literature on online activism was produced between 2009 and 2011, but recently scholars have shifted towards more measured and positive assessments of digital activism. Advocates argue against vilifications of online activism that see it as an inherently substandard form of activism because of its medium. Franklin (2014) argues that slacktivism is not bound to online platforms, with Madison and Kland (2020, 32) echoing this sentiment, asserting that technology is not the root of slacktivism, but rather a convenient scapegoat for criticisms of society-wide low levels of political and civic engagement. Franklin also pushes back against the argument that online activism is unsophisticated, saying that viewing it as a lesser form of activism is "myopic," narrow-mindedly dismissive of the Internet's significance as a tool of mobilization (para. 4). For M. I. Franklin, the relationship between technology and society is unavoidable; moreover, "any sort of serious political or social form of action now has to include an online dimension" (para. 6). In response to arguments about the self-motivated origins of online activism, Nora Madison and Mathias Kland (2020) point out that we do not screen non-digital activists for the same motivational purity.

Digital displays whether they are tributes or activism are, often unconsciously, considered tarnished because of the medium itself (Madison and Kland 2020, 39). Arguably, this is a consequence of the relative newness of the Internet and related technologies; additionally, the mediated nature of the digital world makes activism in this arena seem less tangible and therefore less effectual. But the digital world and the physical world are inextricably linked, and viewing one as detached from the other might be the foundational misinterpretation behind criticisms of clicktivism.

## Moral Balancing and Real-World Activism

Within the dichotomy of "real-world activism" versus clicktivism, the concept of moral balancing commonly informs arguments for the counterproductivity of clicktivism. It argues that when an individual engages in activity they perceive as ethical (e.g., clicktivism), the feeling of satisfaction will prevent future ethical action because the impulse to act has been resolved (Lee and Hsieh 2013, 811). However, the concept of consistency rooted in **cognitive dissonance theory** supports a contrary argument: "partaking in slacktivism may increase people's likelihood of taking related subsequent civic action because people want their behaviors to remain consistent" (Lee and Hsieh 2013, 812).

To study which theory more accurately applies to civic action, Yu-Hao Lee and Gary Hsieh (2013) created an online experiment to test if signing an online petition reduced the likelihood of participants donating to a cause. They concluded that participating in slacktivism does not adversely impact future actions like donations. Indeed, for some participants slacktivism increased their involvement with further action. They also found that people who declined to sign the online petition went on to donate more money to a charity related to the cause (818). So while the theory of moral balancing rings true in some cases, it does not apply wholesale to digital activism (Madison and Kland 2020, 36). Clicktivism is one of the many tools in an activist's toolbox, and rather than foil real-world efforts it often supports them.

## The Universality of Virtue-Signalling Vanity

Considering our collective fixation on personal image, it is no surprise the lengths people go to cultivate online identities. Within the context of the COVID-19 pandemic, this digital image maintenance became even more important given the overwhelmingly digitally mediated nature of our interactions. The explosion of online advocacy movements from BLM to Free Palestine provided clear vehicles for establishing online personal ethos and value systems. As we've established, a key argument made by critics of online activism is that it is motivated by self-interest rather than true altruistic intent. To challenge this argument within a theoretical framework, we introduce impression management theory.

Literature on self-presentation originates in the work of Erving Goffman (1959), who explored the role external presentation played in situating individuals within society. Goffman relied on the metaphor of an actor performing a role to articulate his ideas about how individuals relate to one another on the "stage" of life (Kuznekoff 2012, 16). In short, impression management "refers to the process by which individuals attempt to control the impressions others form of them" (Leary and Kowalski 1990, 34).

Impression management recognizes that individuals are not perpetually responsive to the perceptions of others (Leary and Kowalski 1990, 36). Certain circumstances and scenarios heighten the desire to actively manage one's impression (Leary and Kowalski 1990, 36). Theoretically this idea could extend into the digital realm as well. While browsing on a website, it is unlikely an individual would be attuned to what others may be thinking of them, but when engaging on a particular social media platform, they may be more cognizant of their identity constructions, especially considering the inherently public nature of certain online actions (Leary and Kowalski 1990, 38). Consequently, within the context of online activism, impression motivation would be a desire to be perceived as socially conscious, and impression construction would be the digital steps, such as clicktivism, taken to cultivate this perception (Leary and Kowalski 1990, 36).

Impression management theory gives us the language to refute challenges to the authenticity of clicktivist actions. Despite claims by authors like Morozov (2009) that clicktivist actions are motivated by self-interest and therefore disingenuous, from an impression management perspective, the truth is more complex. Mark R. Leary and Robin M. Kowalski (1990) identify five determinants of impression construction. One is "self-concept," which is the idea that individuals' outward identity construction is comprised of elements they can realistically express without making false claims (41). Inevitably, there are many cases in which individuals present an idealized or deceptive version of themselves online. But even more often, individuals create and maintain online authentic versions of themselves that are not reducible to shifting social mores around concepts such as social justice (Rosenbaum et al. 2012, 36). Anti-clicktivism arguments are often predicated on a simplistic dichotomy between mediated and non-mediated reality, including politics and impression management.

Villainizing the impression management aspect of political activism, online or offline, misses the larger point that these actions are largely unavoidable and inherent to human nature. While performing acts of online activism contributes to the construction of personal identities, it does not necessarily reflect disinterest in the issues. The line between virtue signalling vanity and our innate need to impression manage is a thin one, and of the various online activist movements, some have been successful in encouraging engagement without falling into the identity construction trap. In the following section we explore an example of online activism that demonstrates how online activity can be leveraged to produce meaningful social change.

## Case Study: #iamherecanada

While #blackouttuesday exemplifies key shortcomings of clicktivism, the #iamherecanada movement demonstrates some best practices for online activism. The movement was born from the Swedish counter-speaking movement #jagärhär (#iamhere) created in 2016 by Mina Dennert, a Swedish journalist (Mertz 2020, para. 2; Quan 2020, para. 9). Two years later, Alena Helgeson founded the Canadian branch of the #iamhere movement, whose mandate is to mitigate and neutralize online misinformation and hate speech by countering with facts and positive commentary (Mertz 2020). While the external mission of the group is to combat hate and misinformation, an internal goal is to encourage online participation from those who have traditionally been wary of wading into online spaces out of fear or discomfort (Mertz 2020, para. 6). Entrants to the group must apply to the movement's Facebook group and are vetted before participation (Mertz 2020).

There are three main aspects of the #iamherecanada movement that make it an instructive example of online activism. First, it has a clear mandate and operational guidelines. The movement has a straightforward external goal: to combat online hostility and misinformation with positivity and truth. This mission leaves little room for ambiguity when it comes to the actions members should undertake, in contrast to Morozov's (2009) criticism that online activism is often unfocused. Second, the movement has a clear collective foundation. Members dedicate a certain amount of time to the movement and often work in shifts (Mertz 2020; Quan 2020). This shared responsibility creates a sense of community in the group which combats the individualist tendencies of slacktivism. Finally, the private and gate-kept nature of the group contributes to its social activist function. Interested individuals must translate their interest into action by applying to join the group. The movement does not suffer from a low participation threshold or social loafing; people join intentionally because they want to contribute. Additionally, membership in the group offers limited scope for impression management; #iamherecanada actors move anonymously through the Internet spreading their counter-narratives. This addresses the criticisms of online activism that say it is motivated by concerns around personal representation. While relatively new, the #iamherecanada movement presents a model of what functional and dynamic online activism can look like.

## Conclusion

Dismissals of online activism as "slacktivism" overlook the mobilizational and practical significance of clicktivism and rely on arguments that misunderstand impression management and mediated communication. The "real-world" activism idealized by critics does not stand apart from online engagement, in a world where the digital and the physical are deeply intertwined. While accusations of self-interest in relation to clicktivism too often ring true, it is an essentially unavoidable aspect of online life and does not necessarily translate to an ineffective movement or disinvestment in the cause. During the pandemic, engaging in clicktivism was one of the few ways that many people could take part in social activism, spotlighting clicktivism as a site for social engagement and setting the stage for its continued relevance post-pandemic. Ultimately, the positives of clicktivism far outweigh the potential negatives; as such wholesale dismissals of the practice not only miss the social importance of online engagement but also limit the potential for its continued development.

## Key Words

**Clicktivism/Slacktivism**: Clicktivism/Slacktivism refers to a "low-threshold" (meaning, less risky or costly) Internet-based activism, from "liking"/ sharing posts to organizing online.

**Cognitive Dissonance Theory**: Cognitive dissonance theory argues that humans seek consistency, either by ensuring our thoughts and actions are consistent, or by ignoring or denying inconsistency.

**Impression Management**: Impression management is a theory that posits people communicate so as to create and maintain a specific image of themselves for all external audiences – from people who are familiar to us, to anonymous viewers of our social-media content.

**Moral Balancing**: Moral balancing is a decision-making equation in which previous actions influence the probability of future actions.

**Social Loafing**: Social loafing is a phenomenon in which individual members of a group contribute less to overall group aims.

**Virtue-Signalling**: Virtue-Signalling is when expressions are made in relation to a particular topic with the goal of transmitting a positive moral perception of oneself to others.

## Critical Discussion Questions

1 In recent years, corporations have also been engaging in online activism. Could the arguments of this chapter around the merits of clicktivism, specifically around identity management, be applied to corporations, why or why not?
2 What aspects of activism, and in particular digital activism, make it less susceptible to the theory of moral balancing? What does this say about online identity management?
3 What aspects of social media platforms make them effective sites for activism, and in what ways do these platforms hinder genuine activism?

## References

Buchanan, Larry, Quoctrung Bui, and Jugal K. Patel. 2020. "Black Lives Matter May Be the Largest Movement in U.S. History." *New York Times*. July 3, 2020. https://www.nytimes.com/interactive/2020/07/03/us/george-floyd-protests-crowd-size.html

Franklin, M. I. 2014. "Slacktivism, Clicktivism, and 'Real' Social Change." *Oxford University Press (Blog)*. November 19, 2014. https://blog.oup.com/2014/11/slacktivism-clicktivism-real-social-change/?utm_source=twitter&utm_medium=oupacademic&utm_campaign=oupblog

Goffman, Erving. 1959. *The Presentation of Self in Everyday Life*. Garden City, NY: Doubleday.

Halupka, Max. 2014. "Clicktivism: A Systematic Heuristic." *Policy & Internet* 6, no. 2: 115–32. https://doi.org/10.1002/1944-2866.POI355

Hu, Chih-Wei. 2014. "Health Slacktivism on Social Media: Predictors and Effects." In *Conference on Social Computing and Social Media*, 8531: 354–64. Cham: Springer International Publishing. https://doi.org/10.1007/978-3-319-07632-4_34

Karatzogianni, Athina. 2015. *Firebrand Waves of Digital Activism 1994–2014: The Rise and Spread of Hacktivism and Cyberconflict*. London: Palgrave Macmillan.

Kuznekoff, Jeffery H. 2012. "Chapter 1: Comparing Impression Management Strategies Across Social Media Platforms." In *Social Networking and Impression Management: Self-Presentation in the Digital Age,* edited by Carolyn Cunningham, 15–34. Lanham, MD: Lexington Books.

Leary, Mark R., and Robin M. Kowalski. 1990. "Impression Management: A Literature Review and Two-Component Model." *Psychological Bulletin* 107, no. 1: 34–47. https://doi.org/10.1037/0033-2909.107.1.34

Lee, Yu-Hao, and Gary Hsieh. 2013. "Does Slacktivism Hurt Activism? The Effects of Moral Balancing and Consistency in Online Activism." In *Proceedings of the SIGCHI Conference on Human Factors in Computing Systems*, Paris, 2013, 811–20. https://doi.org/10.1145/2470654.2470770

Madison, Nora, and Mathias Klang. 2020. "The Case for Digital Activism: Refuting the Fallacies of Slacktivism." *Journal of Digital Social Research* 2, no. 2: 28–47. https://doi.org/10.33621/jdsr.v2i2.25

Mertz, Emily. 2020. "Counter-speaking Group Trying to Make Social Media a Better Place." *Global News,* January 17, 2020. https://globalnews.ca/news/6421263/i-am-here-canada-counter-speak-facebook-comments/

Morozov, Evgeny. 2009. "From Slacktivism to Activism." *Foreign Policy*. September 5, 2009. https://foreignpolicy.com/2009/09/05/from-slacktivism-to-activism/

Quan, Douglas. 2020. "How Digital Activists Around the World Are Trying to Change the Tone of Social Media." *National Post*, January 4, 2020. https://nationalpost.com/news/how-digital-activists-around-the-world-are-trying-to-change-the-tone-of-social-media

Romano, Aja. 2020. "#BlackoutTuesday derailed #BlackLivesMatter. A community organizer explains how to do better." *Vox*, June 3, 2020. https://www.vox.com/2020/6/3/21278165/george-floyd-protests-social-media-blackouttuesday-lace-watkins-on-race-interview

Rosenbaum, Judith E., Benjamin Johnson, Peter Stepman, and Koos Nuijten. 2012. "Chapter 2: 'Looking the Part' and 'Staying True': Balancing Impression

Management on Facebook." In *Social Networking and Impression Management: Self-Presentation in the Digital Age,* edited by Carolyn Cunningham, 35–59. Lanham, MD: Lexington Books.

Rotman, Dana, Sarah Vieweg, Sarita Yardi, Ed Chi, Jenny Preece, Ben Shneiderman, Peter Pirolli, and Tom Glaisyer. 2011. "From Slacktivism to Activism: Participatory Culture in the Age of Social Media." In *CHI'11: CHI Conference on Human Factors in Computer Systems, Vancouver, 2011,* 819–22. https://doi.org/10.1145/1979742.1979543

Skoric, Marko M. 2012. "What Is Slack About Slacktivism?" *Methodological and Conceptual Issues in Cyber Activism Research*: 77–92. https://ari.nus.edu.sg/wp-content/uploads/2018/10/InterAsiaRoundtable-2012.pdf#page=83

White, Micah. 2010. "Clicktivism is Ruining Leftist Activism." *The Guardian,* August 12, 2010. https://www.theguardian.com/commentisfree/2010/aug/12/clicktivism-ruining-leftist-activism

Willingham, A. J. 2020. "Why Posting a Black Image with the 'Black Lives Matter' Hashtag Could be Doing More Harm than Good." *CNN,* June 2, 2020 https://www.cnn.com/2020/06/02/us/blackout-tuesday-black-lives-matter-instagram-trnd/index.html

# 5 "Victims of the System"
## Anti-Government Discourse and Political Influencers Online

*Michelle Stewart, Maxime Bérubé, Samuel Laperle, Sklaerenn Le Gallo and Stéphanie Panneton*

Since the beginning of the COVID-19 pandemic, several online movements converged in reaction to health measures enacted by governments internationally and in Quebec, Canada. Some rejected the obligation to wear masks or to confine themselves, others were firmly opposed to vaccines, and still others simply denied the severity of the virus. While this protest movement emerged from diverse, pre-existing groups (antivax, far-right movements, established conspiracy movements, for example),[1] they have united (Darius and Urquhart 2021; Gallagher et al. 2021) to contest what they call the "plandemic," a conspiracy imagining that the pandemic was planned by governments or other shadowy forces in order to control the global population.

In this chapter, we examine the confluence of **microcelebrity** and far-right populism via a portrait of Quebec-based influencers against mask, vaccination, and health measures. Discussions of radicalization in political discourse on social media require a nuanced examination of the processes of radicalization and the terms of participation of those caught up in such movements. While the overwhelming majority of Quebecois (people who live in Quebec and identify as French Canadian) supported the health measures, several influencers built their followings during the pandemic, blurring the lines distinguishing criticism of pandemic management and public health messaging from **anti-government discourse**, **far-right populism**, and a range of **conspiracy theories**. We explore the relationship between online influencers and the communities that develop around them and ask: How does community identity take shape around political issues? Who influences whom? What are the key themes that animated community members in online groups that opposed public health measures during the pandemic?

By the summer of 2020 in Quebec, an online movement contesting mask mandates, lockdowns, and other health measures began to protest in public spaces. This resistance movement of a "fringe minority," in the words of Justin Trudeau, became fertile ground for the organization of the "Freedom Convoy." Indeed, the occupation of Ottawa in February

DOI: 10.4324/9781003310730-7

2022 by the "Freedom Convoy" was funded by some of the same groups and mobilized by some of the same influencers discussed here. The intensity of federal and provincial pandemic responses galvanized populist rhetoric. Populist rhetoric opposes the interests of the "people" and those of the "elites" (understood in a variety of ways – as politicians, journalists, or business leaders), both online and offline.[2] Right-wing forms of populism combine distrust of elites with anti-establishment and anti-democratic sentiment. They often include nationalist, anti-immigration, racist, and sexist currents. Right-wing populist discourses are mobilized and shaped in a specific ways online (Postill 2018; Tanner and Campana 2020). Several researchers note the important role played by "microcelebrities" (Abidin 2015; Lewis 2018). These political influencers skillfully wield the codes of social networks in order to build their status based on "credibility, relatability, and authenticity" with the goal of "destabilizing audience members' world-views" (Lewis 2018). Political microcelebrities build their influence by fostering a "perceived interconnectedness" (Abidin 2015) with their followers. They do this by performing direct communication and suggesting their accessibility and responsiveness via digital features. As we will see here, political microcelebrities do respond, if in limited ways. In so doing, they come to mirror the themes and tone of their subscribers. These seemingly democratic (equal) exchanges enabled by platforms like Facebook or Instagram also offers these microcelebrities the opportunity to fully exploit the populist rhetoric of rejecting "mainstream" media discourses. In effect, the populist opposition to media elites is central in the process, deeming various far-right themes as oppositional or silenced by liberal media and political elites.

This study contributes to an understanding of how populist discourse takes shape online and why it seems to flourish there. As Benjamin Moffitt (2016) emphasizes, "While all contemporary politics are mediatised to some extent, it is ultimately populism that hews closest to the process of mediatisation. The collision between media logic and political logic finds its most pure expression in contemporary populism. As such, media can no longer be treated as a 'side issue' when it comes to understanding contemporary populism" (98). Political microcelebrities echo and reinforce rhetoric pitting the people against a corrupt elite by taking advantage of poor (or reluctant) content moderation and enforcement, as well as recommendation algorithms that favor emotional extremes. While there is strong research tracing the proliferation of disinformation and conspiracy theories online, less attention has been paid to the agency of the followers of these movements and the ways in which they engage with influencers and other subscribers.

Our preliminary research on Quebecois influencers in the QAnon sphere suggests a synergistic relationship between microcelebrity as a performative style and populist discourse. To clarify, QAnon is an

American political conspiracy theory and political movement that began in 2017. In this snapshot of the appeal of Quebec-based microcelebrities during the pandemic, we examine the intersection of populism, conspiracy theory, and microcelebrity. We sketch a model that attends to the "people" solicited by that discourse. Beyond simply examining the topics that engage followers, we are interested in the performative aspects of these videos, the affective and rhetorical dimensions that generate the greatest engagement and suggest the increasing hegemony of microcelebrity as an anti-political discourse with growing resonance and appeal.

**Current Study**

In what follows, we employ mixed methods to analyze two popular anti-mask influencers in Quebec, Daniel Pilon and the Stéphane Blais's Foundation for the defense of the rights and liberties of the people (FDDLP). We chose Daniel Pilon because his Facebook videos exhibited a measurable increase in views and followers over the course of the pandemic. An accountant by trade, Pilon began making videos offering tax and financial advice for Quebeckers beginning in January 2017. From his first tax advice videos 2015 to November 2021, Pilon's audience grew to 70K followers, with many more views. In March 17, 2020,[3] Pilon made his first reference to the pandemic. By August 2020, Pilon was producing videos criticizing pandemic measures with clear references to conspiracy theories. We thus chose Pilon's presence on YouTube as a case study in the production of community around populist terms and conspiracist rhetoric. Pilon assumes the "conspiracy label" with pride and has proposed a rising party of the "conspiracists" (*Les complotistes*).

As a counterpoint, the FDDLP represents itself as a defender against governmental overreach mounting legal challenges to the emergency health measures taken by the Quebec government. A close analysis of the evolution of content and engagement of Pilon's and the FDDLP's videos provide a portrait of a specific and seductive form of antigovernmental discourse and links its success to a particular form of populist appeal that might be better explained in terms of microcelebrity. We will argue that this particular brand of anti-political populism has diffused into the performative, community-building styles of political microcelebrity.

In order to determine key themes for closer content analysis of specific videos, we performed Structural Topic Modeling (STM) on 336 transcripts of Dan Pilon's YouTube videos collected on September 14, 2021, and 37 of the FDDLP's, as well as transcriptions of comments available for 228 of Pilon's videos and 33 of the FDDLP's. Based on these results, we devised coding categories that differentiate between those themes that are political (policy oriented), those that are more epistemological (expertise, sources, beliefs), those that focus more on community identity and consolidation (cohering community, establishing the terms of identity) (see Table 5.1). For each category, we separated approaches to these themes that are more positive/active from those that are more negative/passive (victimization, manipulation). In addition, we identified several codes related specifically to microcelebrity: mobilization (calls to action), self-promotion, fundraising, and references to other influencers (invited guests, laudatory comments, alternate sources, and shared videos). Deploying those codes, we performed close analyses of the top

*Table 5.1* Thematic codes for videos and comments

| Main Themes | Active/Positive | Passive/Negative |
|---|---|---|
| Community | *Microcelebrity maneuvers*: Notable identity production rhetoric or appeals. Praise for the influencer. Linking self with community. Self-defense. Biographical details.<br>*People Citizens-Positive Support* (Appeals to community unity and solidarity) Community self-congratulation for its courage, knowledge, or generosity. | *Elite-Critiques* (establishment of community vs. political, media, economic elites)<br>*Enemies-Others* (Racism, nationalism, fear, community threatened by others who are not elites) |
| Epistemology-Belief | *Alternate information* (reinformation)<br>"*Truth*," appeals to the "real," untold story | *Conspiracy theories* (Great Reset, Plandemic, QAnon themes)<br>*Sheep* (manipulation by "fake news," government, and conformism) apocalyptic themes<br>*Electoral fraud* (2020 American election) |
| Health and Spirituality | *Body sovereignty*<br>*Natural remedies*<br>*Awakening (Consciousness)*<br>*Religious* | *Anti-vaccination* and anti-mask discourse (conspiracy-oriented, not rights-oriented) |
| Political | *Liberty*<br>*Freedom*<br>*Democracy*<br>*Rights*<br>*Sovereignty (political)*<br>*Individual choice* | *Tyranny*<br>*Dictatorship*<br>*Control*<br>*Censorship* |
| Additional codes | *Citation of Other Influencers*<br>*Mobilization*<br>*Fundraising: for the cause, for self-promotion* | |

videos and comments that produced the most engagement, which we define as those videos with the highest number of views, comments, and likes (**Addendum A**).

## Results and Analysis

Our study of the key themes of anti-mask influencers confirmed a certain degree of discursive opportunism. During the pandemic, those influencers who did not previously emphasize conspiracy theories veered from tax advice (Dan Pilon) and populist critiques of government corruption and elites (Stéphane Blais) into more conspiratorial discourses that found at the intersection of the anti-vaccination movement and QAnon. In short, we see movement from critiques of health measures to the mobilization of conspiratorial language linked to QAnon, far-right populism, and anti-vaccination activists.

These results mirrored visible trends on social media across the world (Gallagher et al. 2021). We were particularly interested, however, (1) in gauging how these themes resonated with the followers of these influencers and (2) in identifying the importance of the performances of these political microcelebrities. Addressing these two dimensions required an analysis of the prevalent themes gleaned from the transcripts of videos and related comments, as well as an analysis of the performative elements of microcelebrity.

Thematically and rhetorically, both influencers spend considerable time consolidating community, both by defining the terms and borders of group identity *and* in reinforcing a sense of community with alternative information sources, experts, and ways of knowing. In the videos we analyzed, influencers seem to devote about 7–10% of their videos to self-promotion, either by asking for donations, likes, or selling products. The FDDLP focused consistently on its own cause, whereas Pilon often promoted the causes of his guests (including Blais), in addition to asking for subscribers or donations.[4]

## Daniel Pilon

Pilon produces a sense of group identity rhetorically and performatively, the terms of which tend to be more negative than positive. Speaking directly into the camera, even touching it when he is particularly animated and usually from the familiar and casual setting of his desk. Sometimes he is outside, particularly when doing something of a man-amongst-the-people style of reportage during anti-mask protests. He often drinks on camera, wine or what he calls "café au lait," which casts doubt upon his sobriety, a doubt that Pilon himself treats as an inside joke.

Pilon attributes his popularity to his sense of humor. He does impressions and mocks public figures. He breaks into uncontrollable laughter in response to a letter about the head of Radio Canada getting caught spending the month of December in Florida despite pandemic travel restrictions. He uses Facebook Live features to acknowledge people as they arrive by name, occasionally responding to comments as they scroll live. At the end of some videos, he reads letters from viewers, including correspondence from his critics. This performance cements his status as a target of critics, be they journalists or "sheep." He defends himself by embracing the label of "conspiracist" as a compliment, though he says the criticism hurts. Scrolling comments of support proliferate in these moments, demonstrating the extent to which the microcelebrity's self-defense serves to consolidate community against its critics.

Over the course of our study, Pilon's online performances became more entertaining and unpredictable. They take the form of freewheeling meditations on one to three topics, interspersed with comedic performances and intimate, direct-address. For example, he advises a mother who doesn't want to send her kids to school in a mask. Pilon empathizes and recommends home schooling to protect them from this "genocide." He collapses his own identity with that of the community, asserting that he must speak out because "our lives are danger." This rhetorical move of defensively speaking for and embodying the community constitutes a large proportion of Pilon's online appeal, though the bulk of his videos mobilize community identity in these more defensive, negative terms. To balance this, he closes each video on a positive note, calling his community one of love and "fresh water" (fresh air), telling everyone to get out, enjoy nature, have fun, and signing off by saying, "I love you all."

## Blais and the FDDLP

Blais's videos present a counterpoint that resembles Pilon's subject matter and rhetorical appeals. Given that the FDDLP presents itself as a populist defense of the people's rights, it is notable that Blais's videos move from rights-oriented discourse to more conspiracy-oriented themes over the course of the pandemic.[5] Blais devotes less time than Pilon to building a direct relationship with his audience; rather, he maintains a more measured and formal presentation, representing himself as the defender of the people's rights against incipient tyranny. His guests introduce more extreme positions. For example, in one of Blais's online interviews, Alexis Cossette-Trudel talks about the "la burqa sanitaire" (which he defines as "intentional and damaging limits on gatherings and social dissent"), as well as the techno-health tyranny of pandemic measures. Blais's own discourse becomes more conspiratorial over time. A movement that seemed to brand itself in the active and positive language of rights, liberties and choice at the onset, increasingly deploys the negative terms of tyranny, dictatorship, and censorship.

## Analysis of Comments

Pilon's most popular videos are lightning rods for critical comments (26%) about his content, guests, and those who follow his shows. Those who take up Pilon's themes echo the more negative, populist terms of government tyranny, "dictature sanitaire" (health dictatorship), anti-vaccination and anti-mask arguments (with conspiratorial undertones), as well as populist critiques of political, economic, and media elites. Indeed, these subjects account for more than 50% of comments on Pilon's videos. The more active and "positive" categories of "Alterative Truth," "Liberty, Rights, and Individual Choice," and "Mobilization" account for just under a third of the comments.

Responses to the FDDLP's videos resemble Pilon's, with more negative critiques of elites and conspiratorial themes dominating the comments. The more active and positive language of rights discourse, which makes up the majority of Blais's appeals well into 2020, does not seem to resonate with Blais's audience: Almost half of the comments address populist critiques of elites and assert anti-vaccination and anti-mask sentiment. Yet, the high percentage (36%) of community approbation for Blais and the Foundation's efforts suggests a symbiotic relationship between the performance of the influencer and community response. Blais keeps the FDDLP's channel focused on its court cases and the heroism of the cause, and its (and his) tireless efforts on behalf of "the people."[6]

Two things are interesting here: First, well into 2020, Blais was careful to avoid overtly conspiratorial themes, letting his guests (or featured videos) promote more conspiratorial views (e.g., Dr. Li-Meng Yan, Jean-Jacques Crèvecoeur, and Alexis Cossette-Trudel). His audience praises him for his calm, reassuring manner and his pedagogical and informative presentations, but the videos that receive the most views and comments from his subscribes feature negative emotional appeals by his interviewees or news of the ongoing lawsuits of the FDDLP.

Despite praise for his measured presence, over the course of the pandemic, Blais's discussion of political rights began to move from defending rights, individual choice, and liberty towards critiques of "world government" that reference several conspiracy theories. From 2018 through August 2020, Blais promoted political arguments, such as critiques of government management, calls for transparency regarding taxation, and resisting mask mandates. By fall 2020, Blais clearly articulates conspiratorial tropes about the World Economic Forum, Bill Gates, and the "toxicity" of masks. By November 2021, Blais responds to a news item regarding distracting children getting vaccinated with virtual reality games in less than measured tones. He reposts the item on his Facebook page, calling the news outlet bastards ("salopes") and saying that "one day" they "will pay the price for high treason." In November 2021, Blais hosts Pierre Barnérias, director of the COVID-19 conspiracy documentary,

*Hold On* (2020). The film supports earlier conspiracy theories asserting that the pandemic was engineered by elites to "reset" and control governments globally. In that regard, his increasing references to negative anti-system, populist critiques of elites, and conspiracy theories echo those of his audience.

## Discussion

These results suggest a bi-directional flow of influence between political microcelebrities and their subscribers. Our initial hypothesis focused on a potential shift in populist language from negative, anti-system politics to a more active and positive expression of populist goals, like Blais's, focusing upon citizen's freedom, rights discourse, free speech, and free thought. Similarly, some of Pilon's language seemed to emphasize positivity, e.g., being "anti-vaccination but pro-choice," as well as his loving closing words to his audience.

Our results are more ambiguous, demonstrating a mix of negative and positive sentiment with negative comments prevailing in responses to videos. Community preferences seem to shift the themes and sentiment of political microcelebrity over time as community members adopt the language of influencers. In short, the comments reveal a strong preference for anti-system populism, an illiberal, anti-government discourse that creates something of a negative feedback loop between influencers and their most active audience. This anti-system rhetoric is less issue- or policy-focused than it is existential. The "government" and its representatives are characterized as enemies. Community identity is consolidated around the mobilization of critiques of elites and their efforts to control or manipulate the community. Others are branded "conformists" or "sheep." Epistemological resistance to mainstream arguments defines the community and distinguishes their discourse from mere criticism of government management of the pandemic. Influencers and their followers do raise legitimate critiques of pandemic measures, but the most mobilizing issues are conspiratorial critiques of elites and deep-seated skepticism (if not cynicism) regarding the potential for government reform.

This discourse includes no specific allegiance to established parties, but merges far-right themes with populist critiques of "liberal elites" opposed to "average" citizens, often cast as victims without representation. Political microcelebrities at once self-promote, presenting themselves as privileged defenders of their embattled community and, at the same time, dissolve into "the people," sharing their grievances and their status as outcasts. We would argue that this phenomenon is not fully captured by debates about populism. We prefer the term political microcelebrity as it stresses both the small numbers of influencers and followers and emphasizes the symbiotic relationship between microcelebrity and community.

## Conclusion

Throughout this chapter, we have highlighted the ways in which microcelebrities appeal to their audiences and build group identity. We have shown how microcelebrities, like Pilon, create a sense of equality, accessibility, and shared circumstances. We would like to suggest that analysis of the production of identity around political microcelebrities might be crucial to understanding the divisive politics of our age. The symbiotic social style visible in our study shows political microcelebrities reaching for relevance by testing themes, a discursive opportunism that ends up being less about the issues than about the positioning of the community against elites, "tyranny," and the "system." We see political microcelebrity as an epistemological and identity form: a way of seeking to know the world and a way of seeing one's position in the world. It is a form that is decidedly hospitable to conspiracy theory and illiberalism. QAnon might be understood as the most glaring example of these tendencies, merging anti-system politics and apocalyptic thinking with a strong sense of community identity founded on alternative modes of belief. These trends are visible in the political and cultural movements that coalesced in opposition to vaccinations, masks, and "lockdown" measures.

Microcelebrity as a set of social and rhetorical gestures does indeed resemble "media populism." After analyzing the centrality of the production of small-scale communities of belief (identity, emotion, and action), we argue that further studies of political microcelebrity might provide more clarity regarding this form of cultural politics. A portrait of the workings of political microcelebrity should examine the production of community galvanized around live videos and comments, as well as the ways in which users and audiences perceive their consumption actively, as participation in a community of belief supporting not only certain political views, but a pointed relationship to the consumption of information, as at once embattled and awakened.

## Acknowledgments

This research benefited from the generous support of the Digital Citizenship Initiative of the SSHRC and Canadian Heritage (2021–2023). This article was produced with the invaluable research support of Olivier Santerre, Vicky Girard, Mathias Poisson, and Morad Bkhait.

## Key Words

**Anti-Government Discourse**: Anti-government discourse is an anti-government view or belief is one which stands in opposition to the conventional social, political, and economic principles of a society.

**Conspiracy Theory**: A conspiracy theory is an explanation for an event or situation that invokes a scheme or plot by ill-intentioned and powerful groups, often political in motivation, when other explanations are more probable or truthful.

**Far-Right Populism**: Far-right populism is a political ideology which combines right-wing politics and populist rhetoric and themes. Its rhetoric employs anti-elitist sentiments, opposition to the Establishment, and speaking to and/or for the "regular" or "common" people.

**Microcelebrity**: Microcelebrity is the experience of being well-known to a niche or small, specific group of people, and a practice whereby people present themselves as public personas, create affective ties with audience members, and view followers as fans.

### Critical Thinking Questions

1  How do influencers and commenters define their community?
2  To what extent might influencers be influenced by their followers?
3  Which online dynamics seem to impact the performances of microcelebrities?

### Notes

1  A far-right, conspiracy movement that began online in 2017 and that originally centered upon information coming from an anonymous figure, "Q" who claimed to be someone with high level security clearance in the U.S. government. QAnon adherents would work together to interpret messages coming from Q, called Q-drops. The core belief of the movement was that Donald Trump would save American government from an international ring of "pedo-satanists" led by figures in the Democratic Party and other globalists. The movement exploded in membership during the pandemic and has erupted into real world violence on several occasions. Anti-vaccination movements existed before the pandemic. We use the term "anti-vax" to refer specifically to radical resistance to vaccines based on conspiracy theories. Resistance to 5G phone technology also grew during the pandemic and converged with anti-vax, QAnon, and far-right conspiracists who imagined that vaccines and 5G technology were part of a plan to insert micro-chips (alternatively to track or to control the recipients). Conspiracists imagined different people behind these plans – Big Pharma, Bill Gates, Georges Soros, "global elites," Democrats, or others, depending on the theory.
2  It is important to note the specifics of the response to the pandemic in Quebec. While Justin Trudeau's federal government implemented economic policies to support the population, François Legault's provincial government was responsible for administering the healthcare system and implementing local public health measures, such as masking, containment, and organizing vaccination campaigns.
3  A day after the official announcement of COVID-19 restrictions.
4  Pilon talks about money very openly, but disingenuously, often beginning a plea explaining that he doesn't do his daily chronicle for money, but then lamenting how much it costs in time and energy and suggesting he will have

to stop if viewers aren't generous. Political microcelebrities are distinguished by self-marketing efforts and the need for profitable attention (as opposed to political influence alone).
5 Blais had delved into critiques of "globalists" before 2018, but toned down his rhetoric with the establishment of his political party.
6 Paradoxically, despite promoting himself as the leading defender of the people and going so far as to promise to pay the tickets of protestors given citations for not wearing masks, he will later exhort his audience not to count on him to be their "saviour."

## References

Abidin, Crystal. 2015. "Micromicrocelebrity: Branding Babies on the Internet." *M/C Journal* 18, no. 5. https://doi.org/10.5204/mcj.1022

Darius, Philipp, and Michael Urquhart. 2021. "Disinformed Social Movements: A Large-scale Mapping of Conspiracy Narratives as Online Harms During the COVID-19 Pandemic." *Online Social Networks and Media* 26. https://doi.org/10.1016/j.osnem.2021.100174

Gallagher, Aoife, Jacob Davey, and Mackenzie Hart. 2020. "The Genesis of a Conspiracy Theory: Key Trends in QAnon Activity Since 2017." *ISD Reports*. https://www.isdglobal.org/wp-content/uploads/2020/07/The-Genesis-of-a-Conspiracy-Theory.pdf

Lewis, Rebecca. 2018. "Alternative Influence: Broadcasting the Reactionary Right on YouTube." *Data & Society*. https://datasociety.net/wp-content/uploads/2018/09/DS_Alternative_Influence.pdf

Moffitt, Benjamin. 2016. *The Global Rise of Populism*. Stanford, CA: Stanford University Press.

Postill, John. 2018. "Populism and Social Media: A Global Perspective." *Media, Culture & Society* 40, no. 5: 754–65. https://doi-org.proxy.bibliotheques.uqam.ca/10.1177/0163443718772186

Tanner, Samuel, and Aurélie Campana. 2020. "'Watchful citizens' and digital vigilantism: a case study of the far right in Quebec." *Global Crime* 21, no. 3, 4: 262–82. https://doi-org.proxy.bibliotheques.uqam.ca/10.1080/17440572.2019.1609177

# Addendum A

## Most Viewed, Commented, and Liked Videos on the Channels of Dan Pilon and the FDDLP (July 2020 – July 2021)

### Dan Pilon

Protest (Dec. 2020)
The Ultimate Meeting with Mel, Amélie, and Eve-Marie (Dec. 2020)
The Real Reason for the Curfew (Jan. 2021)
When the Media Go Too Far (Jan. 2021)
The King Is Dead (Jan. 2021)
8 Influencers Speak to Quebecois (Mar. 2021)
Special USA (Jul. 2021)

### FDDLP

Jean-Jacques Crevècoeur at Peaceful Rally for Our Rights (Jul. 2020)
Alexis Cossette-Trudel at Peaceful Rally for Our Rights (Jul. 2021)
News of the Lawsuit & Injunctions with Rocco Galati (Aug. 2020)
Brief Meeting with 2 FDDLP Lawyers (Aug. 2020)
Dr. Li-Meng Yan Tells the Truth About COVID-19 (Aug. 2020)
Stéphane Blais with Alexis Cossette-Trudel (Mar. 2021)
Stéphane Blais Interviews Lucie Laurier (Mar. 2021)

# 6 From Networks to Assemblages
## An Analysis of Feminist Activism against Digital Violence in Mexico

*Marcela Suárez*

In Latin America, the serious situation of gender violence, which may well be expressed in what Rita Segato (2016) has called "the war against women," has resulted in the explosion of **feminist activism**. One of the repertoires of this activism has to do with performances. An important example of this was carried out by the feminist collective Las Tesis entitled "A rapist in your way," which caused social networks and public squares to be filled with videos of new forms of social justice performances making visible the **institutional violence** that traverse them. Another repertoire of this feminist activism has to do with the mobilization of emotions. In performance, women are seen showing they are fed up with the authorities in the face of the prevailing situation of impunity. Women march with banners blaming the authorities, slogans that then become hashtags that circulate in social networks. The most emblematic example is #NiUnaMenos (NotOneLess). Other women display symbolic objects such as crosses, roses, or photos to memorialize murdered women and leave these memorials in some public square as a way of formulating the message that gender violence is a public problem. When there are major events of gender violence such as femicides, the streets, and networks fill up like rhizomes shouting: justice.

In this chapter, I propose to move from the focus on **networks** to one that looks at **assemblages** in order to understand the intertwining of feminist activism between Internet and the streets, but also the digital violence directed towards activists as ways to discipline them. Through an ethnographic follow-up illustrated in the case of the feminist collective Luchadoras, the chapter analyzes forms of feminist activism as political assemblages against digital violence. The argument is that assemblage theory allows us to explore the material dimension in the digital age more broadly in order to understand new forms of feminist activism centered on bodies, as well as the various ways in which they affect and are affected (Deleuze and Guattari 1987).

DOI: 10.4324/9781003310730-8

70  *Marcela Suárez*

## Assembling Networks with Bodies

The theory of assemblages is part of a pluralistic research agenda to analyze multiple relations from and with matter known as the new materialisms (Barad 2007; Coole and Frost 2010; DeLanda 2006). Assemblages can be understood as interactions of heterogeneous entities, people, organizations, or cities (DeLanda 2006). Gilles Deleuze and Felix Guattari (1987) rely on the rhizome metaphor (see below) to unveil its main properties. According to these authors, one of these properties is connection: any point in a rhizome can be connected to another (1987, 7). This means that assemblages can adopt complex connections with ramifications branching in all directions; without having a clear beginning or end, but an intermediate part, i.e. a plateau. This plateau can be understood as a vibrating intensity, a continuum without a fixed goal (Figure 6.1).

Another principle is heterogeneity, which is explained by the form of all entity links (DeLanda 2006). That is, the whole is not just the sum of its parts, and neither can it be explained by the dominance of one entity. The third is the principle of multiplicity. An assemblage changes its nature and expands its connections (Deleuze and Guattari 1987, 8). However, the change cannot be attributed to any single entity (Farías

*Figure 6.1* Feminist rhizomes in the March 8, 2020 protest in Mexico City.

2011). Assemblages are multiple since they mobilize diverse ways of being in the world (Oslender 2017). The fourth principle has to do with rupture: in the words of Deleuze and Guattari (1987, 9), "a rhizome can break, shake itself, but it will regenerate again through old ramifications or create new ones." These ruptures mean, for example, that from an assemblage a counter-assemblage emerges. From this perspective, rather than creating dichotomies, it causes lines to be drawn between the ramifications and their ruptures. The fifth principle is mapping. An assemblage draws its ramifications like a moving map without a predefined structure. This movement has more to do with the capacity of the entities and not with the binary relationships from the various positions of the entities. I contend that the counter-assemblage concept offered by the assemblage theory allows us to better understand the relationship between feminist activism and digital violence.

## Methods

This chapter is based on a **digital ethnography** that can be described as a research strategy for analyzing digital culture (Hine 2015; Pink et al. 2015). Digital ethnography is not limited to what happens online; rather, it seeks to make visible the intertwinings between digital and analog spaces (Murthy 2011). As a process intertwined between on and off site research that were continued online, our digital ethnography began in January 2018 and culminated in March 2020. During that time, the collection of various sources of information was conducted. First, 14 face-to-face interviews were conducted with activist members of various feminist collectives. All interviews were face-to-face and had an open format. On average, they lasted between an hour and an hour and a half. The activists are working on their own collective projects or with non-governmental organizations at the intersection of human rights, technology, and feminisms. The interviews revolved around the following topics: their historical trajectory as feminist activists; their position and notion of self-care, self-defense, digital security; the role that technologies have had in transforming the ways of doing feminist politics, their own meanings of politics, and feminism, as well as meanings of a feminist Internet; the relationship between digital and non-digital violence, the most relevant projects of their activism; the relationship between human rights and digital rights; the relationship and tensions between different feminist positions; legislation against digital violence and the relationship with the state.

Another source of information was ethnographic notes from participant observation of social networks, blogs, and websites of the collectives. These included, first, face-to-face participant observation in workshops on various topics such as digital security, feminist self-defense, feminist Internet, and digital literacy, technofeminism, and documentation through field notes and visual records of the March 8, 2020 protest in Mexico City. Second, online observation of various events such as hacktivism days; the #NoMeCuidanMeViolan protest of August 16, 2019; as well as a series of video interviews called "Hackear/nos." It was possible to collect various audiovisual and textual materials such as reports from collectives derived from web pages.

In this article, the ethnographic approach focuses on the case of the Mexican feminist collective Luchadoras that was created in 2012. They define themselves as a collective that inhabits digital and physical public space (Luchadoras 2020). Their mission is to promote processes of personal and collective political transformation through the creation and dissemination of stories, the appropriation of information and communication technologies, the construction of an Internet free of violence and the creation of meeting spaces that claim knowledge and dignify the knowledge, strength, and power of women (ibid.). One of the political bets of the collective is that digital violence is determined to be "violence" because it has an impact on bodies (Luchadoras, personal communication 2018). As of March 2020, Luchadoras had three members, who could be interviewed face-to-face on four different occasions during the period in which the digital ethnography was conducted. On one occasion, a joint interview was conducted with two of the three members. Various textual and visual materials were also collected from their website, in addition to following up on their social media posts from which field notes emerged.

## Bodies, Affects, and Technologies as Assemblages of Activism

Gender violence has been one of the political causes around for rhizomic collectives emerging throughout Mexico. In that country, there are known to be 10.3 femicides daily, and it is estimated that around 93.7% of the cases are never reported because impunity prevails (Clercq Ortega and Sánchez Lara 2018; Xantomila 2020).

In the interviews, it could be identified that the 2011 mobilizations in Mexico were key for young people to politicize themselves to fight against the manipulation of information by the media. In the specialized literature, the #YoSoy132 movement was celebrated because the multitudes of connected young people mobilized new forms of technopolitics. The mobilization had a wide reach, achieving nationwide protests and international solidarity. However, from these mobilizations emerged an articulated assemblage around an intense and heterogeneous ramification of feminist collectives that marked a clear rupture in their ways of doing politics. These collectives criticized the discourses of the Internet's potential linked to technopolitics to show that gender violence continues within the very same spaces of political mobilization that also extended to the Internet. From there, various collectives began to politicize the

Internet, also by anti-feminist activists. In the interviews, the narrative clearly emerged that the Internet is not only a technology to be appropriated, but also a political space where power relations continue, which had to be occupied in order to resist.

Two moments were experienced that can be characterized as intense moments of mobilizations and creation of counter-assemblages. One of these moments, was on April 24, 2016 with the march #Vivasnosqueremos (#WeWantUsAlive) that multiplied in 40 different cities in Mexico. The march involved actions that extended to the Internet through hashtags of key slogans such as #EstadoFeminicida (#FeminicideState) to hold the state responsible for gender violence.

However, the assemblages of bodies appropriating technologies do not just refer to the feminists. Counter assemblages also emerged of anti-feminist agitators who would send abusive messages to discipline and "correct" the feminists' behavior. The feminist collective Luchadoras (Barrera and Rodríguez 2017) documented the testimonies of eleven of the organizers of the mobilization in which they faced aggressions as a result of the visibility they had on social networks: insults, attempts to hack their devices or accounts. Some of them received threatening phone calls and others even reported aggressions by shock groups that identified them and went to their homes to attack their properties in a clear example of how digital violence is indeed real violence (ibid.). These mobilizations resulted in an explosion of even more feminist collectives that continued to organize to politicize the Internet motivated by their experiences of various ways of being affected by digital violence in response to their political mobilization activities.

In 2019, as throughout Latin America, Mexico experienced another moment of intense feminist mobilizations, following two cases of the rape of women at the hands of four policemen in Mexico City. Women filled public spaces like rhizomes without a beginning or end in 18 cities, as well as the streets of the Internet through photos, performances, and hashtags to demand justice, a stop to impunity, and an end to violence in Mexico. The protest caught the public's attention because the participants relied on multiple affective repertoires guided by rage to carry out acts of civil disobedience such as protests outside the police station and graffiti on historical monuments accompanied by the hashtags #NoMeCuidanMeViolan (#TheyDoNotTakeCareofMeTheyRapeMe) or #MeCuidanMisAmigasNoLaPolicia (#MyFriendsTakeCareOfMeNotThePolice). Following these protests, women activists and human rights defenders themselves experienced waves of digital violence with coordinated actions (Suárez et al. 2022). The hashtags #AsiNoMujeres (#NotLikeThatLadies) and #NoMeRepresentan (#TheyDoNotRepresentMe) began to trend, revealing the expressive dimensions of assemblies to discredit feminist resistance by pointing out that this is not the "proper" way to protest.

The plateaus, as intense moments of rhizomes between the streets of the Internet and those of the public space, have in common the emergence of counter-assemblages that were expressed in forms of digital violence through various formats: corrective threats and discrediting of the cause, ostensibly for the "manner" in which women protested, or the perceived lack thereof.

Thus, key moments of feminist protests in 2016 and 2019 were followed by waves of digital violence visited upon the key collectives. One of these collectives, Luchadoras, then organized a three-day workshop held in 2017 with 25 activists who experienced digital violence after their participation in the march. The aim was to name the affectations they had suffered online. In the workshop, the activists gave testimonies about the various attacks they experienced. They then poured them into a body map. This is a cardboard where activists literally drew a silhouette of each activist's body and marked the impacts of digital violence. A member of the collective recounts her experience as follows "(…) it was the first time that the attendees named and connected the aggressions, with the impacts on their body" (Luchadoras, personal communication, March 9, 2018). Based on the map and the testimonies, Luchadoras made a typology of digital violence, contrasting it with categories from international organizations. Subsequently, they published the typology in the document: "Online violence against women in Mexico" (2020). This document is the first in the country to incorporate the most complete typology of digital violence with a total of 13 categories that include various practices and bodily harm.

Similarly, after the protests carried out in August 2019, the main feminist collectives again experienced digital violence. In the words of a member of Luchadoras (personal communication October 14, 2019), there was a massive wave of hate against feminism from the march. In only two days after the protest, this collective received 300 comments with coordinated actions that had the same mode of operation: making corrective threats with photos of cut-up women's bodies. The effect was a series of affectations in the bodies of the Luchadoras, such as fear, nervousness, desire to vomit, feelings of intimidation, and crying. Luchadoras were not the only ones; in sessions of the Women Human Rights Defenders Network, they realized that several other activists had also experienced digital violence as forms of correction and intimidation, as well as instilling fear with the aim of preventing future mobilization actions. The Mesoamerican Initiative of Women Human Rights Defenders made a statement where it spoke out against the defamation and criminalization campaign alluding to the legitimate right to protest and pointing out that these types of practices only contributed to continue normalizing and justifying the misogyny that prevails in Mexico (IM-Defensoras 2019).

In the workshop organized by the feminist collective, the body was reconnected to the Internet through returning the affectations to bodies

*From Networks to Assemblages* 75

*Figure 6.2* "Somos el grito de las que ya no estan – we are the cry of the ones that are not there no more"

with digital violence: bodily damage (sweating, nausea, crying, back, head, stomach, and kidney pain); emotional damage (nervous affectations, stress, anguish, anger, rage, anger, depression, paranoia, fear, confusion, impotence); damage to reputation, sexual damage, limitations to mobility, invasion of property, loss of identity (Barrera et al. 2018). This mapping was not only an exercise to document violence, it was instead a way to reterritorialize the Internet to create a collective subjectivity and put a name to what they were experiencing. In doing so, they made visible the processes of de/territorialization by counter-assemblages that also operate on the Internet as rhizomes to destabilize their feminist political projects.

Digital violence has consequences not only on women's bodies, but also on their political trajectories. In the case of women activists and human rights defenders, the collective identified coordinated trends of digital violence in the form of viral hate responses to public denunciations on social networks; the expulsion and demolition of the spaces of expression on the websites or social networks of activists, organizations, and media outlets that assume themselves to be feminist; organized attacks; extortion under threat of dissemination of intimate images without consent; state espionage and also smear campaigns (ibid.). These tendencies were clearly aimed at silencing and intimidating them for their political activities.

Both moments of intensity show that, in addition to the appropriation of digital technologies to inhabit the Internet as a political space, one of the main feminist strategies was to put the body at the forefront with a double objective: as the locus of resistance, but at the same time to politicize technologies through giving back the materiality to the digital space by politicizing their bodies and their affectations. These collectives are making visible that digital violence has materiality and causes damage within female bodies. This also vindicates the political potential of female bodies and their affects. Thinking materiality more broadly allows us to understand affects and politics. On the one hand, the fear that is used as a disciplining mechanism after the marches and, on the other hand, the rage and fed-up-ness that women incorporate in their repertoires in the resistance against impunity (Figure 6.2).

## Conclusion

This article has explored the theory of assemblages to analyze forms of feminist resistance in the digital age. It accounts for the strategies of feminist collectives in politicizing that space through assembling bodies to rhizomic networks to make visible the ways in which they are affected through violence, but at the same time exhibiting a capacity for agency central to affects such as rage at the impunity of gender violence. Bodies and technologies formed heterogeneous and multiple assemblages that then caused counter-assemblages. It also shows how the focus on the body allows to broaden the understanding of materiality to articulate a critique of the Internet as a political space of disciplining, violence, and control. In this way, the understanding of materiality is broadened to incorporate the connections between bodies, their affects, technologies, and objects that together forming political assemblages account for new forms of feminist activisms in the digital age.

## Key Words

**Assemblages**: Assemblages can be understood as interactions of heterogeneous entities, people, organizations, or cities (DeLanda 2006).

**Digital Ethnography**: Digital ethnography can be described as a research strategy for analyzing digital culture (Hine 2015; Pink et al. 2015). Digital ethnography is not limited to what happens online; rather, it seeks to make visible the intertwining between digital and analog spaces (Murthy 2011).

**Feminist Activism**: Feminist activism is action grounded in the resistance to systematic forms of oppression, an emotional bond to feminists, and being embedded in political and/or feminist-centered organizations.

**Institutional Violence**: Institutional violence is a form of interpersonal violence resulting from the existence of such institutions as the police and prisons and from the practices of repressive justice.

**Networks**: A network is a social structure that exists between various actors—individuals or organizations. Networks function in order to connect people and organizations through various forms of relations.

## Critical Thinking Questions

1  What challenges face feminist activism in this century?
2  How is it possible to fight digital violence after feminist protest that aims to silence activists?
3  What theoretical challenges make visible the continuum between feminist activism and digital violence?

## References

Barad, Karen. 2007. *Meeting the Universe Halfway: Quantum Physics and the Entanglement of Matter and Meaning.* London: Duke University Press.
Barrera, Lourdes, and Candy Rodríguez. 2017. "La Violencia En Línea Contra Las Mujeres En México." Ciudad de México. https://luchadoras.mx/informe-onu/
Barrera, Lourdes, Anaiz Zamora, Érika Pérez, Ixchel Aguirre, and Jessica Esculloa. 2018. "Violencia Política a Través de Las Tecnologías Contra Las Mujeres En México." Ciudad de México. https://luchadoras.mx/informe-violencia-politica/
Clercq Ortega, Juan Antonio Le, and Gerardo Rodríguez Sánchez Lara. 2018. "Índice Global de Impunidad." *San Andrés Cholula.* https://www.udlap.mx/igimex/assets/files/2018/igimex2018_ESP.pdf
Coole, Diana, and Samantha Frost. 2010. *New Materialisms: Ontology, Agency, and Politics: Diana Coole, Samantha Frost.* Durham: Duke University Press.
DeLanda, Manuel. 2006. *A New Philosophy of Society Assemblage Theory and Social Complexity.* New York: Continuum.
Deleuze, Guilles, and Felix Guattari. 1987. *A Thousand Plateaus Capitalism and Schizophrenia.* Minneapolis, MN: University of Minnesota Press.
Farías, Ignacio. 2011. "The Politics of Urban Assemblages." *City* 15, no. 3, 4: 365–74. https://doi.org/10.1080/13604813.2011.595110
Hine, Christine. 2015. *Ethnography for the Internet: Embedded, Embodied and Everyday.* London: Bloomsbury Academic.
IM-Defensoras. 2019. "MÉXICO/Campaña de Difamación y Criminalización Contra Defensoras Feministas." *Facebook.* 2019. https://www.facebook.com/IMDefensoras/posts/2550376701710012

Luchadoras. 2020. Somos una colectiva feminista que habita el espacio público digital y físico. Retrieved 4 September 2020, from https://luchadoras.mx/nosotras/

Murthy, Dhiraj. 2011. "Emergent Digital Ethnographic Methods for Social Research." In *Handbook of Emergent Technologies in Social Research*, edited by Sharlene Hesse-Biber, 158–79. New York: Oxford University Press.

Oslender, Ulrich. 2017. "Ontología Relacional y Cartografía Social: ¿hacia Un Contra-Mapeo Emancipador, o Ilusión Contra-Hegemónica?" *Tabula Rasa*, no. 26: 247–62. https://doi.org/10.25058/20112742.n26.12

Pink, Sarah, Heather Horst, John Postill, Larissa Hjorth, Tania Lewis, and Jo Tacci. 2015. *Digital Ethnography*. London: Sage.

Segato, Rita. 2016. *La Guerra Contra Las Mujeres*. Madrid: Traficantes de Sueños.

Suárez, Marcela, Yulissa Juárez, and Piña-García-Carlos. 2022. "Toxic Social Media: Affective Polarization After Feminist Protests." *Social Media + Society*. https://doi.org/10.1177/20563051221098343

Xantomila, Jessica. 2020. "ONU: Feminicidios En México Crecieron Diariamente de 7 a 10 En Tres Años." *La Jornada*, 5 March 2020. https://www.jornada.com.mx/ultimas/sociedad/2020/03/05/onu-feminicidios-en-mexico-crecieron-de-7-a-10-diarios-en-tres-anos-8647.html

# 7 Navigating Nii'kinaaganaa (All My Relations) Online

*Joey-Lynn Wabie and Michelle Kennedy*

At the social level, digital media are effective tools for social interaction, operating as a space for conversation and connecting people, but can also act as a window into the lives of others. The harnessing of social and digital media tools allows diverse Indigenous voices to reach Indigenous and non-Indigenous people in Canada and internationally. The flexibility of multi-platformed, conversational learning is that it has the potential to impact both social media users and non-users in a manner that promotes learning and sharing perspectives across the world. In this chapter, we discuss the intricate realities of maneuvering Indigenous knowledges/perspectives online that push past boundaries, shift delivery, and question what should/should be shared from an Anicinabe ikwe and Onyota'a:ka perspective.

> We want to make it clear we do not speak for all Indigenous Peoples since there are many nations across Turtle Island which are all distinct, holding their own languages, traditions, and teachings. We use the term Indigenous within this chapter only for the ease of the reader. We encourage each of you to reach out to the Indigenous people within your territory to learn more.

Indigenous knowledge and ways of being are relational and connected not only to one another, but also with the elements of Mother Earth and the universe. Indigenous peoples have connection to the earth, water, fire, and air elements and are in constant relationship with Grandfather Sun, Grandmother Moon, the stars, and beyond. This is what many Indigenous people refer to as: Nii'kinaaganaa (nee-kuh-naw-guh-naw), which can be translated to "all my relations" (Shawanda 2020, 38). It is part of the Seven Grandfather Teachings (Benton-Banai 1988) where we learn about Humility; to know we can never know everything in its totality, we can only know that we don't, or can't, know everything and accept it. The beyond is something we may never see but we know it's there. With **relationality** and Indigenous ways of being, knowing, and doing, we live our time on Mother Earth in human form trying to come to some sort of agreement with ourselves and all our relations so we can live together, and live well as we are doing it.

*Figure 7.1* The image from Jordain Mirasty's Facebook post shows us how to remember our relations through their use of social media tools: "Company Interests. This painting represents how Canada enforces the rcmp to violently remove Indigenous people from fighting against the pipelines going through our lands; the black snake. What's STILL going on in Wetsuweten is what made me want to make this painting" (@Jordain Mirasty, May 5, 2022).

Over the last thirty years, technology has increased in its ability to connect us to each other through the Internet. Its delivery has improved, moving from dial up connection which required a landline to where we are today: Many people within Turtle Island (Canada, US, Mexico) can access the world wide web from their phones, tablets, laptops, and computers. Our access to others via the world wide web has widened Indigenous relationality guidelines to include a much larger group of people (Figure 7.1).

We, an Alqonquin Anicinabe ikwe and an Onyota'a:ka woman, will describe the technological effects of relationality in this chapter and what it means for Indigenous people. We will share stories along the way which we hope you enjoy, and leave you with a few questions to employ your critical thinking skills. We have arranged our chapter in a circle and within Anishinaabe protocols (which is the territory in the land where we live) we will move clockwise around. In the east, is where we begin and situate ourselves and our topic. We then move to the south and relate our topic to our own experiences, then to the west where we incorporate critical thinking about navigating nii'kinaaganaa (all my relations). We then end in the north, which is the doing stage, where we incorporate the knowledge and chapter content and act on it. This completes the circle for the chapter which can begin again by rereading. A circle never ends.

## East – Where We Always Start

First, let's forget about the notion that Indigenous people must completely return to the old ways in order to be legitimate or taken seriously. A common mainstream perception puts Indigenous cultures at odds with the modern world, although Indigenous peoples have always been adept at fitting new technologies to their cultures (Younging 2018). This is not something that is unique to Indigenous people. All humans have adapted along the years, through the generations, to the spot where you are at right now, reading this chapter. You could be sitting on a bus, in class with your headphones listening to music, lying in bed, or on a plane, all while reading this right now. You might even be listening to it via audiobooks. We have all come a long way from the technological world that our grandparents lived in.

Many Indigenous people have adapted well to new technologies. We think about the beautiful floral beadwork that was created by the Métis when beads became available or the use of canvas on Indigenous built structures such as tipis and wiigwams which increased portability and ease of set-up and take-down. Many positives came from technology shared with the newcomers and vice versa. Unfortunately, there were also catastrophic events that need to be acknowledged about our (Indigenous and non-Indigenous) history including the displacement of Indigenous peoples on their own lands, and the erasure of their culture, identity, and languages through the enactment of Canada's Indian Act policies. These policies included the enforcement of residential schools, the enfranchisement process, the banning of ceremonies up until 1951, among others.

These are the historical realities that Indigenous people have faced, and still experience to this day through systemic and institutional racism, and the present policy enforcement of the amended Indian Act. These historical and current events have had long-lasting intergenerational impacts on our people, although we are still here, strong in our culture, traditions, and way of life. We remain connected. We can, and have the ability to, adapt to many things in the same way non-Indigenous people have adapted. We have also brought many inventions to the mainstream population which are still being used today. Chewing gum, toboggans, canoes, and maple syrup (Toulouse 2018) to name a few.

Now that we have touched on the realities that Indigenous people have historically and presently face, we would like to discuss relationality, what it means for Indigenous people, and how technology has impacted the ways in which we connect and interact with all our relations.

## "Let Me Tell You a Story..." By Joey-Lynn Wabie

When we would go up north (northwestern Quebec) back home that is where I knew who I was. I knew because that is where all of my family was: my cousins, aunties, uncles, and grandma. My cousins were the ones I would run in the bush with, make tipis and build fires, drink spring water, and also get into mischief by throwing rocks at the car windows in the junkyard. We would walk to town to get candy and walk back with sticky fingers on a sugar high. Those were the days before wireless technology when we would be gone for hours and our parents knew we were in the bush or walking to town and didn't think twice about it. Did they know the bush would keep us safe somehow? We shared the bush with all our relations and didn't even realize it. The animals and elements enveloped us and we never asked permission from them; we just did it and never thought twice.

As an adult now, I wish I could go back and ask for forgiveness for taking over a part of their world and mistaking it as mine to use as I wanted. I cringe when I think about the abandoned tipis and scorched earth from the fires we made, the kicking of rocks, the overturned logs, and the breaking of new saplings to forge our paths. I think the bush would forgive me, at least I hope so. All of those things that impacted the earth in my childhood many years ago have healed, but it must remember me though. I would if someone did that to me.

*Why do I share this story?* This story contains unconscious relationality from an adult's perspective about a child who used the bush to play. This child had no idea of the impact their presence had on all her relations. This child grew up, retained these memories, and is now able to relive them through the lens of an adult. The lens has shifted the way the memories are viewed and interpreted.

## South – Relating to One Another

*Why is this significant?* We want you, the reader, to take the concept of **unconscious relationality** and apply it to how you used technology in the past. Maybe it was for school and you put a topic of study into a search engine, or clicked on a link in an email that brought you to a website. Depending on your age, maybe it was texting with friends or playing interactive games via apps. Who were you relating to? Who was impacted by your presence?

There is significance in understanding unconscious relationality and how we can learn from it in the area of technology. Wise practices (Wesley-Esquimaux and Calliou 2010) come from sharing our unconscious relationality experiences with each other. Whether it be through telling our children not to give out their address to strangers in videogame chats, to not sharing passwords with friends; this is all because someone did it in the past with consequences. We learn from our mistakes, make things safer and improve it for others and for ourselves.

Storytelling is important in many cultures; Indigenous peoples have skillfully developed methodology through storytelling which allow for a deeper awareness of experiences to be elucidated, but are scarcely detailed in scholarly, peer-reviewed outlets (Hart 2004; Lavallee 2009; Tachine et al. 2016). It is where our knowledges, morals, ethics, and teachings get passed on to others with the ability to reach many generations at one time. If a grandparent shares a story and the family is listening then there are three generations listening to the story at that moment. Storysharing is one aspect within bundles that many Indigenous people carry with or within them. These bundles can be physical bundles with medicines, drums, and sacred items that can help heal people and other relations. Other types of bundles can be theoretical where the knowledge is known and stored within people as stories, scholarly work, crafting techniques, etc. **Digital bundles** (online Indigenous knowledge projects curated by Indigenous people) were introduced by Wemigwans in 2018. Digital bundles are on the precipice of perpetuating Indigenous resurgence and counteracting the impact of colonization, which continues to attack Indigenous communities today through land appropriation, and the destruction of water and land upon which they rely. Now, we can take our stories, medicines, teachings, lived experiences, etc. and place them in a digital bundle to share with the world via the Internet.

The landscape of sharing our stories, medicines, teachings, lived experiences has shifted once it is moved online. It reminds me of the description of culture under glass, where it is viewed frozen in time, captured in that one way for time immemorial (Antone et al. 2002). If we use the same concept of culture under glass and the sharing of stories, etc. online, it freezes the animate nature of Indigenous people's culture, and ways of being, knowing, and doing. Our stories, when told in person, shift each time they are told, they are never the same, which brings forward the organic and ever-changing nature of our ways. Medicines change with seasons and the impact of climate change can affect plants, which, in turn, may shift the medicinal uses or non-use in that cycle.

## West – Critical Thinking

With the advent of technology and its ability to both reach back and pull forward content that was written years ago is miraculous and daunting. We also grow in wisdom and insight as we age although our words, pictures, and things we share virtually leave an imprint online. Using wise practices, as we fumble through life learning as we go, we now can learn from others through their lessons. We need to think about our intentions with our relationship with the virtual world, understanding that we cannot practice unconscious relationality without consequences. As we interact with virtual realities, being intentional, mindful, and aware of the impact of our presence is imperative. We want to continue having good relations with others, whether they are virtual or in-person. There is someone on the receiving end of the messages we share online, passive or active, who can react.

## Michelle Kennedy's Story

Michelle shares a story below about safe spaces and cultural protocols that can be used as a wise practice online: Working and attending school online has changed the way we interact with one another, how we dress, and even the option of who we talk to. In the fall of 2021, wearing my favorite Zoom suit (pajamas on the bottom with a nice shirt on top) I attended one of my weekly colloquium classes through Zoom as a PhD student in the Cultural Studies program at Queen's University. I had a lot on my mind on this particular day as I found out earlier that week that Dr. Carrie Bourassa had been making false claims of having an Indigenous identity (Pedri-Spade and Pitawanakwat 2022, 23). Many of my colleagues and friends had been affected by the news and were left to pick up the pieces of the fallout that Bourassa left behind.

The day had been filled with reflection on how I can improve my own research relationships by verifying that a person who is identifying themselves as an Indigenous person is telling the truth. As I attended class from the comfort of my home in Sudbury, as did many other students from their respective cities, we started class via Zoom. The organizers had created "breakout rooms" where students would manually be redirected to smaller groups. The purpose of these smaller breakout sessions was to check-in with one another and see how everyone is doing. I briefly shared some of the thoughts I had in regard to false claims to identity within research and academic institutions. A non-Indigenous student in my cohort added to my check-in and mentioned that the ongoing issue of settlers taking up Indigenous identity had been resolved at Queen's University and all accused faculty and employees were verified as Indigenous. The comment created an unwelcoming and stressful learning environment as the quality of conversation dropped drastically after that. This comment was distracting, upsetting, and insensitive as the issue of settlers appropriating identity at Queen's University is not resolved. The remainder of the breakout session was quiet upon returning to the main Zoom room and I was quite irritated by the ignorance of the comment. This provided me with the impetus to reflect and act to restore relationships with other Indigenous students in my cohort.

Keeping this interaction in mind, I reevaluated my level of sharing during the check-in portion with other settler students and faculty. Moving forward, I privately discussed my interaction with the course coordinator and an Anishinaabe-kwe peer and we were able to come to the conclusion that safer spaces need to take place for the benefit of Indigenous students' learning. What followed in the subsequent week was a much more positive interaction that created a safer learning environment. On hearing that a fellow Indigenous peer was struggling with mental health, we organized a breakout room for Indigenous students only. Now, to some this may seem exclusive, but remembering the isolated incident from the previous week, I was not willing to allow other Indigenous students to be a target of senseless comments. Altogether six Indigenous PhD students gathered and did a sharing circle. My peer and I sang a healing song for our classmate, albeit off beat thanks to the timing of Internet connections. While I am never ashamed to sing with my hand drum, I do know that having the Indigenous students' breakout room allowed me to more freely support my classmate in a way I knew how.

Interactions from learning online in a classroom via Zoom have taught me that having control over smaller spaces can be both beneficial and harmful to learners. In one scenario, it was harmful when I did not have control over who was in my space and there was no moderator. In another scenario, where space was taken or specifically created, it had a much better outcome. I also believe that had my initial "check-in" been in-person, the non-Indigenous student would not have made their comment because they had already shared how they were doing, and it is not protocol to interject and add more comments after someone is done speaking, as sharing circles follow a cyclical pattern (Lavallee 2009; Tachine et al. 2016) and there is no Uno card to reverse and get more speaking time.

## North – Doing

So, now what? How do Indigenous people move forward in a virtual world, while still maintaining safe spaces, respecting cultural protocols, and maintaining good relations with one another within a colonial system that was designed to assimilate them? We can use the past and share our wise practices from what we have learned. We would like to ensure they are used as guidelines and not rules. The amazing thing about our ways is that it is based on relationality and all of our relations; it is fluid, ever-changing, and adapting within itself. It does not require validation from other worldviews or perspectives, it stands on its own in power and strength.

When in doubt, go to the original source: Elders. Seeking out advice, knowledge and wisdom from Elders to moderate our intentional or unintentional digital bundles (cultural and spiritual content) is key. We can find Elders in urban areas such as Friendship Centers, cultural centers, or possibly even in post-secondary institutes within their Indigenous student centers. Elders can also be found in First Nation reserves: I would ask that you research ones near you and contact their cultural center or band office. There are protocols when asking advice or working with them, so please ask them! Each Elder is unique and has their own gifts to share.

Creating safe spaces within the virtual world for Indigenous people is crucial to the respectful sharing of content, whether it be spiritual, cultural, or their own individual perspectives. These spaces should be curated mindfully with guidance from each other. Just as Indigenous people create safe spaces offline through circles, gatherings, and ceremonies, the same can be done in the virtual world.

Moving forward with mindful relationality should be taken into account also as we are all navigating virtual spaces that are vast and seemingly unlimited. We should be mindful of our presence online since it can be quite easy to feel like we are shielded and have no impact when we are not in physical relation to one another. The virtual and offline world can intertwine and meet which adds to the complexity of it all. The more we understand we are all connected even if not physically, the more mindful we can be of our actions and presence.

## Conclusion

A new online environment has been made that allows us to share our culture, resist colonial policy, uplift others, and share with each other in ways that many of our ancestors (Indigenous and non-Indigenous) could not have dreamed about. In the east, we situated ourselves for the reader, then shared how skilled Indigenous people are at adapting to new technologies, and the concept of unconscious relationality was introduced via storytelling. We then moved on to the south where we shared a story about how wise practices are learned online, and how the absence of technology (in person, in ceremony) would have changed the group dynamic. In the west is where critical thinking about navigating nii'kinaaganaa (all my relations) online was introduced and discussed. We then ended in the north where we incorporate the knowledge and chapter content and act on it. Our chapter was written using Anishinaabe protocols where we move clockwise around and now find ourselves in the conclusion section. Perhaps this is where you will end your journey within the circle, or you may reread the chapter entering and journey around the circle again.

There are prophecies within Anishinaabe culture that talk about the "black boxes" that people can hold in their hand that will consume them as told to Joey-Lynn Wabie by the kokamig in Algonquin territory. This was told to them by the older generations and is passed down now to us. This prophecy allows us to incorporate wise practices so we are not consumed by the "black boxes," that we put them down and relate to one another face-to-face. We must have balance. This can be found with seeking Elders' wisdom, practicing mindful relationality, and creating safe spaces within the virtual world.

## Key Words

**Digital Bundles**: Digital bundles are online Indigenous knowledge projects curated by Indigenous people (Wemigwans 2018).
**Storysharing**: Sharing stories is a way we connect with each other, find commonalities, and bond as we share a space.

**Unconscious Relationality**: This keyword is described as how we relate to one another and our environment that we are not aware of. This includes the digital environment.

## Critical Thinking Questions

1 Wise practices that derive from unconscious relationality can encompass safety in online interactions but what are the consequences that we have not thought about from the rest of "all our relations"? Who are we missing within all our relations when we share online?
2 If we (Indigenous people, culture and traditions) are forever shifting and changing, then how can online digital bundles be curated in a manner that respects this and not be "frozen" in time and space? Who is receiving this knowledge? What are they doing with it?
3 In creating spaces for Indigenous Peoples online, why is it important to remember that each individual has varying expectations of what topics can be shared, who the topics can be shared with, and how the topics are shared?

## References

Antone, Robert, Diane Miller, and Brian Myers. 2002. *The Power within People: A Community Organizing Perspective.* Desoronto: Peace Trees Technology.

Benton-Banai, Eddie. 1998. *The Mishomis Book: The Voice of the Ojibway.* Minneapolis, MN: University of Minnesota Press.

Hart, Michael. 2004. *Seeking Mino-pimatisiwin: An Aboriginal Approach to Helping.* Halifax, NS: Fernwood Publishing Company.

Lavallee, Lynn. 2009. "Practical Application of an Indigenous Research Framework and Two Qualitative Indigenous Research Methods: Sharing Circles and Anishnaabe Symbol-Based Reflection." *International Journal of Qualitative Methods* 8, no. 1: 21–40. https://journals.sagepub.com/doi/10.1177/160940690900800103

Pedri-Spade, Celeste and Brock Pitawanakwat. 2022. "Indigenization in Universities and its Role in Continuing Settler-Colonialism." *Janus Unbound: Journal of Critical Studies* 1, no.11: 12–35. https://journals.library.mun.ca/ojs/index.php/JU/article/download/2377/pdf_1

Shawanda, Amy. 2020. "Baawaajige: Exploring Dreams as Academic References." *Turtle Island Journal of Indigenous Health* 1, no. 1: 37–47. https://doi.org/10.33137/tijih.v1i1.34020

Tachine, Amanda R., Eliza Yellow Bird, and Nolan L. Cabrera. 2016. "Sharing Circles: An Indigenous Methodological Approach for Researching with Groups of Indigenous Peoples." *International Review of Qualitative Research* 9, no. 3: 277–95. https://doi.org/10.1525/irqr.2016.9.3.277

Toulouse, Pamela. 2018. *Truth and Reconciliation in Canadian Schools.* Winnipeg, MB: Portage & Main Press.

Wemigwans, Jennifer. 2018. *A Digital Bundle: Protecting and Promoting Indigenous Knowledge Online.* Regina, SK: University of Regina Press.

Wesley-Esquimaux, Cynthia and Brian Calliou. 2010. *Best Practices in Aboriginal Community Development: A Literature Review and Wise Practices Approach.* Banff, AB: The Banff Centre.

Younging, Gregory. 2018. *Elements of Indigenous Style: A Guide for Writing By and About Indigenous Peoples.* Edmonton, AB: Brush Education.

# 8 Virtually Authentic?
## Digital Bodies, "Blank" Squares, and Staring Online

*Victoria Kannen*

What does your online body look like? What does it feel like? Maybe you haven't taken the time to think about it, but I'd like you to take a moment and imagine your online body.

Picture it in your mind.

Now, is your online body authentically *you*? This question may seem like an odd one but stay with me. Next question: Is your offline body authentically you? How can you tell?

We'll return to these later.

In the pandemic, our relationship with virtual **identity** was magnified by so many folks switching to primarily learning and working online. In meetings, online classrooms, and social interactions, we stare at screens which often include a view of ourselves. As a professor, I have pivoted from teaching in a classroom, where I rarely see myself to staring at my own face and shoulders, while simultaneously staring at my students – who are often empty, "blank" squares (see Figure 8.1). I am self-focused. I stare at my hair, my face, my nervous twinges, all while I am listening to my voice – recognizing it is being recorded. Although this is not new behaviour for many people, this is a novel, and sometimes, overwhelming world for the rest of us. Millennials and Gen Z (aka Zoomers) are often slotted into the judgment-full categories of narcissists, the self-obsessed, and the "me" generation. However, if you are on social media or use technology to facilitate connections online, you too are curating an online identity. So, let's ease up on judging folks for thinking about how their bodies are being presented. This isn't easy.

When opening Zoom or Microsoft Teams or any other number of communication apps, there is this moment where you have to decide if you want to show your face or not. If you do "Start Video," do you share your background, blur it, or use some sort of cat wallpaper? Do you fix your hair? Change the lighting? Adjust your clothes? These are split-second decisions, but they have become a mainstay of online interactions with the increasing use of video conferencing/collaboration platforms. Our **digital bodies** matter now more than ever and our relationships to them offer new identity formations. We are staring at ourselves, we are staring at avatars, and often we are staring at "blank" squares, but maybe we are

DOI: 10.4324/9781003310730-10

also reflecting on our bodies in ways that have been neglected: considering our online interactions with others, while also distanced from them, and recognizing the (im)materiality of our identities. In this chapter, I explore how reimagining our presentations of self can allow for new understandings of living online. When we curate our online appearances, where can we locate our authentic selves? What is the relationship between authenticity and online identity, anyway?

## The "Real" Me: Authenticity Online

George E. Newman and Rosanna K. Smith (2016) argue that authenticity is a fragmented concept. They say – in general – "authenticity is a concept aimed at capturing dimensions of truth or verification" (610). They go on,

> [a]nd yet, reflecting on the many ways in which people use the term authenticity reveals the limitations of this very broad definition. For example, even when evaluating the same entity, people may use very different criteria to evaluate authenticity; a diner from Iowa may define 'authentic Mexican food' very differently than a diner from Texas. Dutton (2003) highlights the complexities of this issue when he refers to authenticity as a 'dimension word' – a word whose specific meaning is uncertain until one knows which dimension of authenticity is being discussed.
> 
> (Newman and Smith 2016, 610)

Considering our relationship to authenticity online is incredibly challenging as so many of our interactions are mediated by filters, edits, deletions, fakes, and misleading curations. However, the "live" element of video conferencing enables some of those mediations to be eliminated via its synchronous elements. Are we, perhaps, more ourselves when synchronously video conferencing? Are our online engagements more real?

The inspiration for this chapter came from a recent teaching experience that I had. I returned to in-person teaching at my university, but we were all still wearing masks. As we were approaching the mid-way point of the semester, I decided to offer my students a synchronous virtual class instead of the in-person one that week. Everyone agreed. Most students noted how much they missed the familiarity of Zoom classes that they had been taking for the last few years. I, reluctantly, agreed with them because I missed teaching and being online too. For me, the most interesting moment that happened was when two students noted in the Zoom chat that it was so nice to see me, *the real me*. These comments stayed with me. Was the "me" that was standing in front of them for the last 6 weeks, not the real me? As I was unmasked and in my home, did the mask impact who I was that much or the physical space that I was in? Or, was it something else?

I have a few guesses. The position of my body in a virtual class is equalized to my students. We, presumably, are all sitting down. When standing, I am 6'3" tall. Even with my self-awareness of the potential to be intimidating and my best efforts at mitigating that, my stature is imposing. When I sit while teaching, I am on the same ground as them (so to speak).

Next, with my mask off, my facial expressions come through more clearly. They can see the position of my mouth, see my smile, and, perhaps, read my lips when necessary. This can make teaching more accessible, or, at the very least, comforting.

I also teach from home. While I am sitting in a fairly plain home office, a spatial intimacy is created when a glimpse at my home-life is offered. Some things about me are shared and learned.

Even the format of virtual synchronous teaching is also an implicit acknowledgement that we have all been through something, together. The format of the space is predicated on the pandemic we have all lived through and that sharing of an online experience can be comforting.

All of my guesses as to why these students felt they were seeing the real me are digitally **embodied**.

## What Is a Digital Body?

Before we can think about what it means to appear as a digital body, it is crucial to think through the connections between bodies, identities, and technologies. A body, in general, is a representation of who and how we are. It is the surface and structure through which our entire interactions, from birth to death, exist. Our bodies are made through our relationships with one another. "Our bodies exist within the boundaries of cultural structures and it is not possible for us to separate them from our social lives" (Kannen 2021, 6). In 2003, Susan Bordo a prominent feminist thinker on the politics of bodies, wrote that the body is "a powerful symbolic form, a surface on which the central rules, hierarchies, and even metaphysical commitments of a culture are inscribed and thus reinforced through the concrete language of the body. The body may also operate as a metaphor for culture" (165). This is referring to how our bodies are material objects, but they are also deeply symbolic and carry meanings with them that can change and differ throughout our lives and experiences. Digital bodies are challenging to define. The complex understanding and ever-changing idea of who and how we are via technological meditations is incredibly difficult to pinpoint. Below, I explore three key areas of understanding regarding what a digital body might be: an avatar, the Internet of Bodies, and/or politicized (re)imaginings of self.

Most of us have used avatars, at one point or another, to stand-in for our bodies in online spaces. As a reminder from the introduction, an avatar can be "a graphical representation of a person or character in a computer-generated environment, *esp.* one which represents a user in an interactive game or other setting, and which can move about in its surroundings and interact with other characters" (Oxford English Dictionary 2022) When we choose an avatar for ourselves it is an intentional element of our online existence. When considering our performances of self online, the intentional choices that we make when selecting an avatar, a profile picture, and so on to function as the representation of our selfhood (whether this is an idealized version or otherwise), which is meaningful both to ourselves and to how we foster relationships online. While an avatar can function as a representation of our online body, it might also reflect something completely disconnected from a body entirely.

According to Ulrike Schultze, "...users rely on their avatars as a medium for experiencing not only the virtual world but also themselves in it" (2014, 85). When thinking about our online bodies, these intentional elements are important to reflect on, as well as reflecting on how our bodies and identities are received and exist beyond our control. For example, Donna Z. Davis and Karikarn Chansiri (2019) explore the role of presentation of self online for disabled people and the ways that they navigate how to present themselves via avatars in various online spaces. They note, "[f]or all the participants, the ability to choose their avatar appearance was fundamental to their experience" (Davis and Chansiri 2019, 501). Their study showed that online freedom of expression encouraged disabled people to explore new forms of embodiment, reconnection, reconstruction, escape, opportunity, connection, community, fit, and engagement.

Next on our quest to define digital bodies, we could discuss the recent idea of the Internet of Bodies. This concept is based on the billion-dollar industry of personal devices that monitor physical bodies, usually for the purposes of health, and transmit the data collected to Fitbits, Apple watches, smart pacemakers, and so on. These devices are "worn, ingested, or surgically implanted in a human body, allowing the body to transmit information via the Internet. Based on this information, the body or device can in some cases be directly modified (as in the case of a smart pacemaker or insulin pump)" (Casey 2021, n.p.).

However, digital bodies may also be framed as enabling a new relationship to our physical embodiment. In a discussion of a virtual reality (VR) space, Carina Rogl claims,

> The feeling, while sometimes a bit dizzy-ing, is unlike anything else. When we enter virtual reality worlds, we genuinely feel we are there and our concept of our bodies shifts. In technical terms, we call this "embodiment." "Embodiment" is the possibility in VR to visually substitute a person's real body by a life-sized virtual one, seen from the person's own first-person perspective. In other words, when we place a VR headset on, our virtual bodies at least momentarily

substitute our real bodies. When we move, our virtual bodies move, and everything feels the same, even when we see our virtual bodies reflected in virtual mirrors. All of this induces a strong illusion of ownership and agency over the virtual body, which has proved to more broadly influence physiology, behaviour, attitudes and cognition. Embodiment is also the most advanced aspect of VR and it means that we can create experiences that are impossible to replicate in real life...

(Rogl 2020, n.p.)

Our digital bodies are also political representations. In keeping with the discussion of conferencing/collaboration platforms, we can think about how technology is mediating our understandings of appearance and language, and the choices that we make when we choose to present ourselves to others online. Ahmet Atay (2020) wrote a compelling personal essay entitled "Digital Eco System: Cyber Bodies, Cyber Lives, and Cyber Narratives." In it, they craft a narrative of their digital body that is deeply connected to their art, voice, and the power of narrative.

I thus situate myself as a transnational queer diasporic body, living in our highly digitalized U.S. culture in order to make sense of the different elements of my interactions with technology. I discuss the ways in which I embody the digital culture and perform my digitalized identities as I digitally narrate my stories and make sense of these stories as a life-writing method. Mine is a culturally-infused transnational and diasporic queer digital story. I am also a queer storyteller, a digital body.

(Atay 2020, 318)

A digital body can be best understood as an extension of our offline bodies. The technological effect on our body is enabling our bodies to extend their reach, while retaining their material properties. Maurice Merleau-Ponty (2003) describes this extension in his example of a blind person and the extension of the person's sense of touch through their use of a walking stick or using other tools. The Internet is the tool through which our digital body is manifested. Its form and shape are altered, crafted, and potentially ever-changing.

## Staring and "Blank" Squares Online

To be "blank" implies that something is bare, empty, or plain. It's not quite right to say that the squares we see in video conferencing where people do not turn on their cameras are "blank," but what are they? They often contain a name, either a generic avatar, or a photo that someone has chosen to present themselves.

94  *Victoria Kannen*

*Figure 8.1* Default "blank" avatar in Zoom.

There could be a wide variety of reasons that people choose to keep their cameras off during a video conference. Are we to presume that this "blankness" is them showing us who they really are? No, but what might be the impact of "blank" squares?

For those of us who choose to always be on camera when in a meeting or class, there can be a self-consciousness about what we look like and how we are seen – at least, from the waist up. This is also why so many people decide to not start their videos in the first place (amongst a variety of other reasons, such as classism, racism, and sizeism to name a few). What we are talking about is a digital presentation of self or the absence of one. The stare that being visually present online engenders can be an unsettling one. As Rosemarie Garland-Thomson notes, "[w]e relish looking, produce endless images, and root our understanding of the world in observation. Indeed, most information comes to us through sight in this intensely technological world saturated with advertising and crowded with computer, television, and video screens" (2009, 25). Whenever we stare at the face and bodies of other people, the relationship that is created has consequences – in terms of communication, meaning-making, and the emotions it fosters in both the starer and the staree. The basis for a stare is simple. Garland-Thomson states, "[w]e stare when ordinary seeing fails, when we want to know more. So staring is an interrogative gesture that asks what's going on and demands the story. The eyes hang on, working to recognize what seems illegible, order what seems unruly, know what seems strange" (2009, 3). Our world is highly organized through visual understanding as we depend on sight as the primary sensory outlet that structures our being in the world, even when it is problematic to do so.

Online staring can be a relatively safe outlet because the very foundation of conferencing platforms is staring-based; all participants are staring towards those people who turn their cameras on (as the squares are often organized with video imagery taking precedence). We stare to connect, we stare to relate, we stare to understand, but what is the impact?

Remember earlier when I asked if your online body was authentically you? Consider this: Jenny L. Davis (2012) notes that online authenticity is verified through at least three criteria. These indicators posit that you must project your identity consistently, you must stay committed to your personal values, and that you appear to be spontaneous, but natural in social interactions. All of these guidelines are intended for you to offer an impression that your self is one "that appears to be, rather than a self that is accomplished" (Davis 2012). In the decade since these guidelines were created, I argue that our online selves should always be understood as both of these ideas – they are who we are *and* they are accomplished. We create what our digital bodies and identities are, much more so than we often can offline. As Garland-Thomson states, "while social rules script staring, individual improvisation can take the staring encounter in fruitful directions. Staring, in other words, makes things happen between people" (2009, 33). We are watching ourselves being watched by others and this gives us some control over the act of looking. We also have more control over the virtual frame (think: square Zoom box) through which that looking occurs *or doesn't*. The digital presentation of self that I craft is the authentic version of me in the moment I present it. I accomplish that self through my online decision-making and this can be a very empowering act of creating my digital body. It is who I am and, perhaps, the version of me that is most "real."

## Key Words

**Digital Body**: A digital body can be best understood as an extension of our offline bodies. The technological effect on our body is enabling our bodies to extend their reach, while retaining their material properties.

**Embodied/Embodiment**: Embodiment is the expression or representation of our bodies in a readable, material, or visible form. It is the process of given a concrete form to an abstract idea.

**Identity**: An identity is some element of who we are that we understand in relation to someone or something else. Kannen defines identity as, "…a relational process through which we understand ourselves/others/groups at any given time in any given place" (2013, 179). This means that identity is not a neutral or absolute fact, but identities are actually variable and context-dependent.

## Critical Thinking Questions

1. What is your relationship to being on or off camera when you are online? How does it make you feel?
2. Has this chapter challenged you to consider or reconsider what form or shape you imagine your digital body to be? Why or why not?

## References

Atay, Ahmet. 2020. "Digital Eco System: Cyber Bodies, Cyber Lives, and Cyber Narratives." *International Review of Qualitative Research* 13, no. 3: 317–31.

"avatar, n.". OED Online. September 2022. *Oxford University Press*. https://www-oed-com.librweb.laurentian.ca/view/Entry/13624?redirectedFrom=avatar (accessed November 20, 2022).

Bordo, Susan. 2003. *Unbearable Weight: Feminism, Western Culture, and the Body*. Berkeley and Los Angeles: University of California Press.

Casey, Cat. 2021. "The Internet of... Bodies?" EDRM Blog. Accessed August 3, 2022. https://edrm.net/2021/01/the-internet-of-bodies/

Davis, Donna Z. and Karikarn Chansiri. 2019. "Digital Identities – Overcoming Visual Bias through Virtual Embodiment." *Information, Communication & Society* 22, no. 4: 491–505.

Davis, Jenny L. 2012. "Accomplishing Authenticity in a Labor-Exposing Space." *Computers in Human Behavior* 18, no. 2: 1966–73.

Garland-Thomson, Rosemarie. 2002. *Staring: How We Look*. Oxford: Oxford University Press.

Kannen, Victoria. 2013. "Pregnant, Privileged and PhDing: Exploring Embodiments in Qualitative Research." *Journal of Gender Studies* 22, no.2: 178–91.

Kannen, Victoria. 2021. *Gendered Bodies and Public Scrutiny: Women's Stories of Staring, Strangers, and Fierce Resistance*. Toronto: Women's Press.

Merleau-Ponty, Maurice. 2003. *Phenomenology of Perception*. Translated by Colin Smith. New York: Routledge.

Newman, George E. and Rosanna K. Smith. 2016. "Kinds of Authenticity." *Philosophy Compass* 11, no. 10: 609–18.

Rogl, Carina. 2020. "What is 'Embodiment' in Virtual Reality?" *Virtual Bodyworks*. Accessed August 3, 2022. https://www.virtualbodyworks.com/posts/what-is-embodiment-in-virtual-reality

Schultze, Ulrike. 2014. "Performing Embodied Identity in Virtual Worlds." *European Journal of Information Systems* 23: 84–95.

# 9 From a Group of Friends to a Mainstream Audience
## *Critical Role* and New Media Publics

*Betsy Brey and Elise Vist*

While **technological determinism** would have us believe that every cool and new thing that happens on the Internet (or new media in general) brings us to a more advanced, more prosperous future, digital media is not the "final form" of progress. There is more give-and-take between new media and traditional media depending on what the medium allows users to do. For example, a highly digital community, the previously **intimate public** of *Critical Role* (CR) has now become a mainstream, traditional media property. In other words, a **public** that is no longer an intimate public.

First, we'll explain how CR, a live-play tabletop role-playing *Dungeons and Dragons* game streamed on platforms like Twitch and YouTube, initially developed an intimate public online, making use of digital affordances to create a unique culture and community distinct from traditional *Dungeons & Dragons* (D&D). This intimate public supported different modes of play that prioritised role-playing, identity, emotional connections and relationships between players and characters. Because this was so different from traditional D&D culture, CR reshaped the public perception of D&D to match its values of play and digitality. Now that CR is canonised as official content within both D&D official merchandise and within its own media empire, it is no longer a unique intimate public. What this shows us, then, is that the relationship between digital media and traditional media is not one-way, but instead that these two media inform, interact, and build upon each other.

## The Affordances of Publics and Intimate Publics Online

The ways we interact with technology is shaped by the specifics of its design elements, otherwise known as affordances. Affordances, according to Don Norman (2013), are the sets of actions provided to users of an object by the design of the object itself. Because online spaces and digital media have different affordances than physical spaces and physical media, communities can form in different ways online than we do in person. One way of understanding how groups of people interact with their media, whether that's physical or digital, is the concept of publics. Although

DOI: 10.4324/9781003310730-11

we could use the term audience to describe the "active, critically aware, and discriminating" viewers of popular media, scholars sometimes use the term publics to emphasise the power that this audience has (Jenkins 2006, 135). Offline, in physical spaces, scholars have understood publics to be a group of citizens in a public space who express, develop, and share opinions and "articulat[e] the needs of society and the state" (Habermas 1991, 176). However, as a result of the affordances of digital spaces, "networked technologies reorganise how information flows and how people interact with each other," so online publics work differently than those in physical spaces (Boyd 2010, 41). Where offline publics are restricted to those people who can meet in generally the same time and space (like at a protest), online publics are not limited by time or geography and can exist asynchronously on social networking sites like Twitter.

What's particularly special about online spaces and publics, though, is that these spaces afford both publicity (in that anyone can join them) and privacy (not everyone can see what's happening). In other words, we can form intimate publics online (Morrison 2011). Intimate publics online are distinct from publics online because they are relatively small, reciprocal communities made up of people that don't quite fit into the public. Instead of retreating to the private space of a home when you don't fit into the larger public, you can instead find an intimate public of people who are similarly unwelcome in the public and share a desire to interact with you and others like you. Intimate publics are more likely to form when a small online space affords emotional intimacy through the following: two-way communication and reciprocity, both synchronous and asynchronous interaction, and both searchability and privacy simultaneously (Morrison 2011).

Certain communities benefit more than others from this reciprocal two-way communication, a combination of synchronous and asynchronous interaction, all in a space that is findable but not entirely public. For example, although a large, public fandom like Star Wars makes use of social media that support those affordances, they don't need them in the same way that the queer fans and fans of colour do. That is, if a fan likes Star Wars in all the expected and traditional ways, there's no risk in posting about their fandom online. However, if a fan wants a queer main character in a Star Wars movie, or believes that there should be Asian and Black characters on screen, they are likely to experience gatekeeping from other fans "largely to reinforce traditional norms" (Coddington and Holton 2014, 242). When you say something outside the norm of a public or fandom, it puts you at risk of being (at best) asked to leave and (at worst, but still quite likely) harassed and threatened with violence. It makes sense, then, that the people who make use of the affordances of intimate publics online are frequently those whose desires are out of line with the public fandom, and who need a community where they can find people who relate to the feelings they have. Necessarily, then, their communities are relatively small and highly protective: its members are used to being shamed by outsiders, so they group together for safety and care.[1]

## Critical Role as Intimate Public of D&D

Dungeons and Dragons (D&D) is a table-top role playing game where players take on the personality and actions of a character in the fictional game designed by the Game Master, or GM. Players interact with each other and the GM in a fantasy-based setting. D&D was originally published in 1974 by Gary Gygax and Dave Arneson, and in the five decades since, it has developed a public of players, GMs, and fans worldwide. Originally modelled after wargames that were popular during the 1970s, D&D was a fantasy-genre reimagining of playing out a conflict between two or more players, all commanding opposing armed forces in a simulation of a battle. D&D was originally a very competitive, antagonistic kind of game where a GM would set up challenges and the players would fight to the last in order to beat those challenges. Traditional D&D rewards what is called the hegemony of play, "a complex layering of technological, commercial and cultural power structures have… creat[ed] an entrenched status quo which ignores the needs and desires of 'minority' players" (Fron et al. 2007, 309).

Although the stereotypical D&D player is a "nerdy" boy in his teens, the contemporary reality of D&D players is far from its stereotypical roots and portrayal in popular culture. While the white, straight, cisgender male is still a dominant voice in D&D culture, it's not because they are the most numerous. Players are, of course, more diverse, but many are excluded from this public, because "geek culture" itself is often thought of as the domain of the perceived straight, white, cis male players (Salter and Blodgett 2017). So, when it comes to D&D's public, it has been in the best interest of Wizards of the Coast, the company that now owns and sells D&D, to keep a normative expectation. Basically, it is in the company's best financial interests to keep acting like the stereotypical player makes up their player base and create products for them accordingly.

However, the show *Critical Role*, an actual-play D&D show, initially aired on Twitch, was not made up of – or for – that stereotypical player. Initially, the affordances of Twitch live streaming allowed CR to create quick, low-budget weekly content that, in turn, created the community that would soon develop around this "bunch of friends playing RPGs in their living rooms" (Critical Role n.d.a). Although CR was not the first nor the last actual-play D&D show, they offered a different kind of D&D and thus invited in different kinds of D&D fans: fans who were excluded and thus needed the intimate public.

CR creates different expectations for D&D players both in terms of gameplay and game content. Because of CR's players and GM, many

D&D players now expect a more theatre-like gameplay, with heavy emphasis on role-playing. With a table of prolific voice actors, CR's table is less concerned with the minutiae of rules and more with collaborative storytelling and worldbuilding. In addition, CR offers fans a more diverse D&D world, with multiple queer playable characters, and their players representing gender expressions not always seen at the traditional D&D table. The women at the table are treated by the rest of the cast as full players, not oddities to be gawked at. Additionally, in behind-the-scenes interviews, male cast-members frequently discuss their own strained relationships to traditional masculinity. In combination, these relatively queer expressions of gender and sexuality create a D&D fandom in which feminism, queerness, and a gentler masculinity are considered the norm.

As a result, the fans that watched CR at the beginning of the show were not your normal D&D fans, and in many cases *weren't even D&D fans to start with*. For many in the CR audience, it was their first encounter with the game: either they'd been pushed out of D&D by its traditional fans, or just assumed it wouldn't appeal to them because of its public fandom. Through the small, relational community that developed around CR, its fans and cast-members soon became their own intimate public.

Although CR now boasts millions of viewers, its early streams celebrated their new viewers one by one as they joined the synchronous live chat. With this smaller number of viewers, the livestream's chat could hold conversations, which often included cast members, as fans reacted to the events in the game as they happened. Cast members had their phones or tablets open to the chat, and would comment on things "*The Chat*" was talking about or even solicit help from their more informed audience. This reciprocal, two-way communication created the feeling that both cast and audience were part of the same community.

However, even fans who did not participate synchronously could still interact with the show, especially those who create "fanworks." Cast members collected fanart from various social networking sites to display on the official CR website, during the weekly stream, and eventually in published art books. Another popular feature was the "GIF of the Week" competition that celebrated the often funny GIFs that fans would create and rewarding those fans who took time to make them. Because of the reciprocal, asynchronous communication between fanartists and cast, fans of CR had the ability to shape not just their own interpretation of the show, but that of other fans *and* the cast. This ability to shape the fandom made it feel more like an intimate public than a media fandom. Combined with the more inclusive norms, being a fan of CR at this time felt intimate and special, unlike traditional publics. Can you imagine feeling like you were friends with Stan Lee and had input on Tony Stark's suit design? This is how it worked in CR in its early years.

## The Publics Today: CR and D&D

The intimate public of CR was so drastically different from the traditional public that it revitalised and renewed popular culture interest in D&D as a whole. Because it attracted such a different audience, D&D fundamentally changed to better reflect its new public (Sidhu and Carter 2020, 4). Since its days as a wargame, D&D has been reproduced in new editions of the game, each with slightly different rules and systems. The traditional public of D&D would emphasise combat and exploration, minimising the role of social interaction. However, the most recent edition's emphasis on social interactions reveals a large shift away from the traditional public (Sidhu and Carter 2020, 4) seemingly creating a game that is more inclusive and less agonistic. It is crucial to note, however, that such changes to the game itself are not led by the publisher, but by players themselves, who create different kinds of play in their own games based on the set rules (Bryant 2009). Highly visible disruptions to the hegemony of play, like CR, act to represent the new public of D&D.

This looks like a new D&D format, one that takes advantage of the affordances of digital media and challenges the old hegemony, building on and overtaking the old D&D. Although CR does not represent the *traditional* public of D&D, it now represents D&D's current public. And as part of the popularisation of geek culture, D&D has shifted from its heavily combat-focused roots to a game with more focus on social and role-play aspects--in addition to fighting off hordes of goblins, of course (Bryant 2009). That is, where CR used to be on the edges of D&D fandom, a weird group of friends playing a weird game of D&D for their weird fans, CR now represents what is normal – or soon to be normal – in the public of D&D. Wizards of the Coast now publishes official CR content and acts as a permanent sponsor for CR's main show. CR's audience is now a main target audience for D&D.

While this sounds like a case of new media overcoming old media, what is happening in the publics of CR is the opposite. Its popularity and success mean it can no longer sustain the small, relational – and therefore intimate – public of its early days. Cast-members, now also executives of the CR company, make business choices that expand their media presence. As their fandom grew, CR separated from its former parent-company in 2018 (Rachel 2019), and changed how they could relate to their fandom. After their record-breaking Kickstarter for their animated series, CR began to attract a larger audience. In 2019, *Amazon Studios* picked up the animated show for 2 seasons (Spangler 2019). Soon after, in 2020, CR collaborated with *Hot Topic* and *Funko Pops* to sell official CR merchandise in physical stores, allowing non-CR fans to see (and potentially purchase) their products (Bloodgood 2020; Christina 2020).

Partnering with *Amazon, Hot Topic,* and *Funko Pops* took CR beyond the confines of weird Internet content and into mainstream geek culture.

Now, CR streams their shows but no longer airs them live, making it a broadcast rather than a live stream (Critical Role n.d.). This change makes the once-intimate public of CR no longer possible, since the fandom is not only split across multiple broadcast platforms, but also loses the relationality of the live stream. This choice benefits CR as a media broadcast, since their audience now includes non-fans – much like any other mainstream television show. The loss of the live stream, however, in addition to the loss of fan competitions like GIF-of-the-Week, empties the stream and fandom of any potential reciprocity between cast, crew, and fans. In other words, the cast of CR is no longer a part of CR's intimate public.

Because CR is much more like a traditional media fandom, it now has power and responsibility that it did not have as a small, weird, intimate public online. Fans have criticised CR as early as 2019 for its lack of racial diversity, citing CR's popularity as one of the reasons they must be held accountable (Hall 2019). A show that a bunch of friends throw together with a single camera around a table has much less at stake than a mainstream, high budget broadcast pre-recorded in a studio (@queerdnd 2019). As a result, although CR's main cast remains the same eight white actors, they have begun introducing actors of colour as guest cast members. Mica Burton, Khary Payton, Sumalee Montano, and Erika Ishii joined as guest cast members for multiple episodes. Both Aabria Iyengar and Lou Wilson have also taken on roles as player characters (PCs) in the series of extended universe campaigns known as *Exandria Unlimited*, with Iyengar also running a miniseries as a GM. While *CR* could have invited guest members as an intimate public, they no longer have the excuse of being a small, low-budget stream made up of a group of friends around a table and must continue to increase the diversity of their cast. Since CR now stands for mainstream D&D fandom, fans can demand that they continue to better represent the diversity of the public they now stand in for.

Although digital media can create new interesting wild spaces, as it did with CR in its early days, they can also develop more normative, profitable media publics. Making use of the affordances of digital media to develop an intimate public leads, in this case, directly to turning all that into a profitable, traditional media company that makes use of old media platforms: broadcast, published books, television, physical merchandise, etc. As CR became more popular, it lost its intimate connection with its fans, but the commodification of an intimate public creates, in turn, a public that has power. What CR shows us, then, is that new media does not automatically replace and improve upon old media; instead, the relationship between the two is more dynamic than technological determinism might suggest.

## Key Words

**Intimate Public**: Intimate publics online are small groups of people who gather in relatively private spaces online to express often queer desires and opinions that may not be safe to express in a wider public.

**Public**: Publics are physical or digital gatherings of otherwise private citizens who share, articulate, and express their interests, opinions, and desires for the society they live in. A public can gather in a town square or in a hashtag on Twitter.

**Technological Determinism**: Technological determinism is the idea that technology shapes social change and not the other way around. It argues that changes in technology brings forward new phases of human history. It's a really common way of thinking about the world, but it's got distinct faults so it's important not to reduce human society to its technology only!

## Critical Thinking Questions

1. When an intimate public becomes a public, what responsibility do they have to politics of inclusion/to the politics of their previous intimate public?
2. In your online spaces (e.g. social networking services) what affordances exist? Which ones help you create community? Are all those affordances intended by the designer?
3. How does an online public construct community and identity? Is it different from offline publics?

## Note

1 It is important to note that just because a group is in a safe, intimate, protective space does not mean that they themselves cannot do harm to others: "non-dominant groups or communities can be essentialist in choosing for their own kind, whether or not as a reaction against exclusion" (Essed and Goldberg 1070). In other words, these small, relational communities can be exclusionary, partly from necessity (e.g. excluding those who would seek to mock or shame them) but also from fear. For instance, intimate fandom spaces that are ostensibly made for and by women are often themselves exclusionary of Black women fans, ostracizing and harassing those fans who call out anti-Black racism in their fanworks.

## References

@queerdnd. 2019. "An Open Letter to the Cast of *Critical Role*." *Medium*. Accessed July 1 2022. https://medium.com/@queerdnd/an-open-letter-to-the-cast-of-critical-role-5275288fc9a2

Bloodgood, Kat. 2020. "Critical Role Merchandise Comes to Hot Topic!" *That Hashtag Show*. Accessed July 1, 2022. https://www.thathashtagshow.com/2020/02/06/critical-role-merchandise-comes-to-hot-topic/

Boyd, Danah. 2010. "Social Network Sites as Networked Publics: Affordances, Dynamics, and Implications." In *Networked Self: Identity, Community, and Culture on Social Network Sites*, edited by Zizi Papacharissi, 39-58. New York: Routledge.

Bryant, Rebecca. 2009. "Dungeons & Dragons: The Gamers are Revolting!" In *Games as Transformative Works*, edited by Rebecca Carlson, Special Issue. *Transformative Works and Cultures*, no. 2. https://doi.org/10.3983/twc.2009.083

Christina. 2020. "Vox Machina Funko Pop! Collectibles Are Coming Soon!" *Critical Role*. Accessed July 1, 2022. https://critrole.com/vox-machina-funko-pop-collectibles-are-coming-soon/

Coddington, Mark, and Avery E. Holton. 2014. "When the Gates Swing Open: Examining Network Gatekeeping in a Social Media Setting." *Mass Communication and Society* 17, no. 2: 236–57. https://doi.org/10.1080/15205436.2013.779717

Critical Role. n.d.a. "About Us." *Critical Role*. Accessed July 1, 2022. https://critrole.com/

Critical Role. n.d.b. "What Is Critical Role?" *Critical Role*. Accessed July 1, 2022. https://critrole.com/what-is-critical-role/

Fron, Janine, Tracy Fullerton, Jacquelyn Ford Morie, and Celia Pearce. 2007. "The Hegemony of Play." *Situated Play, Proceedings of DiGRA 2007 Conference*, 309–18.

Habermas, Jürgen. 1991. *The Structural Transformation of the Public Sphere: An Inquiry into a Category of Bourgeois Society*. Cambridge, MA: MIT Press.

Jenkins, Henry. 2006. *Fans, Bloggers, and Gamers Exploring Participatory Culture*. New York: New York University Press.

Morrison, Aimée. 2011. "'Suffused by Feeling and Affect': The Intimate Public of Personal Mommy Blogging." *Biography* 34, no. 1: 37–55. https://doi.org/10.1353/bio.2011.0002

Norman, Don. 2013. *The Design of Everyday Things, Revised & Expanded*. New York: Basic Books.

Rachel. 2019. "Critical Role and Talks Machina Updates." Critical Role. Accessed July 1, 2022. https://critrole.com/critical-role-talks-machina-broadcast-updates/

Salter, Anastasia, and Bridget Blodgett. 2017. *Toxic Geek Masculinity in Media: Sexism, Trolling, and Identity Policing*. Cham, Switzerland: Palgrave Macmillan.

Sidhu, Premeet, and Marcus Carter. 2020. "The Critical Role of Media Representations, Reduced Stigma and Increased Access in D&D's Resurgence." *Proceedings of DiGRA 2020*, 1–20.

Spangler, Todd. 2019. "Amazon Orders Two Seasons of Critical Role's Animated 'Legend of Vox Machina Series." *Variety*. Accessed July 1, 2022. https://variety.com/2019/digital/news/critical-role-amazon-prime-video-legend-of-vox-machina-1203388522/

# Section II
# Games & Play

# 10 Not All Fun and Games in #mypokehood

## The Politics and Pitfalls of Universal Game Design in Pokémon GO!

*Kiera Obbard and Abi Lemak*

In the midst of the COVID-19 pandemic, game developers of augmented reality (AR) mobile apps have been pushed to evolve and adapt to global lockdowns and user concerns over moving safely through public space. Pokémon GO has been no exception to these changes, evolving game play in response to the COVID-19 pandemic and framing these changes in the context of focusing on user safety and well-being.

Members of the Black and Latinx communities have been raising concerns over the disproportionate risk marginalized players face when playing Pokémon GO in public space since the game came out in 2016—but to no avail. In light of more recent #BlackLivesMatter calls for action, our chapter examines Pokémon GO's response to the COVID-19 pandemic to better understand how the pandemic has influenced AR game design, development, and play.

Drawing on **intersectional** understandings of **digital redlining**, **universal design**, and the social ecology of public space, this chapter examines the following questions:

- How has game play and development been affected by the global pandemic?
- How does the concept of "user safety" intersect with identity in ways that make game play and development complex, both during and outside of the pandemic?
- What can we learn from these enhancements to user safety for future game design?

## What Is Pokémon GO?

Pokémon GO is a location-based AR mobile game developed by American software company Niantic, Inc. in 2016. It uses mobile device GPS functionality and encourages users to walk outside to complete actions like capturing Pokémon, visiting PokéStops and Gyms, battling Team Rocket, and hatching eggs. Although some of these actions can be completed from a user's home (particularly, catching Pokémon), the ability

DOI: 10.4324/9781003310730-13

to engage in certain aspects of the game without walking outside largely depends on whether a user lives close to PokéStops and Gyms—which, as we will discuss later, largely depends on the user's geographic location.

**Niantic's Response to COVID-19**

Niantic regularly issues updates to Pokémon Go, which typically introduce new features, fix bugs, or announce special events or new Pokémon. When the COVID-19 pandemic began and lockdowns and stay-at-home orders were imposed globally, the creators of Pokémon Go implemented several features designed to help users play at home and maintain their social distance. These updates were primarily released in March 2020, with updates to address the pandemic released sporadically throughout 2020. Specifically, on March 12, 2020, Niantic, Inc. posted the following on Twitter in response to the pandemic (Figure 10.1).

Some updates implemented during COVID-19 enabled basic remote play without any associated in-app purchases. For example, the updates on March 20, 2020 to the GO Battle League enabled players to more easily battle against random remote trainers ("GO Battle League Temporary Updates" 2020). Previously, the GO Battle League required users to walk a certain distance to "unlock" battle opportunities; this was removed on March 20. In addition, the updates on March 23, 2020 to "Gifts" enabled your Pokémon "buddy" to travel to nearby PokéStops and bring back

**Niantic, Inc.**
@NianticLabs

**The safety of our global player community is our top priority. COVID-19 is challenging us and the world to adjust. We're putting our focus on expanding features and experiences in our games that can be enjoyed in an individual setting and that also encourage exploration!**

8:20 PM · Mar 12, 2020 · Twitter Web App

**394** Retweets   **64** Quote Tweets   **3,030** Likes

*Figure 10.1* A screenshot of a twitter post from March 12th, 2020 from Niantic that writes: "The safety of our global community is our top priority. COVID-19 is challenging us and the world to adjust. We're putting our focus on expanding features and experiences in our games that can be enjoyed in an individual setting and that also encourages exploration!" (Niantic 2020)

gifts for you to send to other players, rather than requiring users to walk to and spin PokéStops ("Increased Daily Bonuses, Changes to Gifts, and Rotating 1 PokéCoin Bundles" 2020). Typically, gifts include items like Pokéballs, berries, potions, and more, and users send gifts to other players in their friends list and receive experience points for doing so. Instead of focusing on motivating users to move through and interact with each other in the physical world, these updates demonstrate a clear shift to a "play from home" model.

However, some updates to the game were temporary and simply added additional safety measures to "real-world" play. On March 31, 2020, Niantic doubled the Gym interaction distance ("Temporary Changes to Pokémon GO" 2020). The Gym interaction distance is how close a player needs to be to a Gym to interact with it. Although expanding the Gym interaction distance may have allowed players to stay more socially distanced, it still required users to go outside and potentially interact with other players at the Gym (unless they happen to live close to a Gym).

Other changes to the game required in-app purchases. For example, remote play options like remote raid passes and tickets to participate in special remote events were introduced during the pandemic; however, these items must be purchased through the app with PokéCoins. PokéCoins can be purchased for a fee in the app or can be collected by walking to a Gym and leaving your Pokémon there to "defend" the Gym (again, requiring users to go outside). The paid remote play options like remote raid passes and special remote events are the primary way for users to catch rare or higher-level Pokémon; users who are able to access these remote play options are, thus, often at an advantage over other players.

Because it is a commercial game, the motivations for these changes may be focused on maintaining the Pokémon GO user base (and revenue) rather than on ensuring user safety. Pokémon GO's business model is largely based on in-app purchases, and VentureBeat reported that Pokémon GO's in-app purchases have increased during the pandemic, with "global player spending reach $23 million during the week of March 16, according to mobile market researcher Sensor Tower" (Minottii 2020; Williams 2020).

In addition, these one-size-fits-all changes that are meant to help all users are an example of universal design. Universal design is a concept that was developed by architect Ronald Mace, which describes "the concept of designing all products and the built environment to be aesthetic and usable to the greatest extent possible by everyone, regardless of their age, ability, or status in life" (Center for Universal Design 2008). Advocating for the use of universal design in the humanities, George Williams observes that if more projects employed the concept of universal design, our final products would serve "the needs of those with disabilities as well as those without" (2012). Arguably, then, adopting universal design in Pokémon GO game design should help ensure gameplay meets the needs of marginalized groups.

However, as Richard H. Godden argues, "the 'Universal' in [universal design] can carry with it some unintended and unexpected assumptions about normalcy and our physical orientation to the world" (Godden and Hsy 2016). In the case of Pokémon GO, the one-size-fits-all approach to enabling safe play in public spaces does not take the lived, embodied experiences of marginalized groups into account, and updates to the game continue to be built on existing problematic structures that privilege the safety of some players over others.

## Oh No, Pokémon GO!

When Pokémon GO! was first developed, Niantic used a map from a previous AR game called Ingress, which was built from a combination of crowdsourced data from a Historical Marker Database, and crowdsourced data from early Ingress players. Both the database volunteers and Ingress players tended to be young, English-speaking males, which had unintended consequences (Huffaker 2016). As Christopher Huffaker explains:

> [T]he locations of pokéstops and gyms are taken from the locations of 'portals' in Niantic's previous augmented-reality GPS-based game, Ingress. And Ingress's portals, while not available as an exportable list, are viewable on a world map, making it possible to compare city demographics to the distribution of Ingress portals.
> 
> (Huffaker 2016)

Huffaker used the available data from Ingress' portals to compare city demographics and found that there tend to be significantly more "locations"—PokéStops and Gyms—in white, affluent neighbourhoods (and in downtown cores) than in Black neighbourhoods and rural areas. Living in an area with lots of PokéStops and Gyms means that you can gain more experience points, collect items, fight in Gyms, leave your Pokémon to defend a Gym (which gives you PokéCoins, which can then be exchanged for items in the in-app store), and more. In other words, it gives you an advantage over players who don't live in areas with many PokéStops or Gyms.

A 2019 report on racial literacy in tech demonstrates that "seemingly neutral technologies are deeply affected by race" (Daniels et al. 2019). Using a map that privileges locations in white, affluent neighbourhoods and downtown cores, and provides fewer gameplay opportunities in Black neighbourhoods and rural areas, is an example of how **unconscious bias** can further entrench inequalities or, as the report phrases it, "recreate old divisions" (Daniels et al. 2019). If, as Anne Balsamo argues, "technological innovations have cultural consequences," then game designers have a responsibility to consider the consequences of their biases (or the biases of the data they are using) in game design (2011).

## The Politics and Pitfalls of Universal Game Design in Pokémon GO!

In addition, for players who have to travel to different neighbourhoods in order to access PokéStops or Gyms, this can present a number of problems—from accessibility issues to fear of being stopped by police, as board game designer and equity advocate Omari Akil wrote in 2016:

> When my brain started combining the complexity of being Black in America with the real world proposal of wandering and exploration that is designed into the gameplay of Pokemon GO, there was only one conclusion. **I might die if I keep playing**.
>
> (Akil 2016, emphasis in original)

Critiques over the structural inequalities and unconscious bias built into the game are certainly not new, and a number of users and scholars have previously critiqued how Pokémon GO engages in digital redlining (Akhtar 2016; Bogado 2016; Juhász and Hochmair 2017).

### Digital Redlining, Unconscious Bias, and Pokémon GO

Digital redlining is when digital technologies perpetuate inequalities and inequities between already marginalized groups. Digital redlining is an extension of redlining, which was a practice employed by banks to assess the risk of granting loans to potential homeowners "on the basis of neighborhood demographics (specifically race and ethnicity), rather than individual creditworthiness" (D'Ignazio and Klein 2020).

In 2016, Aura Bogado posted a photo on Twitter demonstrating that there are way more PokéStops and Gyms in areas that do not look like her predominantly Latinx/Black neighbourhood in Los Angeles, and asked others to share their neighbourhoods and racial identities using #mypokehood (Akhtar 2016) (Figures 10.2 and 10.3).

Researchers have also taken up this question of the location of PokéStops in various neighbourhoods. According to Urban Institute researchers, there are an average of 55 PokéStops in predominantly white neighbourhoods, in stark contrast to the 19 in predominantly Black neighbourhoods. This pattern was also found to repeat itself in Black neighbourhoods within Detroit, Miami, and Chicago (Akhtar 2016).

In 2017, Levente Juhász and Hartwig H. Hartwig conducted a geographic analysis of Pokémon GO locations, demonstrating a lack of PokéStops and Gyms in disadvantaged neighbourhoods, effectively restricting gameplay for residents. The research compares metropolitan Downtown Miami and Hialeah, a closeby municipality with a significantly higher Hispanic population (Juhász and Hartwig 2017). What these reports indicate is that that crowdsourced map used by Niantic to develop Pokémon GO engages in digital redlining and perpetuates inequalities and inequities between already marginalized groups. Thus, although the game developers have made changes to Pokémon GO to make game play safer during the COVID-19

*Figure 10.2* A screenshot of a twitter post from July 18th, 2016 from Daisy that writes: "@aurabogado Outer section of East Oakland. African American, inner city, and low income. Spotty cell. #mypokehood" Pictured is an empty PokemonGO! vista.

pandemic, these changes continue to be built on an unequal playing field and do not account for the lived realities of marginalized players.

## Conclusion: What Can We Learn from Pokémon GO?

On June 3, 2020, Niantic shared an internal memo to their blog site titled "Taking Action." The memo was sent from Niantic CEO John Hanke to Niantic employees outlining the company's commitment to change in light of the global #BlackLivesMatter movement.

As noted in the memo, Niantic's existing model for effecting sustainable, long-term change was to:

> …encourage players to explore the world around them and connect with their local community through physical interaction to build a strong body and mind through exercise, and to build positive connections with fellow human beings through real-world social interactions.
> (Hanke 2020)

## The Politics and Pitfalls of Universal Game Design in Pokémon GO! 113

*Figure 10.3* A screenshot of a twitter post from July 18th, 2016 from Rianne Olde Keizer that writes: "Welcome to San Francisco Lower Nob Hill. #mypokehood looks like this every night. No need to even leave my house." Pictured is a bustling PokemonGO! Vista (Olde Keizer 2016).

Moving forward, the company committed to "fund[ing] projects from Black creators" so that they may share their own "characters, story, and points of view that validate the lives and experiences of the Black community" (Hanke 2020).

Although Niantic's push to fund Black creators is no small gesture and certainly a step in the right direction, there are also in-game changes that could be made to improve the quality of play and safety of Black Pokémon GO players. There seems to be a critical blindspot around gaming and politics here, one that ignores biased, built-in game design principles that require immediate attention—something that Black, Hispanic, and other racialized Pokémon GO players have been pointing out since 2016.

Although we acknowledge that Niantic has implemented some important in-game changes within Pokémon GO in response to the pandemic and, more recently, corporate changes in response to the #BlackLivesMatter movement and protests around the world, these changes fail to bring lasting, meaningful change towards safer gameplay if the underlying conditions and unconscious bias built into the map continue to go unaddressed.

In a 2016 article for *The Atlantic,* academic and videogame designer Ian Bogost wrote that when AR games were first becoming popular in the early-to-mid 2000s, "pervasive and alternate reality games promised to offer a different way to see and understand the physical, material world" (Bogost 2016). This optimistic view of AR games as providing a new way to see and understand—and, perhaps, experience—the physical world is only possible if AR game designers adopt an intersectional approach to identity[1] that offers a more inclusive model of player safety in public spaces (Crenshaw 1991). Adapting Tara McPherson's call to design for difference, what might it mean to design AR games, from conception, "from a feminist concern for difference"? (McPherson 2014).

To address the bias built into Pokémon GO, game designers could consider the following suggestions towards a safer gaming experience for all players, now and in a post-COVID-19 landscape:

1. Extend all remote play options to non-paying users
2. Revise the language on the safety warnings on the opening screen in order to include prompts that better protect marginalized members of their community
3. Extend the ability to suggest new PokéStops and Gyms to all users, regardless of rank
4. Conduct a review of the distribution of PokéStops and Gyms in rural versus urban areas, white versus marginalized communities, etc.

With these changes, the projected outcome would be a more accessible and safe app to play for marginalized members of the Pokémon GO community. In this model, rather than reinforce digital redlining or neighbourhood stereotypes, players would be able to judge for themselves when and where is safest for them to play, and disabled players as well as low-income players in disadvantaged areas would also be afforded equal playing opportunity.

## Key Words

**Digital Redlining**: Digital redlining is when digital technologies perpetuate inequalities and inequities between already marginalized groups.

**Intersectionality**: Intersectionality is an analytical framework for examining how aspects of identity (e.g., race, gender, sexual orientation, class) create intersecting layers of oppression (Crenshaw 1991).

**Unconscious Bias**: Unconscious biases, sometimes referred to as implicit biases, are biases, prejudices, or social stereotypes that are ingrained at a deep, unconscious level.

**Universal Design**: Universal design is a one-size-fits-all approach to design that is intended to meet the needs of all users.

## Critical Thinking Questions

1  What challenges are associated with universal design?
2  What does it mean to design from a feminist concern for difference?
3  What is digital redlining and why is it harmful to players?

## Note

1  There are many examples of mobile gaming apps that apply principles of intersectional feminism in productive, reparative ways. For more on the intersections between race and technology, see:
   - Sweetgrass AR
   - DOHR (Digital Oral Histories for Reconciliation)
   - Elizabeth LaPensée's games
   - 99% invisible podcast episode: "Map Quests: Political, Physical and Digital"
   - The Radical AI Podcast
   - All Tech is Human
   - Centre for Race and Digital Studies
   - Black Software, by Charlton McIlwain

## References

Akhtar, Allana. 2016. "Is Pokémon Go Racist? How the App May Be Redlining Communities of Color." *USA Today*, August 9, 2016. https://www.usatoday.com/story/tech/news/2016/08/09/pokemon-go-racist-app-redlining-communities-color-racist-pokestops-gyms/87732734/

Akil, Omari. 2016. "Warning: Pokemon GO Is a Death Sentence If You Are a Black Man." *Medium*. July 13, 2016. https://medium.com/mobile-lifestyle/warning-pokemon-go-is-a-death-sentence-if-you-are-a-black-man-acacb4bdae7f

Balsamo, Anne. 2011. *Designing Culture: The Technological Imagination at Work*. Durham, NC: Duke University Press. https://doi.org/10.1215/9780822392149

Bogado, Aura. 2016. "Gotta Catch 'em All? It's a Lot Easier If You're White. | Grist." *Grist* (blog). July 19, 2016. https://grist.org/justice/gotta-catch-em-all-its-a-lot-easier-if-youre-white/

Bogost, Ian. 2016. "The Tragedy of Pokémon Go." The Atlantic. July 11, 2016. https://www.theatlantic.com/technology/archive/2016/07/the-tragedy-of-pokemon-go/490793/

Center for Universal Design. 2008. "Center for Universal Design NCSU - About the Center - Ronald L. Mace." 2008. https://projects.ncsu.edu/ncsu/design/cud/about_us/usronmace.htm

Crenshaw, Kimberlé. 1991. "Mapping the Margins: Intersectionality, Identity Politics, and Violence against Women of Color." *Stanford Law Review* 43, no. 6: 1241–300.

D'Ignazio, Catherine, and Lauren F. Klein. 2020. *Data Feminism*. Strong Ideas Series. Cambridge, MA: The MIT Press.

Daniels, Jessie, Mutale Nkonde, and Darakhshan Mir. 2019. "Advancing Racial Literacy in Tech: Why Ethics, Diversity in Hiring & Implicit Bias Trainings Aren't Enough." *Data & Society*. https://datasociety.net/wp-content/uploads/2019/05/Racial_Literacy_Tech_Final_0522.pdf

"GO Battle League Temporary Updates." 2020. *Pokémon GO* (blog). March 20, 2020. https://pokemongolive.com/post/gobattleleague-updates/

Godden, Richard, and Jonathan Hsy. 2016. "Universal Design and Its Discontents." In *Disrupting the Digital Humanities*, edited by Dorothy Kim and Jesse Stommel, 91–115. https://library.oapen.org/bitstream/handle/20.500.12657/25400/1004695.pdf?sequence=1#page=92

Hanke, John. 2020. "Taking Action." *Niantic* (blog). June 3, 2020. https://nianticlabs.com/en/blog/blacklivesmatter/

Huffaker, Christopher. 2016. "There Are Fewer Pokemon Go Locations in Black Neighborhoods, but Why?" *Belleville News-Democrat*, July 14, 2016. https://www.bnd.com/news/nation-world/national/article89562297.html

"Increased Daily Bonuses, Changes to Gifts, and Rotating 1 PokéCoin Bundles." 2020. *Pokémon GO* (blog). March 23, 2020. https://pokemongolive.com/post/updates-20200323/

Juhász, Levente, and Hartwig H. Hochmair. 2017. "Where to Catch 'em All? – A Geographic Analysis of Pokémon Go Locations." *Geo-Spatial Information Science* 20, no. 3: 241–51. https://doi.org/10.1080/10095020.2017.1368200

McPherson, Tara. 2014. "Designing for Difference." *Differences* 25, no. 1: 177–88. https://doi.org/10.1215/10407391-2420039

Minotti, Mike. 2020. "Sensor Tower: Pokémon Go Revenues Increase as Coronavirus Lockdowns Spread." *VentureBeat*, March 25, 2020. https://venturebeat.com/2020/03/25/sensor-tower-pokemon-go-revenues-up-almost-67-week-over-week-as-coronavirus-shutdowns-spread/

Niantic – GONE EXPLORING #MeetYouOutThere. 2020. Twitter post. June 3, 2020, 11:02am. https://twitter.com/NianticLabs/status/1268196386454949888

Olde Keizer, Rianne. 2016. Twitter post. July 18, 2016, 1:10am. https://twitter.com/RianneOK/status/754906124063678464

"Temporary Changes to Pokémon GO: Gym Interaction Distance Has Been Doubled." 2020. *Pokémon GO* (blog). March 31, 2020. https://pokemongolive.com/post/gyminteractionupdate-20200331/

Williams, George H. 2012. "Disability, Universal Design, and the Digital Humanities." In *Debates in the Digital Humanities*, edited by Matthew K. Gold, NED-New edition, 202–12. Minneapolis, MN: University of Minnesota Press. http://www.jstor.org/stable/10.5749/j.ctttv8hq.15

Williams, Roberts. 2020. "'Pokémon Go' Spending Jumps 67% after Indoor Play Adjustments." *Mobile Marketer*, March 26, 2020. https://www.mobilemarketer.com/news/pokemon-go-spending-jumps-67-after-indoor-play-adjustments/574910/

# 11 Lip Dubbing for Fido

## Listening to the Internet through Viral Pet Video Memes

*Kate Galloway*

In 2019, the independent videogame developer House House released *Untitled Goose Game* and viral playing, sharing, and waddling ensued. This form of play began generating **musicking** viral media that responded to its idiosyncratic animal gameplay, environmental sound design, amongst composer Dan Golding's procedural remixing of Debussy (2021). This is not the first-time human listeners have responded in fascinating ways to nonhuman animal musicking through playful participatory remixing, sharing, and listening on **social media**. Christopher Small famously coined the term "musicking" to highlight that music is not a static thing (e.g., the musical "work"), but rather a broad and inclusive "activity, something that people do" (1998, 2). He wrote, "to pay attention in any way to a musical performance, including a recorded performance, even to Muzak in an elevator, is to music" (1998, 9). I extend musicking to include practices of moving to music, responding to sound, sonic communication that is reframed by human users as musical, and audiovisual remix involving the nonhuman animal. Internet memes and viral videos that use pre-existing music and the sonic environments of the nonhuman animals pictured on the user's screen are also used as a method of relating to the nonhuman animal, particularly those who live alongside us in our homes as pets.

In this chapter, I examine Internet musicking, theorized by musicologist Paula Harper as a distinctly twenty-first century musical practice (2019), through the lens of animal memes. I focus on video memes that repurpose pre-existing popular music to create new networks of musical meaning and connect with the domesticated nonhuman animals in our lives. I illustrate the musicality of pet memes by examining the Internet musicality of one such case study, the participatory "Sometimes I Think About You" trend where past and present photos or videos of a user-creator's pet is scored to "Heat Waves" by Glass Animals. Although Animal Studies is a rapidly growing interdisciplinary field devoted to examining, understanding, and critically evaluating the complex relationships between humans and other animals, including Margo DeMello's *Animals and Society* (2012), Kari Weil's *Thinking Animals: Why Animal Studies Now?* (2012), and Lori Gruen's *Entangled Empathy: An Alternative Ethic*

DOI: 10.4324/9781003310730-14

*for Our Relationships with Animals* (2015) followed by the collection *Critical Terms for Animal Studies* (2018), among others, the scholarship in the field has rarely drawn on the sonic and musical elements of these multi-faced relationships to understand how nonhuman animals figure in our lives and we in theirs in cultural practices of making music. Textual and visual analysis grounds many of the existing critical approaches to the study of animals and their representation, including John Berger's foundational chapter "Why Look at Animals" in *About Looking* (1980). But what can the inclusion of sound, music, and listening contribute to the studies of animals and their representation and how these representational politics have been used to support and perpetuate systems of human difference? I use this viral TikTok and Instagram trend case study to illustrate the ways in which pet owners use pre-existing music and forms of participatory audiovisual Internet media to articulate their deep connections to the nonhuman animals in their lives and connect with other active user-creators in the digital space that is now known as "Pet" Instagram and TikTok.

## Listening to the Internet

How do people listen to the sounds and music they encounter in the digital spaces and screens while online? Listening in this context involves people taking in, making sense of, reacting to, and sometimes creating and recreating sounds and music made by other media makers and by the technologies that circulate these digital audiovisual objects. These digital audiovisual events are not just sounds and music that we listen to alongside associated still and moving images and icons, they are framed and shaped by the technologies that we use to listen. Here are a few examples of digital media listening and listening to the Internet: How do we imagine the voices in a film's use of subtitles? How do we hear the voice of a loved one on the other side of a text message or even a stranger in an Instant Message (IM) from an online dating app? Do different fonts and styles "sound" different – that is to say, does bold face Comic Sans "sound" different than Arial (let alone Wingdings) when we read it aloud or silently in our heads on the screen, and why/why not? Even when sound isn't playing from the many screens in our lives, we are still listening to the Internet and listening online. Even before these forms of listening to screens became commonplace, people were silently listening to the voices and soundscapes in novels, poetry, short stories, comics, news stories, and graphic novels as they imagined characters, narratives, and places in their head.

When we watch a viral video of an Australian Shepherd wiggling its rear end, greeting its human parents after they arrive home from a short trip to the grocery store or one of many remixes of a javelina, an animal similar to a wild boar southwestern North America, Central America,

South America, and some regions of the Caribbean, exuberantly running down the streets of Tucson to Rebecca Black's equally viral classic "Friday," we are listening to the Internet. When we listen to **social media** and while using the Internet we are participating in what film and media scholar refers to as "ubiquitous listening" (Kassabian 2013). Ubiquitous listening is prevalent in urban and suburban environments, places where people are listening while they do other things (e.g., traveling on the subway of walking to work while listening to an iPod, turning on the radio while driving, the Muzak or mood music playing in the mall and its individual stores). In all of these instances, including listening to digital media on the Internet listening occurs alongside and during other, often quotidian activities (Kassabian 2013, 9). A number of modes of listening are enfolded into ubiquitous listening, Anahid Kassabian argues, and listening in this context involves "a *range of engagements* between and across human bodies and music technologies" (2013, xxi).

The sound design of audiovisual memes draws on the conventions of **compilation film scores**, where unlike an original score where the music is composed specifically for the film it is used in, a compilation score in film composition re-purposes pre-existing music composed for other purposes. Thus, the music used in a compilation score brings to the film all of the meanings and memories associated with a piece of music that a viewer has accumulated from previous listening contexts. The re-use of preexisting song in audiovisual media, which includes our listening encounters in the moving images and sounds we encounter across the ubiquitous digital spaces of the Internet, is a material example of what Michel de Certeau (2011) terms "manipulation by users who are not its makers" (xiii). It is an active interpretation and use of culture articulated within a volatile matrix of creative will, industrial imperatives, and strictures of licensing and synchronization. As such, compiled scores of pre-existing music are byproducts of social events (for which there can often be an oblique historical record) in which industry figures interpret, within commercial and legal parameters, how music can coherently speak alongside moving images. As Kassabian argues, the compiled score can offer "affiliating identifications" for viewers that "depend on histories forged outside the film scene," presenting a collision between a song's existing socio-cultural meanings and the meanings of the images and narratives with which it is joined (Kassabian 2001, 2; See also Donnelly 2001, 152–66; Powrie and Stilwell 2006).

## Listening to Pet TikTok and Instagram and the "Sometimes I Think About You" Viral Video Trend

Let us listen now to TikTok and Instagram through a viral video trend that used pre-existing popular music to listen to the cute expressive ecology of pet TikTok and Instagram. The Internet is saturated with

120  *Kate Galloway*

pictures, videos, and GIFs of cute pets posted and shared by users on their own account or on an account specially created for their pet and on Pet Influencer accounts, such as, the golden retriever Tucker Budzyn (@tuckerbudzyn), who was voted by the American Influencer Awards as the 2021 Pet Influencer of the Year in the Lifestyle category. Many of these digital artifacts playback sound and pre-existing music. In the case of a TikTok or Instagram video, however, the original track is truncated and in some instances this truncated sample is further remixed by an indie artist is made to launch a video trend. A successful video trend relies heavily on musical response. Each time a piece of music is reused in a new context, all previous meanings and associations from where that piece of music was previously encountered are carried with it. Like a palimpsest, a material like a manuscript page that is reused yet it continues to retain visible traces of the original image or writing that was effaced to prepare for new content, listeners scrape away these networked sonic associations to form new meanings and relationships with the music. However, while listeners recall many places where they have heard this music before, they rarely have a comprehensive knowledge of all instances where a piece of music has been replayed (e.g., who is the listener who knows every social media context where "Bohemian Rhapsody" is reused?).

On July 16, 2021, TikToker @sevier.edits posted a montage of romantic footage from the second season of the popular Netflix teen television series *Never Have I Ever* set to a remixed excerpt of "Heat Waves" by Glass Animals' that was slowed down and feature postproduction reverb effects (Soto 2021). The "Sometimes I Think About You" viral trend popular during the summer of 2021, also uses a remix of Glass Animals "Heat Waves" (*Dreamland* 2020) popularized by the Netflix coming-of-age dramedy *Never Have I Ever*. The track was a summer 2020 radio hit making it immediately identifiable to the target audience of the series. This post launched the "Sometimes All I Think About Is You" viral lip dub trend, a type of music video used frequently in social media trends that combines lip synching and audio dubbing. In their "Sometimes All I Think About Is You" videos, TikTokers lip synched to the lyrics "sometimes all I think about is you" to show that they miss someone when away from them, as described by on-screen text and dubbed over the recorded video audio in post editing with the audio from the original song. User-creators first daydreamed and lip synched along to images and video montages of loved ones in their life, some of which they hadn't seen in a long time. It was not long before those loved ones became the dogs, cats, hedgehogs, and other cuddly pets in their lives (Figures 11.1 and 11.2).

A central plotline of the series explores the romantic relationship between the protagonist Devi and one of her love interests, Paxton. In episode 9 of season 2, Devi is alone in her bedroom and Paxton secretly visits late at night through her bedroom window. He is soaking wet from the rainstorm and Devi cautiously asks him, "are you here to study, or?"

*Listening to the Internet through Viral Pet Video Memes* 121

*Figure 11.1* The "Present Day" (Adult) and (Screenshots by the Author).

As her unfinished question trails off, Paxton moves closer and closer to Devi. After several anticipatory moments of relationship uncertainty presented to viewers as a classic "will they won't they" situation, this scene is the first time that they kiss. The build-up to their kiss is simultaneously visual *and* audible. The entire song is not replayed in the scene, only the chorus is showcased and aligned with narrative tension between Devi and Paxton. The song gradually fades in on the lyrics "sometimes all I think about is you… late nights in the middle of June" that focuses on the chemistry between the two characters as the scene builds in audiovisual tension which is released as they kiss. The drop is strategically synched to the moment of the kiss that breaks the narrative tension.

Across social media on platforms such as TikTok, Instagram, and Facebook, user-creators used the #AllIThinkAbout trend remix of "Heat Waves" to score then-and-now throwback photos and videos of their pets, adapting the "Sometimes I Think About You" trend to their furry friends. Even the lead singer of Glass Animals, Dave Bayley participated, sharing images of his beloved dog Woody on the band's official TikTok account (@glassanimalsofficial). This time user-creators emphasize the "sometimes all I think about is you" portion of the lyrics to emphasize

*Figure 11.2* "Throwback" (Puppy) frames of the "Sometimes All I Think About is You" Pet Video trend.

the importance of their pet in their lives, but also their obsessive documentation of their cuteness. Although many of these videos use video editor pre-sets that display the lyrics of the song fragment on screen, these videos frequently feature a "sound on" or "unmute this" directive. These videos are meant to be listened to in order to reveal the full choreography between sound and image. As Paula Harper (2019) has examined, "sound on" or "unmute this" videos invite (and sometimes even demand response, action, and, ultimately, participation through the use of bold or italic typeface and the excessive use of exclamation marks). The "sound on" or "unmute this" directive also carries with it the implied promise that this modest user labour of just tapping the screen or clicking on the video will result in a sonic surprise and satisfying listening experience that will encourage the user to re-listen and recirculate the musical meme (Harper 2019, 7–23). This brief set of instructions that might appear as a text overlay edited into the video by the creator or written by the creator or the reposter in the comments calls for scrolling platform users to switch from passive to active listening and literally turn on the sound (or turn up the volume) on a piece of media's sound. This request of the user carries with it the implied promise that this modest user labour will result in a sonic surprise and satisfying listening experience that will encourage the user to re-listen and recirculate the musical meme (Harper 2019).

On TikTok and Instagram, many content creators who are also pet owners created a versioning of the "All I Think About Is You" video trend featuring their own pets. In this video trend, the cuteness reveal of their pet when it was a puppy or kitten of only a few weeks or months old is synchronized with the same audible structural marker of the drop that is synchronized with the moment when Devi and Paxton kiss for the first time. Each video follows a similar formula. The sample hook of Glass Animals' "Heat Waves" as the listener looks at a still image or video of the content creator's pet in the present day, often as an adult dog or cat. There is a superimposed line of text in one of the standard text styles offered by the audiovisual streaming platform that reads "Don't miss the puppy stage. It was too much work." In one video, I watched an adult Pembroke Welsh Corgi was chewing on its leash and in another a full-sized Harlequin Great Dane staring out an open front door on a sunny day wagging his tail, the sun streaming into the hallway. On the drop and the lyric "Sometimes all I think about is you" the photograph or video switches to one of the pet when it was a baby from one of it in the present, a process of remembering and reflecting on when their dog or cat first arrived in their lives as a puppy or kitten. The Corgi is now in its puppy-stage with ears that were once too large for its body, looking up at the camera with its puppy dog eyes soliciting love and affection (and forgiveness for puppy training mistakes), while the Great Dane is a much smaller puppy, standing in the same position looking out the very same door in similar weather conditions. When the cute puppy is revealed, the lyrics "Sometimes all I think about is you" are superimposed on screen by the user-creator who is more often than not the featured pet's owner. Sometimes when you see a throwback picture of your dog as a puppy you forget the hard work involved in the puppy stage. In the episode of *Never Have I Ever* that the musical hook used in the video trend references, Devi forgets with one kiss from Paxton all the times before that Paxton ignored and disrespected her.

## Conclusion

The cultural compulsion to engage in the mediated anthropomorphizing of pets is not new, as Jessica Maddox points out in her study of the cute economy of Pet Instagram where images of pets serve as communicative **social media** actions (2021). Listening to and during our activities online interacting with digital media, specifically the ways in which we listen and react to pet-themed groups, accounts, and content on **social media** platform is a form of ubiquitous listening that needs to be taken more seriously. Listening to the Internet is a prevalent form of listening in the daily lives of the majority of North Americans in the twenty-first century.

## Key Words

**Compilation Score**: A compilation film score, sometimes often referred to as a soundtrack rather than a score, is one comprised of pre-existing music. In contrast, an original film score, which features music specifically composed for the film it is featured in. The music in compilation scores was composed for a previous purpose and often viewers have heard this music before and bring all previous listening experience and meanings to the film's narrative, which is often why a song is intentionally used by the music director.

**Musicking**: The music scholar Christopher Small coined the term musicking to position music making as an active process and something that people do rather than a static object. His use of the term musicking also extends music making and whether something or someone is musical to include both musical and extra-musical elements, in that musicking involves the performers on the stage, but it also includes the physical and aural architecture of the performance space, the process of buying a ticket to the performance and the person or computer system who sells you that ticket.

**Social Media**: Social media is a kind of interactive technology and digital community and circulation space with technological features and affordances that facilitate the participatory sharing and creating of ideas, media, information, and other forms of digital culture and expression.

## Critical Thinking Questions

1 Listening to Glass Animals' "Heat Waves" in a viral video on TikTok is different from listening to the same song on Spotify. People listen to these platforms in different ways. How do you find new music and what platforms do you use? How do you listen to streaming music in different and similar ways to when you listen on social media platforms? How does the interface of the platform shape our listening?
2 Using a video on a social media platform of your choice that uses pre-existing music, examine the techniques used to edit and remix the music to attract the viewer's attention. How do these techniques influence the viewer to listen to, like, comment on, and share the video, or even make their own version of the video?
3 In a viral video trend that incorporates a pre-existing piece of music, how might different people interpret the message or meaning of the video differently based on their previously exposure to the piece of music in different contexts?

## References

Berger, John. 1980. *About Looking.* New York: Pantheon.
de Certeau, Michel. 2011. *The Practice of Everyday Life.* Oakland, CA: University of California Press.

DeMello, Margo. 2012. *Animals and Society: An Introduction to Human-Animal Studies.* New York: Columbia University Press.

Donnelly, Kevin J. 2001. "Performance and the Composite Film Score." In *Film Music: Critical Approaches*, edited by Kevin J. Donnelly, 152–66. Edinburgh: Edinburgh University Press.

Golding, Dan. 2021. "Finding Untitled Goose Game's Dynamic Music in the World of Silent Cinema." *Journal of Sound and Music in Games* 2, no. 1: 1–16.

Gruen, Lori. 2015. *Entangled Empathy: An Alternative Ethic for Our Relationships with Animals.* New York: Lantern Books.

Gruen, Lori, ed. 2018. *Critical Terms for Animal Studies.* Chicago: University of Chicago Press.

Harper, Paula. 2019. "'Unmute This': Captioning an (audio)visual microgenre." *The Soundtrack* 9, no. 1, 2: 7–23.

Kassabian, Anahid. 2001. *Hearing Film: Tracking Identifications in Contemporary Hollywood Film Music.* New York: Routledge.

Kassabian, Anahid. 2013. *Ubiquitous Listening: Affect, Attention, and Distributed Subjectivity.* Berkeley: University of California Press.

Maddox, Jessica. 2021 "The Secret Life of Pet Instagram Accounts: Joy: Resistance, and Commodification in the Internet's Cute Economy." *New Media & Society* 23, no. 11: 3332–48.

Powrie, Phil and Robynn Stilwell, eds., 2006. *Changing Tunes: The Use of Pre-Existing Music in Film.* London: Routledge.

Small, Christopher. 1998. *Musicking: The Meanings of Performing and Listening.* Middletown, CT: Wesleyan University Press.

Soto, Tianna. 2021. "TikTokers are Daydreaming in the 'All I Think About is You' TikTok Trend," *Her Campus*, September 9. Accessed January 10, 2022. https://www.hercampus.com/culture/all-i-think-about-is-you-tiktok-trend-explainer/

Weil, Kari. 2012. *Thinking Animals: Why Animal Studies Now?* New York: Columbia University Press.

# 12 'Turn Off That Friggin' Radio!'

## The Canadian Soldier Figure and Identity Formation in Videogames

*Jason Hawreliak and Venus Torabi*

While all questions of national identity are nebulous and often self-contradictory, this seems doubly so for Canadians. "Not quite American, not quite English or French" is a common refrain which speaks to Canada's position in navigating dominant cultural influences. However, not only is this definition by negation unsatisfactory, it entirely neglects foundational aspects of the country, most notably the historical and contemporary role of Indigenous peoples, and the many influences from outside of Europe. This chapter does not attempt to settle the question of what makes Canadian identity unique, as it is not an answerable question to begin with. Rather, we examine how one version of Canadian-ness is discursively constructed through videogames, and war-themed videogames in particular.

In this chapter, we offer potential strategies for analyzing meaning in videogames. We examine the figure of the Canadian soldier in war-themed videogames and argue that it is a powerful rhetorical device for encapsulating key characteristics of nationhood and identity. Although the Canadian public does not quite share the same degree of reverence for the soldier as the American public, the Canadian soldier remains a generally positive figure in Canadian imagery, embodying many desirable traits, including duty, honor, strength, resilience, and excellence (Brush 2021). Representations of the soldier figure can therefore illuminate important insights as to what constitutes a particular idealized version of identity.

As a starting point, we take it for granted that presentations of identity online affect how we understand identity offline, and that the lines between the two are both blurry and mutually constitutive (Gray 2020; Shaw 2014). Furthermore, we recognize that identity formation is messy, non-linear, and that there are many factors which contribute to individual and group identity formation. We focus on the Canadian soldier figure not to suggest a one-to-one relationship between online representation and "real" identity formation; rather, we take the Canadian soldier figure to be the embodiment of one particular vision of what it means to be Canadian, which, in turn, impacts how individuals may form their own identities.

DOI: 10.4324/9781003310730-15

## The Canadian Soldier Figure

The relationship between the military, videogames, and propaganda is well established (Halter 2006; Hawreliak 2013; Payne 2016). War-themed videogames often rely on advisors and consultants from Western militaries to ensure accuracy (Stahl 2009), for instance. Furthermore, most big-budget military-themed games depict (Western) soldiers as brave, fierce fighters who are honorable, compassionate, and act out of a sense of duty to their country and comrades. Outside of videogames, myths surrounding the Canadian soldier in popular narratives depict the Canadian military as small but comprising innovative, courageous soldiers (Gordon 2014). Stories of Canadian bravery in battles such as Vimy Ridge in WWI, Juno Beach in WWII, and most recently, the Afghanistan war have been the subject of major films (e.g., *Passchendale* 2008, *Hyena Road* 2015).

Whether in film, television, or videogames (Figure 12.1), the Canadian soldier figure is typically presented as courageous, resourceful, and strong, but also white, masculine, and **heteronormative**. As we

*Figure 12.1* Canadian WWII propaganda poster (Canada: Department of National War Services).

demonstrate in our analyses below, this is also the case for videogames. It need not be this way. There are stories worth telling from other perspectives; for example, Black and Indigenous soldiers have fought for Canada in essentially every conflict, including WWI, WWII, and most certainly the recent war in Afghanistan (Government of Canada 2022). Furthermore, there is precedent for these stories, as numerous big-budget titles have recently centered stories around Black soldiers in WWI, e.g., the "Harlem Hellfighters" in *Battlefield 1* (DICE 2016), and WWII, e.g., Arthur Kingsley in *Call of Duty: Vanguard* (Activision 2021). Whether popular videogames are the best way to honor Black and Indigenous service members—who often faced racism and oppression upon their return— is a separate question, but the fact that so few of these stories exist in popular videogames is telling. Indeed, this is especially curious given the high-profile stories of Black and Indigenous soldiers serving in the Canadian Forces, perhaps most famously, Sgt. Tommy Prince, one of Canada's most decorated soldiers from the Second World War (Government of Canada 2020). Examples of female Canadian soldiers in games are even less evident. According to the Canadian Department of National Defence (2022), as of 2022 women made up 16.3% of total members in both Regular and Reserve Forces, and 13.8% of Army members, or roughly 1 in 7 Army service members. While those in combat roles are likely even fewer, there are clearly enough women in combat roles that they warrant inclusion in videogame representation.

Why then, are representations of Canadians in videogames so uniformly white, male, and heteronormative? At least part of the answer lies in wider industry trends. In games where players do not have the option to create their own character, the vast majority of playable protagonists continue to be white, cisgender, heterosexual men (Lahti 2016). There are exceptions, of course, and the trends are getting better (Petit and Sarkeesian 2020), but it remains a problem. A key contributor to the lack of representational diversity in videogames is the composition of videogame studios themselves. The demographic make-up of workers in the major game industry centers outside of Asia, such as Canada, the US, UK, and Australia continues to be homogenous (IGDA 2021).

## Method

In our analysis, we examine a number of war-themed games which feature Canadian soldiers from the two World Wars and the war in Afghanistan. Although our sample size is relatively small, it is representative given the dearth of games which represent Canadian soldiers. To identify games featuring Canadian soldiers, we conducted an Internet search of war-themed games which feature Canadian troops as playable characters.

Below is a non-exhaustive list of some of the more popular games/franchises featuring Canadian soldiers:

- *Battlefield 1942* (DICE 2002)
- *Call of Duty 3* (Activision 2006)
- *Valiant Hearts* (UbiSoft 2014)
- *Squad* (Offworld Industries 2015)
- *Rainbow Six: Siege* (UbiSoft 2015)
- *Verdun* (Blackmill Games 2016)
- *Battlefield 2042* (DICE 2021)

We found that the vast majority of Canadian soldiers were featured in multiplayer mode only, which means they do not typically come with much of a narrative frame (backstory). In the above list, only *Call of Duty 3* and *Valiant Hearts* had any narrative focus on Canadian soldiers at all.

In our analysis we primarily looked at games which feature the infantry experience, most of which are First-Person Shooters (FPSs). We do not include games which feature Canada in a militaristic role but are not military-themed games per se, such as strategy games, or games which primarily focus on air or tank combat. Future study into how the Canadian military is represented in videogames at large is an area of inquiry for the authors.

To examine these games, we adopt a **multimodal** approach, which examines how various aspects of representation (e.g., image, text, music, speech) come together in a single **semiotic** event to convey meaning (Bateman et al. 2017; Jewitt 2009; Kress and van Leeuwen 1996). A multimodal approach is useful for examining videogame representation as videogames utilize a high number of semiotic modes simultaneously (Burn 2021; Ensslin 2011; Hawreliak 2018). This approach thus allows us to better understand the entirety of a particular representation instead of just one component, such as visual appearance. Videogame developers can draw on a wide range of semiotic resources to communicate all kinds of meaning, from indicating where a player should go on a map, to intentionally or unintentionally encoding ideological views (Hawreliak 2020). In addition to established semiotic modes such as image, music and text, researchers in game studies also examine how a game's rules and mechanics express meaning through procedurality (Barnes 2019; Bogost 2007; Hawreliak 2019; Murray 1997; Russworm 2018). In the context of war-themed videogames, procedurality translates to weapon damage rates, movement speed, and win/loss conditions, which are usually determined by capturing objectives or which team has the most kills. In our analyses below, we comment on a wide range of representational components so that we can better understand the totality of how Canadian soldiers and Canadian-ness are depicted in videogames.

## Case Studies

The majority of games which feature Canadian soldiers are within the First Person Shooter (FPS) genre, which means that the player does not see their avatar very often. Nevertheless, we do get glimpses of avatars in FPSs in a number of ways, including **paratextual** elements like loading screens, menus, marketing materials, character selection, and so on. Additionally, the player can see other players too (e.g., teammates), who often belong to the same unit as the playable character.

In our research, we found that the overwhelming majority of Canadian soldiers depicted in videogames were white and male. The one exception is found in *Squad*, detailed below, which also features Black Canadian soldiers. However, we did not find a single instance of a female soldier in our scan. This does not mean that they do not exist, but it speaks to a severe gender disparity, nevertheless. We have conducted brief analyses of several games below in order to provide an overview of how Canadian soldiers are depicted.

### *Verdun* (Blackmill Games 2016)

In *Verdun*, players can take the role of Canadian soldiers in WWI in a number of classes. *Verdun* is a typical objective-based FPS wherein players are divided into two teams and must capture and hold territory, primarily by shooting and eliminating players on the other side. The game is centered around the Battle of Verdun in France, and mostly consists of fighting through trenches, in villages, and across fields. The player can play as a soldier from a variety of nations on both the Central Powers and Triple Entente sides. The Canadian soldiers are represented via a variety of semiotic modes, though they share a number of markers with British and American character models. All Canadian character models are white and male, and while it is certainly true that the vast majority of frontline soldiers in WWI were white men, there are high-profile stories of Black units, for example, who also served (Government of Canada 2022).

Visually, Canadian soldiers are differentiated by their uniforms, which are brown/green with a gold maple leaf lapel pin and, depending on the soldier class, a cap with a maple leaf emblazoned on the front. Canadian soldiers also use historically accurate weapons, such as the Lee-Enfield rifle, a bolt-action rifle fixed with a bayonet, which makes it suitable for long-range shooting as well as close encounters in enemy trenches. Musically, their theme – played after a round ends – is "The Maple Leaf Forever," which pre-dates Canada's current national anthem. The Canadian soldiers do not have any distinctive speech when compared with other Entente powers and, in fact, use the same voiceover as the British soldiers, i.e., with a British accent. In terms of gameplay or procedurality, there is not much that distinguishes Canadians from the other Entente soldiers. Although players can choose from a variety of weapon classes (like Medic, Machine-Gunner, and Assault) apart from the weapons noted above, there is no uniquely Canadian play-style here.

### *Call of Duty 3* (Activision 2006)

Of all the games surveyed, the popular FPS, *Call of Duty 3* (*CoD 3*), features the largest quantity of in-game representation of Canadian soldiers. *CoD 3* dedicates an entire section of its single-player campaign on a Canadian unit, with the others focusing on American and British units. The Canadian campaign follows the exploits of Corporal Joe Cole, a soldier with the Argyll and Sutherland Highlanders. The single-player campaign provides additional content than we see in the primarily multiplayer games: in addition to combat with other players online in the multiplayer component, there are heavily scripted cutscenes, Canadian-specific dialogue and voice-acting, and the settings of historically accurate battles.

Visually, Canadian soldiers are signified through their uniforms, which are a beige/tan color and include unit-specific markings, such as arm-patches. They are differentiated from American uniforms by the inverse chevrons for non-commissioned officers (i.e., pointing downward instead of upward), and by the brimmed helmets typical to British and Commonwealth units. For the mode of speech, the game attempts stereotypical Canadian accents and turns of phrase. For example, one of the soldiers calls his comrade a "piss-ant" while in an argument, and a sergeant tells his troops to "turn off that friggin' radio!" before battle. Cole's platoon leader, Lt. Jean-Guy Robiechauld has a Quebecois accent and uses occasional French phrases, such as "mes amis." In terms of procedurality, Canadian soldiers are outfitted with historically accurate Canadian weapons, such as the Bren machine-gun, but otherwise the gameplay does not meaningfully change between the various playable units. Nevertheless, like all games in the *CoD* series, the game requires players to enact a procedural rhetoric of heroism (Hawreliak 2013) by forcing the player to lead the charge: in certain sections, if the player does not move forward on the map, the enemies will continually respawn and the game will not progress.

Generally speaking, the soldiers are depicted as brave – with one exception – and willing to die for their countries. At one point Lt. Robiechauld tells his troops that death and glory await them, which his troops meet with good humor. The fighting has the soldiers charge head-on into heavy fire with seemingly no regard for personal safety. They are willing to sacrifice their lives for the cause of defeating Nazi Germany and liberating Europe, and one soldier receives a posthumous recommendation for the Victoria Cross, the Commonwealth's rarest and most prestigious commendation for bravery.

Again, all Canadian soldiers are white and male. It is true that the vast majority of soldiers in combat units for the Canadian military were white men; however, there are a number of highly decorated soldiers whose story could have been told, as noted above.

## *Battlefield 2042* (DICE 2021)

*Battlefield 2042* is another FPS, this time set in the future. There is no single-player campaign, so all characters appear in online multiplayer only. Like other games in the genre, the player can choose from multiple characters and each character boasts unique skills and abilities. One of the playable characters is Webster MacKay, a member of the elite Canadian special operations group, JTF-2. Visually, MacKay is white and male, and his uniform is contemporary Canadian camouflage (CADPAT). In terms of speech, there is not much to differentiate MacKay from other operators, as he only has a few lines (e.g., "reloading"). For procedurality, MacKay has two unique abilities: a grappling hook, which allows him to quickly traverse the map and more easily gain the high ground, and Nimble, which gives him increased movement speed when aiming down his weapon sights. These abilities do constitute a procedural expression of Canadian military prowess, fitting into the narrative that smaller armies need to be able to move quickly and use strategy instead of brute force in battle.

## *SQUAD* (Offworld Industries 2015)

The *CoD* and *Battlefield* series are blockbusters which prioritize action over realism. *Squad*, on the other hand, is a team-based tactical FPS that can be categorized as a military simulation or "mil-sim"; this genre is typified by its attention to realism in various representational facets, such as ultra-realistic weaponry, a focus on tactics, and realistic environments. The game is set in contemporary times and so contains contemporary weapons and technologies. Visually, the Canadian uniforms and weapons look extremely accurate: the uniforms use the CADPAT pattern with TAC vest, accurate helmet shape, and so on. The weapons are also accurate, as the infantry use the C-7 assault rifle, complete with the chevron style sight. Unlike the other games examined, *Squad* does have Black character models, which makes it an outlier and is likely a result of the game's attention to realism. There are no female character models, and a glance at the community forums illustrate that there is both a desire for this but also typical resistance. For instance, in a 2018 Reddit thread, a user asks if the game will feature female player models, but the comment is met with replies such as,

> Squad is about being realistic, so sure. They can drive supply vehicles, stay in the FOB [Forward Operating Base] doing paperwork, and comprise less than 3% of the combat infantry units in the game.
> (wysoft, Reddit user 2017)

Other comments in the thread are similar in tone. In terms of procedurality, apart from the Canadian weapons (which are very similar to American weapons), there is no play-style that differentiates Canadians from other units. *Squad*'s setting in contemporary wars also means that it plays a part in reinforcing ideas surrounding the enemy as other (e.g., an "insurgent" from Afghanistan), which is a key component of setting up in-groups and identity formation.

## Conclusion

Military service members continue to hold an honored place in Canadian society, and the soldier figure is a powerful rhetorical tool for constructing national narratives regarding ideals, values, and desirable traits. The soldier figure is an important rhetorical device not because it is illustrative of any objective or immutable "Canadian-ness," but because it represents the dominant view of ideal Canadian-ness which reinforces the status quo, i.e., masculine, physically strong, dominant, and protective. As we have demonstrated in our analyses, this is certainly the case for how Canadian soldiers are depicted in many war-themed games. With only a few exceptions, they are depicted as honorable, brave, capable of heroic feats, and they are demographically homogenous. The media we consume are one aspect of how we come to learn how to act and how to be; alternative depictions of soldiers and other societally revered figures could go a long way in changing attitudes, especially as they pertain to the mutually constitutive realms of white supremacy and toxic masculinity.

For future studies, a more comprehensive analysis of how Canadian-ness (and Canada) is represented in videogames across genres would be most welcome. To our knowledge, this remains a vastly under-explored topic. Videogames, even war-themed videogames, need not be predictable perpetuators of the status quo; they can also play a role in constructing more inclusive and healthy ideals to strive towards. As a ubiquitous medium played by people of all ages, videogames play an important part in the media landscape and therefore of individual and group identity formation.

## Key Words

**Heteronormative/Heteronormativity**: Heteronormative/Heteronormativity is the view that heterosexuality and strict gender binaries are "normal," ideal, and natural. Sexual orientations and gender identities which deviate from this norm are thus deemed to be abnormal, undesirable, and unnatural.

**Semiotics**: Semiotics is the study of meaning through the examination of signs, which include letters/words, images, sounds, and so on. A semiotic event is any sign or combination of signs which communicates meaning.

**Multimodality**: An area of semiotics called multimodality examines how semiotic modes (e.g., text, image, speech, music, gesture) come together to create meaning. For instance, the tension in a horror film is produced by visual images on-screen, but also by the film's musical score.

**Paratext**: Elements outside of or peripheral to the main text are referred to as a paratext (e.g., the cover or table of contents of a book, or marketing materials for a videogame).

## Critical Thinking Questions

1 What other sorts of messages and ideals might we find in popular videogames?
2 Are there videogames which feature Indigenous peoples in Canada? How do these games represent Indigenous people?
3 How might you use multimodal analysis to interpret videogames in other genres?

## References

"2021 Developer Satisfaction Survey COVID-19 Report – IGDA." Accessed June 28, 2022. https://igda.org/resources-archive/2021-developer-satisfaction-survey-covid-19-report/

Barnes, Katerina. 2019. "Agniq Suaŋŋaktuq and Kisima Inŋitchuŋa (Never Alone)." *First Person Scholar*, July 24, 2019. http://www.firstpersonscholar.com/agniq-suannaktuq-and-kisima-innitchuna-never-alone/

Bateman, John, Janina Wildfeuer, and Tuomo Hiippala. 2017. *Multimodality: Foundations, Research and Analysis - A Problem-Oriented Introduction*, Illustrated ed. Boston: Mouton De Gruyter.

Bogost, Ian. 2007. *Persuasive Games: The Expressive Power of Videogames*. Cambridge, MA: The MIT Press.

Brush, Stephen Lloyd. 2021. *Canadian Military Identity Constructions: Examining Civil-Military Relations in Canada*. PhD diss., University of Calgary.

Burn, Andrew. 2021. *Literature, Videogames and Learning*. 1st ed. New York; London: Routledge.

Department of National Defence. 2022. "Women in the Canadian Armed Forces," https://www.canada.ca/en/department-national-defence/services/women-in-the-forces.html

Ensslin, Astrid. 2011. *The Language of Gaming*. New York: Springer.

Gordon, Neta. 2014. *Catching the Torch: Contemporary Canadian Literary Responses to World War I*. Waterloo, ON: Wilfrid Laurier Press.

Government of Canada. "Tommy Prince," 2020. https://www.veterans.gc.ca/eng/remembrance/people-and-stories/tommy-prince

Government of Canada. "Black Canadians in Uniform: A Proud Tradition," 2022. https://www.veterans.gc.ca/eng/remembrance/people-and-stories/black-canadians

Gray, Kishonna L. 2020. *Intersectional Tech: Black Users in Digital Gaming.* Illustrated ed. Baton Rouge: LSU Press.

Halter, ed. 2006. *From Sun Tzu to XBox: War and Video Games.* New York: Public Affairs.

Hawreliak, Jason. 2013. "'To be Shot at Without Result:' Gaming Gaming and the Rhetoric of Immortality." In *Handbook of Research on Technoself: Identity in a Technological Society,* edited by Rocci Luppicini, 531–53. Hershey, PA: IGI Global.

Hawreliak, Jason. 2018. *Multimodal Semiotics and Rhetoric in Videogames.* New York: Routledge.

Hawreliak, Jason. 2019. "On the Procedural Mode." In *Approaches to Videogame Discourse: Lexis, Interaction, Textuality,* edited by Astrid Ensslin and Isabel Balteiro, 227–46. Indiana: Bloomsbury.

Hawreliak, Jason. 2020. "Experiential Rhetoric: Game Design as Persuasion," in *What Is a Game? Essays on the Nature of Videogames,* edited by Gaines Hubbell, 19–34. Jefferson, NC: McFarland.

Kress, Gunther, and Theo van Leeuwen. 1996. *Reading Images: The Grammar of Visual Design.* New York: Routledge.

Lahti, Ida. 2016. *Representation of Primary Characters in Narrative-Based Games.* PhD diss., Uppsala University.

Murray, Janet H. 1997. *Hamlet on the Holodeck: The Future of Narrative in Cyberspace.* Cambridge, MA: The MIT Press.

Payne, Matthew Thomas. 2016. *Playing War: Military Video Games After 9/11.* New York; London: NYU Press.

Petit, Carolyn, and Anita Sarkeesian. 2020. "More Video Games Featured Women This Year. Will It Last?" *Wired,* https://www.wired.com/story/women-video-games-representation-e3/

Russworm, TreaAndrea M. 2018. "Computational Blackness: The Procedural Logics of Race, Game, and Cinema, or How Spike Lee's Livin' Da Dream Productively 'Broke' a Popular Video Game." *Black Camera* 10, no. 1: 193–212.

Shaw, Adrienne. 2014. *Gaming at the Edge: Sexuality and Gender at the Margins of Gamer Culture,* Illustrated ed. Minneapolis: University of Minnesota Press.

Stahl, Roger. 2009. *Militainment, Inc.: War, Media, and Popular Culture,* 1st ed. New York: Routledge.

wysoft. 2017. "How About Female Player Models?" *Reddit.* https://www.reddit.com/r/joinsquad/comments/8kbq0i/comment/dz74m7y/?utm_source=reddit&utm_medium=web2x&context=3

# 13 Inventing with Zoom

## How Play and Games Uncover Affordances in Digital Environments

*Jacob Euteneuer*

Nails raked across a chalkboard. A metal fork scraping against a ceramic plate. Your own voice played back to you on a recording. There are sounds that make us physically recoil in horror, terror, or even physical pain. While few beyond horror movie directors and annoying younger siblings actively seek out these sounds, a whole range of beautiful and wonderful noises also exist. The calm babbling of a brook, the infectious laughter of a baby, the cheerful notes of a hermit wren's song. It should come as no surprise then that when designers and engineers are attempting to create the next viral app, they seek to make the whole experience – from the soft, welcoming chimes that play on launch to the clickable buttons that audibly pop when pressed – as positive as possible. This is a form of what Thomas Rickert terms **ambient rhetoric**. Ambient rhetoric is "an ensemble of variables, forces, and elements that shape things" (Rickert 2013, 7). While this may seem like a vague definition, it helps us to consider many of the unseen or unnoticed aspects of our environments that influence our emotions and decisions. The world around us is constantly trying to persuade us in ways we might not always consider, from a draft prompting you to close a window to a robin persuading you not to sleep in.

Nowhere is this ambient rhetoric more prevalent than in the sights, sounds, and touches of digital technologies. As an example, Rickert looks at an all-too-common sound: the startup noise for the Windows operating system. He traces the development of the early beeps and boops of personal computers to the customized and composed sounds developed to welcome users into the exciting world of Windows '95. Multiple Grammy award winner and influential composer Brian Eno was hired to develop the sound effects played as users started up Windows, launched programs, and put the PC to sleep. Combined with the blue sky and gentle cloud backgrounds, Microsoft's push to make personal computers feel a bit more at home with us worked, and people stopped associating computers solely as objects for the workplace or office. Modern apps and software now finetune every note to get the right impact on the user. But sometimes things don't always go as planned.

DOI: 10.4324/9781003310730-16

In the spring of 2020 as communities responded to the COVID-19 pandemic, a now-familiar noise rose up across the globe: the drippy "bwoop" of Zoom's five-minute notification and the chirpy "ding-dong" upon entrance to a virtual Zoom room. These noises were designed to be fun and welcoming, but their eventual replacement of the more familiar sounds of books on desks or bookbags being unzipped, left many students, teachers, and employees feeling "Zoomed out." All the beautiful noises, sounds, and poppy animations Zoom had designed soon started to become a bit too familiar as every class turned into a long Zoom meeting. For most, the crash-course introduction to Zoom consisted of getting the software downloaded and installed, testing your mic and video, and then begging people to please remember to mute themselves. In fact, beyond the trifecta of launching meetings, joining meetings, and muting mic or video, most users found themselves in a comfortable but ultimately boring position.

Is that really all there is to Zoom, though? Or can we dig in and discover more about how Zoom works, how we use Zoom, and what Zoom could be? I argue that we can. In fact, not only can we begin to create and invent with any piece of software from AllRecipes to Zoom, but doing so can reconfigure the emotional attachments that turned the once pleasurable act of hopping on to chat with your classmates or cooking up a nice homemade dinner into the dread of having to turn your video on for attendance or the drudgery of cooking another day's meals.

So, how do we perform the magical act of turning software made for "productivity" into software we want to open and engage with? We can look to the way children are able to manage the hundreds of things they are compelled to do daily. The child turns regular, necessary behavior into the "unnecessary" but oh-so-fun behavior of play. During a boring trip to the grocery store, the child joyfully hops over cracks in the parking lot. Or during the trip, the child tries to keep track of all the shoppers wearing a hat and, through their staring and counting, ends up getting an understanding of who smiles back at them and who looks away. Play can turn anything into a game, and in doing so, it helps us reestablish our relationship with whatever we are playing.

It's not just kids that can use play to reconfigure the world around them, though. While our minds might leap to kids when we hear the word "play," adults end up doing plenty of play themselves. From sports to videogames to a deck of cards, adults are also constantly playing. We play primarily for one reason: because it's fun. But what is it that makes games fun? It's not a question that can easily be answered, definitively or objectively, but game designer and author Raph Koster has come up with a pretty good idea for what we humans find fun in our games. Koster (2013) argues, "Fun from games arises out of mastery. It arises out of comprehension. It is the act of solving puzzles that makes games fun. In other words, with games, learning is the drug" (40). All the things we commonly associate with what makes a game fun – the story, the challenge, the competition – can be summarized as an act of learning. Figuring out what is behind the next door or working out the best strategy to knock off the top opponent are acts of learning.

We take joy in mastering a skill, and games feed us a constant stream of new skills to develop. If you are still skeptical that what we commonly call "fun" is just a way of talking about learning, Koster uses the example of tic-tac-toe to drive his point home. Many of us played the game when we were little and had fun. However, once you have played enough games, simple strategies emerge, and every game quickly becomes an unbreakable tie. The game has been solved, and it is no longer fun to play. A game like chess on the other hand, with a board seven times bigger and with six times as many variable pieces, takes a lot longer to "solve" and estimate every potential move or strategy. Chess remains fun because there is always more to learn. That's why we have a lot of chess competitions but very few tic-tac-toe tournaments.

Games and play can help us engage deeper with the world around us and motivate us to learn to the point where we conflate learning with fun. That is amazing, but it doesn't address the whole problem with Zoom: that feeling of your stomach filling with dread when you hear the Zoom ding-dong for the sixtieth time in a single day. Games help us reengage with people and technology, reworking our emotional attachments to the world through the act of playing. When we play games, we actually adopt a new identity. Sometimes this means we put on a whole new uniform. Other times it just means that you get to go out, compete, leave it all on the floor, and then go back to regular life. The end effect of this identity shifting is that we can try out new things, fail, and still keep moving forward. When we play and take on a new role, we are more willing to try new things and are more comfortable with failure.

Feminist scholars such as Judith Butler (1990) have helped theorize how we shift and change between these ideas through the concept of performativity. As we move through our day, we adopt and perform different aspects of ourselves and our identities. These identities can overlap or butt against each other. The different ways we express our identity – and the identities that are forced on us – lead to interesting intersections. Kimberlé Crenshaw (1989) used these intersections to call attention to the important ways discrimination and prejudice can often go uncovered or ignored. A deeper understanding and awareness of your own intersectionality can help call attention to the often unseen or unspoken experiences of others.

Digital scholar Kishonna Gray (2020) brings these ideas of intersecting identities to the Internet to demonstrate how technology and videogames have perpetuated unjust systems. However, they also have the power to disrupt and subvert those systems. While we are always able to become more conscious of intersectionality and how we perform our identity, play is one way to quickly bring these concepts to the forefront of your mind. Play may even make you more willing to log onto Zoom, if you know it doesn't have to be "you" on Zoom the whole time. It could be a version of You the Player and not just You the Student. You would probably be even more willing to be involved as well because of the interactive nature of games.

Games demand our active participation, and because we are forced to act, games are able to target a wider range of emotions, especially social emotions like camaraderie, empathy, or shame. Games researcher Katherine Isbister (2016) argues that "because players make their own choices and experience their consequences, game designers have unique powers to evoke emotions—such as guilt and pride—that typically cannot be accessed with other media" (40–1). The negative emotional relationship formed between Zoom and its users can be flipped into a positive through social play. Isbister (2016) also goes on to demonstrate how playing with other people gives us more of that wonderful fun feeling we seek from games. We can learn about the game and those we play with simultaneously. The result is a better connected and more positive environment for education. That is an enviable goal in and of itself, but play is not just some abstract, philosophical concept. We have to play *something*. We play ball. We play violin. We play roles in theatre *plays*. And what we play is what we learn about. So, how do we play with Zoom and what can such play help us learn about Zoom, software, and our digital world?

Inventing games to be played on Zoom allows for the discovery of new ways of relating to the software, new connections with other users, and a greater understanding of the processes and possibilities of "productivity" apps. Engineer, psychologist, and designer Don Norman (2013) defines the relationships and ways of interacting with a particular piece of technology as **affordances**. Norman's (2013) formal definition of an affordance is "a relationship between the properties of an object and the capabilities of the agent that determine just how the object could possibly be used" (11). A mug with no handle can still be held, but a mug with a handle affords the user the ability to hold on to a hot cup of coffee without getting too hot. Affordances are about the relationships we form with objects around us. Norman argues it's the designer's job to make these relationships as clear and obvious as possible. He examines ice cube makers, circuit boards, lawn mowers, and more to demonstrate the importance of being able to quickly and confidently identify affordances. With physical products like artist Jacques Carelman's "masochists' coffee pot" – featured below (Norman 2018) and on the cover of Norman's 2013 *The Design of Everyday Things,* the affordances are often obvious or easily discoverable through simple use. However, when we move from the physical world to the ever-evolving digital world, discovering affordances can be a lot harder.

Discovering affordances in the digital world may be the most important and most difficult task of developing a twenty-first-century digital literacy. Traditional literacy – reading and writing – has been associated with upward mobility and a developed society. Digital literacy is no different, but the skills needed to thoughtfully create and critically consume media on the Internet changes at a much quicker pace. While it may be a hard task, play and games can help us develop digital literacies, have fun, and build strong social relationships essential to a sound learning environment. Play and games work particularly well because of what game designer Bernard De Koven calls the "**play community**." De Koven invented games and taught them to camp counselors, P.E. teachers, and YMCA coaches across the country and always noticed the same thing. De Koven (2020) saw that when we play games with each other, we form stronger and more intimate social bonds. When most people complain about Zoom or other distance learning options, it is the lack of those social bonds that is the biggest complaint.

Making games can help us build those social bonds and critique the software we often uncritically rely on for everyday life. To help my students in writing and communication classes develop their digital skills, I tasked them with developing games using the many features of Zoom. They worked in groups with individual roles to develop a series of documents including rules, analysis of potential audiences who could play the games, and evaluation of the problems they faced with digital communication. Their creative results helped us all develop a more positive relationship to the software and a better understanding of the app's affordances. As a group, we decided to start with a game of screen grabs. One player would count to three, and then everyone else would make a funny pose or silly face while the original player took a screenshot of the panel of faces. From there, the player would crop the photo and add some quick text to their favorite pose and make a meme. Students loved the game and immediately felt more like a community. They laughed and joked with each other. Students turned their cameras on early to chat with classmates or stayed after class to wave or make goofy faces as the field of participants slowly dripped out of existence. It is easy to see why. Isbister (2016) notes that "researchers have found that enhanced bonding and mutual good feeling more reliably arises from coordinated physical activity involving mutual gaze" (96). Intentionally looking at each other and moving around were central to playing. In our little game, students ended up working with photo editing software like PowerPoint or GIMP to make small memes, exploring ideas of genre and circulation on the Internet, and strengthening their emotional bonds with their classmates. But, that was just the start.

While the students were having fun, some immediate questions started to arise in our discussion. Students wondered if it was ethical to take pictures of other people's faces without their consent or even their knowledge. If we could take pictures of people making funny poses, then someone else could be taking your picture at any time and pasting it all over the Internet. Our exploration of the affordances of Zoom brought up important questions about digital ethics and good digital citizenship. It is interesting to note that while Zoom allows every user to take pictures of anyone, it does have the technology to stop people from viewing others' screens when copyrighted material is playing. For example, if someone shares their screen, Netflix will not display on other users' Zoom screen. Playing with our software allows us to more deeply interrogate how it works and whom it serves.

You probably haven't spent much time thinking about how Zoom decides to arrange its panels of participants' faces. That is totally normal. But, if you were tasked with making a game out of how those panels were arranged, it would be important to figure out exactly whose face is going to be where. This is how one group of students discovered the affordances of Zoom's panel and gallery view beyond merely thinking about the size of the face talking to you on the screen. The students were trying to make a game where players had to take on certain roles – pirate, astronaut, etc. – depending on their position on the Zoom screen. Unfortunately, they were unable to ever reliably figure out who would appear in what position. And it turns out that this kind of hidden affordance – deciding whose face goes where on your computer screen – can have a real negative impact on some students. Researchers Janet Rankin and Ryan MacDowell (2021) at MIT noticed that Zoom favored users' faces in prominent positions when that user spoke often. That makes sense, but it also means that students that speak less may not even be on the screen. The researchers also cite studies which show men talk more often and earlier in class than women, potentially pushing female students off the front page at an unequal rate.

Other researchers have noticed this phenomenon as well. In an examination of academic conferences, researchers noticed that when a man was first to ask a question, women were less likely to participate in the discussion or ask a question of their own (Carter et al. 2018). Combine this tendency with Zoom's preference for highlighting the most recent speaker and you have a regressive cycle where only male students are speaking and sharing their perspective. Even the most attentive professor may end up putting the rest of the students out of sight, out of mind. But, because play has the potential to jostle us and make us reconsider our current context, play can be a way to find these potentially hidden inequities buried in our software and digital experiences.

The games students created ranged from adapting existing board games like Apples to Apples to creating their own cave-exploring, spelunking live action roleplaying game where dark sections required participants to turn their cameras off. The students explored the various affordances of the software to see what could be used for game mechanics. The ability to blur backgrounds led to simple "Guess Where I Am?" games. More important features such as the chat function led to more complex games as students tinkered and explored with the display names, the interplay between video and text, and the ability to message privately and publicly across breakout rooms or whole sessions. From these elements of the software, students forged games about detectives searching for hidden messages and a series of riddles where player names were changed to colors. Through designing, crafting, and writing about games, students were able to learn and gain a better understanding of the software they were using, including exploring important issues like privacy and catfishing, all while having fun. That shouldn't be much of a surprise, though. Learning really is just another form of having fun. If we can take the everyday, mundane technologies we use and turn them into tools for playing, we can reshape our relationship with technology. As our world becomes increasingly digital and the total time we spend online begins to eclipse the total time we spend offline, it will be more necessary than ever to maintain healthy relationships with our apps. Play and games are one way to build that positive relationship with the added benefit of broadening our skills and digital literacy.

## Key Words

**Affordance**: The relationship between an object and its user that defines its possible uses or indicates how the object can or should operate is referred to as an affordance. An object or app's affordances are the total sum of different ways someone could use it.

**Ambient Rhetoric**: The ambient rhetoric is the total sum of the environmental aspects that influence our actions and decisions. This includes all sensory detail and types of information present, both human constructed and natural.

**Play Community**: The bond formed among a group of people as they work toward a common goal can be called a play community. This social community exists most intensely during acts of play but persists even after play ends.

## Critical Thinking Questions

1. How has your relationship with Zoom, Microsoft Teams, or other similar apps changed over the last year? What types of apps or programs do you look forward to opening or using and how do they differ from the types of apps you dread clicking?
2. When was the last time you created a new game or even a new rule for an old game? If it's been a while, why do you think adults rarely make their own games? Can inventing new games help us be more creative, or is play really just a waste of time?

3   How does the composition of a group affect your participation in that group? With what types of communities, topics, or people are you more likely to participate? Does that type of community building and participation have an effect on your education or social life?

## References

Butler, Judith. 1990. *Gender Trouble: Gender and the Subversion of Identity*. New York: Routledge.

Carter, Alecia J., Alyssa Croft, Dieter Lukas, and Gillian M. Sandstrom. 2018. "Women's Visibility in Academic Seminars: Women Ask Fewer Questions Than Men." *PLoS One* 13, no. 9: e0202743. https://doi.org/10.1371/journal.pone.0202743

Crenshaw, Kimberlé. 1989. "Demarginalizing the Intersection of Race and Sex: A Black Feminist Critique of Antidiscrimination Doctrine, Feminist Theory, and Antiracist Politics." *University of Chicago Legal Forum* 1, no. 8: 139–67.

De Koven, Bernard. 2020. *The Infinite Playground: A Player's Guide to Imagination*, edited by Celia Pearce and Eric Zimmerman. Cambridge, MA: MIT Press.

Gray, Kishonna L. 2020. *Intersectional Tech: Black Users in Digital Gaming*. Baton Rouge, LA: Louisiana State Press.

Isbister, Katherine. 2016. *How Games Move Us: Emotion by Design*. Cambridge, MA: MIT Press.

Koster, Raph. 2003. *A Theory of Fun for Game Design*. Sebastopol, CA: O'Reilly Media.

Norman, Don. 2013. *The Design of Everyday Things, Revised & Expanded*. New York: Basic Books.

Norman, Don. 2018. "Unusable Objects." *JND.org*, last modified November 12, 2018. https://jnd.org/unusable-objects/

Rankin, Janet, and Ryan MacDowell. 2021. "How to Overcome Zoom's Algorithmic Bias." *MIT Teaching and Learning Lab*. Accessed October 27, 2021. https://tll.mit.edu/how-to-overcome-zooms-algorithmic-bias/

Rickert, Thomas. 2013. *Ambient Rhetoric: The Attunements of Rhetorical Being*. Pittsburgh, PA: University of Pittsburgh Press.

# 14 Interfaces and Their Affordances
## Critical Game Design, Identity, and Community in MMORPGs

*Chris Hugelmann*

Digital games have become a mainstay in the entertainment industry, given the rise in home console gaming since the 1980s, as well as mobile, or casual, gaming (Juul 2010). Much of gaming gains its value from time spent working towards mastery of the mechanics in a game, and high levels of mastery are commonly associated with genres like massively multiplayer online role-playing games (MMORPGs), where players compete against one another in player vs. player (PvP) and player vs. environment (PvE) activities. In many role-playing games, identity, agency, and immersion are vital aspects of gameplay and offer a social space to explore new identities and social interactions. This facet of gaming can be especially meaningful for people who are unable to enact these social or identity realities in their everyday lives.

This chapter highlights the importance of identity and community in online digital games and analyses MMORPGs as well as contemporary game scholarship on social values, identity play, in-game interfaces, community, and their intersections. **Critical play** is highlighted as an essential component for creating games that allow for identity and community creation. Specifically, the *interfaces* that players engage with are highlighted as the means to enable identity and social play online. Finally, **modding**, the act of modifying a game's code in ways that players deem useful, is discussed. To conclude, this chapter discusses how players engage in these practices, and encourages critical reflection on the importance of who they are and how they engage online.

### Identity and Community in Online Digital Games

Creating one's character, or avatar, in-game is paramount in one's attempt to "perform and present different identities" (Bullingham and Vasconcelos 2013, 102). The player has agency in creating their avatar, which allows them to explore new identities whether it's an idealized version of themselves, or an identity that oscillates between the online and offline self (102). In reference to digital games, Victoria McArthur et al. (2015) define **affordances** as "action possibilities" (232) that a player can

DOI: 10.4324/9781003310730-17

enact within the game world. While many games offer the opportunity to create or customize one's character or avatar, not every game offers the same affordances. Thus, affordances refer to an object's ability to convey what it is designed to do through a technology's "qualities, features, or cues" (Nagy and Neff 2015, 2). Avatars can alter and shape a player's behaviours in-game (Ayiter 2010), highlighting the importance of the affordances of in-game interfaces to provide flexible customization to enable diverse player representation.

Scholarly work on digital game interfaces has focused on the character creation process. Beyond identity play, many of the social aspects of MMORPGs rely on the formation of groups or long-term **guilds** in order to complete difficult end-game content. Guilds or clans in MMORPGs can offer more than a means to an end; they are also places where social interactions occur. Whang and Chang (as cited in Zhong 2011) point out that online games should be considered "a social place where new types of human relationships are created" (2352). These social interactions can be formed through matchmaking within the game itself (Nardi 2010, 15) or organically through common interests (301).

Many guilds form from groups of friends that want to play together and socialize online. Social bonds can help "gamers redefine their own goals and what enjoyment they could/should attain from playing" (Eklund and Ask 2013, 6), where players navigate the tension between enjoying time spent with others while trying to complete challenging end-game missions. Especially for *hardcore* players – those who complete end-game content – many games offer social capital through *reputation*. In *World of Warcraft* (Blizzard Entertainment 2004), this reputation system highlights a player's trustworthiness and progress throughout the game, encouraging "others to cooperate with them" (Bainbridge 2010, 122). This is showcased through the designed division and specialization of in-game tasks within typical MMORPG classes: tank, damage per second, and healer (Bainbridge 2010, 125). This interdependence implies that forming groups can serve to "increase gaming efficiency" (Ducheneaut et al. as cited in Zhong 2011, 2353). Typically, in-game goals become set expectations for new guild members. These expectations, however, are not always part of the in-game interfaces. In this way, the interface may prevent new membership, as the information that it affords may be lacking based on its underlying design.

In William Sims Bainbridge's (2010) ethnography within *World of Warcraft,* an informant noted that some "[p]eople have different values, and some place a higher value on winning points than winning friends" (133). This is also noted as a distinct shift "from 'friendly guild' to 'raiding guild'" (Eklund and Ask 2013, 5), where progressing through missions becomes a more powerful draw than friendly social spaces. This is especially prevalent in extraludic spaces – spaces related to the game but that exist outside of the game itself, like web forums. If the in-game interface feels lacking, players will seek other avenues to find players, such as within *Destiny 2*'s (Bungie 2017) looking-for-group forums. This becomes vital when creating and maintaining a large group of individuals working to achieve similar goals within a gameworld.

Authors have noted that through game design changes over *World of Warcraft*'s development, most socialization occurs within end-game content. Once players have reached end-game content that requires coordinated groups of individuals, groups can be created through matchmaking without speaking with others (Ducheneaut et al. as cited in Braithwaite 2018, 120). This means that forming groups only when it is needed for a specific purpose is a viable strategy in earlier parts of the game, allowing for more organic groupings to occur. However, closer to the end when "missions get too resource and time demanding," obstacles tend to "no longer be dealt with by teams built up on an ad-hoc basis" (Daneva 2017, 57). Thus, longer term social groups like guilds are generally linked with difficult end-game missions.

There is a need to explore how social aspects are built into the gameworld and understanding how to support player interactions. Game designers and developers must be aware of this, as they are the ones who "make the rules by which [the game] society operates" (Castronova as cited in Braithwaite 2018, 123).

## Critical Play, Critical Game Studies and Its Significance to Game Design

Critical game design posits that games can take on the intricacies of cultural and social life (Flanagan 2009, 6). Critical game design, aims to position game designers as individuals who imbue specific aspects of life into digital games, not only from a narrative standpoint, but also through mechanics and rules. Mary Flanagan's early work entitled *Critical Play: Radical Game Design* (2009) showcases a perspective on game design and game practices that she calls critical play, which proposes:

> an alternative, or 'radical,' game design [... that] investigates games designed for artistic, political, and social critique or intervention, in order to propose ways of understanding larger cultural issues as well as the games themselves.
>
> (2)

The focus of critical game design is to convey "human concerns, identifiable as principles, values, or concepts" (257) into the game. Flanagan pushes critical game designers to consider how all of the elements and processes of game design can be made to serve the interventionist or cultural goals of the game. This centralization of values and human concerns is essential, as the interfaces of online digital games play an important role in accessibility and community formation, given the global nature of games in the MMORPG genre. A critical play methodology to reconfigure game interfaces can offer a flexible and immersive way to play with notions of identity and community in digital games. As Flanagan describes it, "games designers have yet to grapple with the full range of inequities ingrained [...] in most of today's games" (225). Even something as seemingly benign as a choice of race for the player's character, can offer an opportunity to reflect on the notion further such as a permanent penalty for choosing a High Elf avatar in *Skyrim*.

As described by Flanagan, the critical play methodology can be viewed as a subversive intervention into normal digital game tropes and genres, driving games to "engage with political or social issues – a 'stepping in' or interfering [...] to affect its course or issue" (11). Improving aspects of identity and community within online digital games through their interfaces through a critical play mentality can afford more flexibility and accessibility for players to *play with* identity and community.

Ultimately, critical game design and the critical play method are important in understanding how games engage with social and cultural issues, even within the interfaces of an MMORPG. Utilizing this approach can help designers explore the ways a game's design can be altered to better support and empower players to play in potentially subversive ways. In terms of the interface design of MMORPGs, critical play can reveal how even something as simple as changing the typical gender binary option in the character creation interface to a slider can allow the player to critically engage with ideas about the social construction and fluidity of gender. As digital games continue to invite play, community, and membership, these spaces should be investigated as a "site for play and struggle" which are constantly negotiated, and "contain the possibility for social [...] transformation" (253).

## The Role of Designers and Modders

Mods have long been the way that players take control over assets in a game. Tanja Sihvonen (2011) describes modding as an activity "where the player tweaks, adds, alters, and deletes existing game code to transform her own gameplay experience" (39), and adds that modding is "both a subcategory of game creation as well as [...] hobby" (155). One needs to only look at social formations of modders, such the website Nexus Mods, to see how modders work together and create social spaces.

Many contemporary digital games are created with game engine platforms like Unity and Unreal Engine. In fact, "Unity [alone] is responsible for more than half of all videogames published on commercial platforms" (Nicoll and Keogh 2019, 35). Because of their relative simplicity, these game engines are an important tool for scaffolding the work of developers. Sometimes argued as "lowering the barrier of entry to becoming a videogame developer" (Nicoll and Keogh 2019, 104), this scaffolding and utilization of pre-made assets can help to "avoid unnecessary repetition so as to focus resources and labour towards [other] aspects of development" (Nicoll and Keogh 2019, 105). This is similar to the ways in which modding communities alter digital games and allows players to create better ways to enable identity play and community formation in digital games. Mods can be simple tweaks to lighting or textures like in *Dragon Age: Inquisition* (BioWare 2014) (Collins 2020, 26–31; Sihvonen 2020, 162–166), while others create entirely new games, sometimes called "total conversions" (Johnson 2009, 50) such as the original *Counter-Strike* (Cliffe, Le, and Gray 1999). Through the use of these popular game engines, one takes on a **modder stance**, by working within the confines of the engine or development platform while actively attempting to restructure, rework, or modify the ways digital games are created. This also means aligning games with what users are searching for in terms of accessibility, usability, identity and community support, and positive player experience. This brings a sense of collaboration and community back into digital games through user-generated content and mods.

Many games rely on mods to extend their lifecycle and provide elements that were lacking in the original game, such as *The Sims* having nearly 90% of its content created by users (Hayes and King as cited in Jones 2020, 95). Mods are "likely to be motivated by the players' desire to improve and upgrade their own gameplay experience" (Sihoven 2011, 38). Modders have increasingly been the subject of academic research due to their "agency and their complex and mutually beneficial relations with the game industry" (Sotamaa 2010, 240), which further highlights the need for developers to maintain relevancy as well as the demand from consumers to have improvements to their favourite games. This points towards a "redefining of developer responsibility" (Miele 2020, 146), where the critical play mentality for accessibility and representation should fall on the developer. *The Elder Scrolls V: Skyrim* (Bethesda Softworks 2011), for example, offered a tool for developing mods called the "Creation Kit" (Miele 2020, 134), which gave modders the tools they needed to implement user interface, texture, and gameplay changes. This indicates "that developers are, perhaps, looking at what modders have identified as problematic" (145) which were then modded, translating into a marked increase in avatar customization options, given that many of the mods of Bethesda's previous games revolved around the ability to alter a player's avatar's appearance to include things such as natural hair styles or different body shapes (136–9).

## Being the New You with Your Crew, or How You Are Already Performing Online

Overall, reflecting on critical game design literature, as well as the work of modders, is vital to investigating how identity and community can be better supported by game developers and modders within digital games. In many ways, those who engage with MMORPGs are constantly negotiating their identity and community performances without noticing; the avatars that they create and the groups they play with result from how they want to enjoy and play the game. The identity and community of players are mediated through the game mechanics – such as needing several different types of characters to take on end-game bosses – as well as the interfaces the player is presented with – what types of identity they can create with the character creation interfaces.

The mediation of identity and community through in-game interfaces continues to be studied at length, offering ways to improve these interfaces for practitioners, like game designers, and to critically assess what these interfaces do for players' sense of sociality in-game. Modding has been the predominant way to reconfigure these interfaces for players (Targett et al. 2012), while others request flexibility and customization from designers to allow for "developers and users to collaborate and cooperate in the creation of user preferred UI" (Hui and See 2015, 1932). It is vitally important to be aware of the affordances that interfaces offer players in creating their identity and social circles in-game, and to consider how these interfaces can affect or limit in-game play. Every design choice creates new realities for players, and both designers and players should be cognizant of these when engaging with contemporary digital games.

## Key Words

**Affordances**: Though argued to have been overused to the point of being misleading in communication studies (Nagy and Neff 2015), affordances have been discussed as the possibilities for actions that are understood through the design of the object or interface. For instance, in Norman's famous example, a door handle affords a person to pull a door, whereas a horizontal bar on the door affords a person to push it.

**Critical Play**: Critical play is a concept and book (*Critical play: Radical game design*) conceived by Mary Flanagan (2009) that works to push game design towards the avant-garde, and creates a process by which designers can create "artistic, political, and social critique" games to better understand the larger social or cultural world through the media of digital games (2).

**Guild**: A long-term social formation within a digital game is referred to as a guild. Its name is taken from historical groups of merchants, artisans, or tradespeople that shared a similar practice, such as locksmiths or shoemakers. Guilds in digital games offer a similar social space for players that share common interests or goals within a game.

**Modder Stance**: A type of game design that utilizes the scaffolding of knowledge that is enabled by pre-built assets in game development platforms such as Unity or Unreal Engine in much the same way that modders utilize a game's code to alter it into something new.

**Modding**: Modding is the act of modifying a game's code in ways that players deem useful.

## Critical Thinking Questions

1 In what ways has your gameplay changed based on the avatar you were given/created? Was this change intentional?
2 How do social experiences with players you've been automatically paired with compare to those that with friends or people you know?
3 If you were to take the design of a character creation interface and a guild creation interface within an MMORPG and alter it, what would you include? What would you remove? Why?

## References

Ayiter, Elif. 2010. "Embodied in a Metaverse: Anatomia and Body Parts." *Technoetic Arts* 8, no. 2: 181–88. https://doi.org/10.1386/tear.8.2.181_1

Bainbridge, William Sims. 2010. *The Warcraft Civilization: Social Science in a Virtual World*. Cambridge: MIT Press.

Bethesda. Elder Scrolls V: Skyrim. Bethesda. PC/Xbox/PlayStation/Nintendo. 2011.

BioWare. Dragon Age: Inquisition. BioWare. PC/Xbox/PlayStation. 2014.

Blizzard Entertainment. World of Warcraft. Blizzard Entertainment. PC/Mac. 2004.

Braithwaite, Andrea. 2018. "WoWing Alone: The Evolution of 'Multiplayer' in *World of Warcraft*." *Games and Culture* 13, no. 2: 119–35. https://doi.org/10.1177/1555412015610246

Bullingham, L., and A. C. Vasconcelos. 2013. "'The Presentation of Self in the Online World': Goffman and the Study of Online Identities." *Journal of Information Science* 39, no. 1: 101–12. https://doi.org/10.1177/0165551512470051

Bungie. Destiny 2. Bungie. PC/Xbox/PlayStation. 2017.

Cliffe, Jesse, Minh Le and Richard Gray. Counter-Strike. PC/Mac/Xbox/PlayStation. 1999.

Collins, Jennifer. 2020. "'And nothing he has wrought shall be lost': Examining Race and Sexuality in the Mods of Dragon Age: Inquisition." In *Women and Video Game Modding: Essays on Gender and the Digital Community*, edited by Bridget Whelan, 9–35. Jefferson, NC: McFarland & Company.

Daneva, Maya. 2017. "Striving for Balance: A Look at Gameplay Requirements of Massively Multiplayer Online Role-Playing Games." *Journal of Systems and Software* 134: 54–75. https://doi.org/10.1016/j.jss.2017.08.009

Eklund, Lina, and Kristine Ask. 2013. "The Strenuous Task of Maintaining and Making Friends: Tensions between Play and Friendship in MMOs." In *DiGRA 2013: DeFragging Game Studies, Conference Proceedings*. Atlanta Georgia, USA.

Flanagan, Mary. 2009. *Critical Play: Radical Game Design*. Cambridge: MIT Press.

Hui, Sarah Low Tze, and Swee Lan See. 2015. "Enhancing User Experience through Customisation of UI Design." *Procedia Manufacturing* 3: 1932–7.

Johnson, Derek. 2009. "*StarCraft* Fan Craft: Game Mods, Ownership, and Totally Incomplete Conversions." *The Velvet Light Trap* 64, no. 1: 50–63. https://doi.org/10.1353/vlt.0.0041

Jones, Shelly. 2020. "Simulated Ableism: The Sims and the Lack of Disability Representation." In *Women and Video Game Modding: Essays on Gender and the Digital Community*, edited by Bridget Whelan, 90–113. Jefferson, NC: McFarland & Company.

Juul, Jesper. 2010. *A Casual Revolution: Reinventing Video Games and Their Players*. Cambridge: MIT Press.

McArthur, Victoria, Robert John Teather, and Jennifer Jenson. 2015. "The Avatar Affordances Framework: Mapping Affordances and Design Trends in Character Creation Interfaces." In *CHI PLAY '15. Conference Proceedings*, 231–40. London: ACM Press. https://doi.org/10.1145/2793107.2793121

Miele, Cara. 2020. "Simulated Ableism: The Sims and the Lack of Disability Representation." In *Women and Video Game Modding: Essays on Gender and the Digital Community*, edited by Bridget Whelan, 126–50. Jefferson, NC: McFarland & Company.

Nagy, Peter, and Gina Neff. 2015. "Imagined Affordance: Reconstructing a Keyword for Communication Theory." *Social Media + Society* 1, no. 2: 1–9. https://doi.org/10.1177/2056305115603385

Nardi, Bonnie A. 2010. *My Life as a Night Elf Priest: An Anthropological Account of World of Warcraft*. Technologies of the Imagination. Ann Arbor, MI: University of Michigan Press.

Nicoll, Benjamin, and Brendan Keogh. 2019. *The Unity Game Engine and the Circuits of Cultural Software*. New York: Springer International Publishing.

Sihvonen, Tanja. 2011. *Players Unleashed!: Modding The Sims and the Culture of Gaming*. Amsterdam: Amsterdam University Press.

Sihvonen, Tanja. 2020. "Game Characters as Tools for Expression: Modding the Body in Mass Effect." In *Women and Video Game Modding: Essays on Gender and the Digital Community*, edited by Bridget Whelan, 151–71. Jefferson, NC: McFarland & Company.

Sotamaa, Olli. 2010. "When the Game Is Not Enough: Motivations and Practices Among Computer Game Modding Culture." *Games and Culture* 5, no. 3: 239–55. https://doi.org/10.1177/1555412009359765

Targett, Sean, Victoria Verlysdonk, Howard J Hamilton, and Daryl Hepting. 2012. "A Study of User Interface Modifications in World of Warcraft." *Game Studies* 12, no. 2: 1–38.

Zhong, Zhi-Jin. 2011. "The Effects of Collective MMORPG (Massively Multiplayer Online Role-Playing Games) Play on Gamers' Online and Offline Social Capital." *Computers in Human Behavior* 27, no. 6: 2352–63. https://doi.org/10.1016/j.chb.2011.07.014

# 15 Better than the Real You? VR, Identity, Privacy, and the Metaverse

*Iain Macpherson and Adiki Puplampu*

> *Kentarō rolls off his futon, tired and bleary with the sluggishness that comes from prolonged virtual exertions; he'd spent all yesterday recumbent in his VR lounger. He'd attended two computing conferences, via his favourite handsome-geek avatar. Then he partied all night at a Fortnite-hosted rave. At the sink, he puts in his smart-lens contacts, blinking twice to bring up the weather and start the coffeemaker.*
>
> *He heads out for a bike ride. Beautiful day, but he can't stand the ravine anymore; its homeless encampments are getting bigger every week. An upper-left eye roll, and now he's cycling through the Japanese countryside outside his childhood hometown. As he stops atop the hill, an ad rolls across his view, for Zuckerbeerg Ale, featuring the Meta CEO hydrofoiling on a lake before quaffing a cold one. One blink, and Kentarō has ordered a case.*

If tech-sector CEOs from firms like Meta and Microsoft, plus industry hypers and investors, get their way, then days and nights like Kentarō's will become commonplace. This future is heralded under a banner-word **the metaverse**, envisioned as a blending of virtual and physical realities that will profoundly alter how people experience everyday life, from entertainment to work to relationships. Think 'augmented reality' (**AR**): So, these are computer visuals overlaid by screen or lens onto the actual world – but re-imagine this as a more seamlessly immersive experience, in which we intensify or reduce, at will, our envelopment in virtuality. Meta CEO Mark Zuckerberg recently described the metaverse as an "embodied Internet, where instead of just viewing content, you are in it" (as cited in Newton, 2021, para.11). This metaverse will depend on advances and convergences across a vast technological array: 5/6G telecommunications, computer processing/graphics, VR, AR, artificial intelligence, social media, the mobile Internet, 'smart' glasses/lenses, body tracking and face recognition, holograms and deepfakes, blockchain and cryptocurrency, and 'the Internet of Things.'

If this massively, multi-user, multimedia metaverse comes to pass, there will be ramifications for everything from the economy and politics to psychology and relationships. This chapter explores implications for human identity, in three senses: psychological well-being, a deeper 'sense of self,'

DOI: 10.4324/9781003310730-18

## VR, Identity, Privacy, and the Metaverse 153

and digital privacy. In each case, we highlight negative and positive discoveries and potentials regarding existing and emergent technologies. Our conclusions are tentative, since findings on 'virtual identity' remain debated, and the metaverse isn't here yet, but this chapter will equip you to decide whether you approach its subject with worry, wonder, or doubt that **virtual reality** (VR) will transcend niche interests any time soon.

### Definitions/History: VR, AR, the Metaverse

Historians trace the origins of **VR** – technologically rendered artificial environments – to the 1830s invention of 3D stereoscopes. The VR abbreviation is specific to computer-powered technologies, typically based on 'head-mounted displays' (HMDs) or projections onto the wall-screens of a chamber or room. Usually, the medium renders a 3D audio-visual experience that is low-resolution and cartoony or videogame-like, though more photorealistic offerings are increasingly common. **AR** refers to less immersive 'augmented reality': digital information layered onto the real world seen through a viewfinder. Pokémon Go is its most famous example. The first VR contraptions appeared in the 1960s, with names fun to know: Sensorama! The Sword of Damocles! However, these alternatives to real reality were too crude, their interfaces too ill-fitting, if not painful or nausea-inducing, and their cost too high, for mass adoption. VR/AR at this time did achieve significant advances in professional usage, from flight simulation to military training. Such successes have continued to this day, branching out into health care and education.

However, the same flaws frustrating VR's earliest backers – lack of realism, comfort, and affordability – have persisted, impeding the technology's popularization. VR's history is one of hype cycles, fuelled by its capture of popular imagination in cyberpunk fiction, from 1984s *Neuromancer* to 1999s *The Matrix*. VR faddishness swelled during the 1990s, amidst fascination with Internet-mediated 'cyberspace,' but this was short-lived, with emblematic flops like Nintendo's Virtual Boy console. VR re-entered the limelight with Second Life's mid-2000s boom, proving people would pay big to buy digitally rendered real estate and advertise to avatars. VR/AR interest resurged after 2010, peaking with Facebook's 2014 purchase of VR-headset company Oculus.

In 2020, Facebook released Oculus Quest 2. This proved successful by many measures, with approximately 8 million units sold worldwide, more than 170 thousand in Canada (Roettgers 2021). Many credit the product with finally, or nearly, mainstreaming VR. They attribute this to the headset's $400 CAD affordability, untethered lightness, and social media compatibility – plus COVID-19 lockdowns making VR more appealing and less strange relative to its real counterpart. Oculus' perceived potential was a central factor in Facebook's October 2021 rebranding as Meta.

Meta formerly Facebook aims to spearhead a tech-sector shift towards the **metaverse**, a term minted by Neal Stephenson in his 1992 cyberpunk novel *Snow Crash*. With its sci-fi overtones, and not-yet status, the buzzword *metaverse* remains defined variously and vaguely, often as some evolution of the Internet. Many imagine it as the physical world smoothly synchronized with VR, through technological advancements from holograms, AI, and the miniature-computerization of, well, everything (including humans), to ever-more inconspicuous interfaces such as 'smart glasses' now rolling out, and the AR contact lenses being prototyped.

## Virtuality and Identity

For our purposes, dictionary definitions of identity generally suffice, e.g., "the qualities, beliefs, etc., that make a particular person or group different from others" (Merriam-Webster). Below, we focus on three aspects of identity key to understanding how it's influenced by VR/AR: (1) mental wellness, from a psychological perspective; (2) a more philosophically conceptualized 'sense of self'; and (3) privacy, as in control over digital information identifying us to others.

### *Virtuality and Well-Being*

Most mass-market VR platforms are now *S*VR – Internet-connected social media – also offering VR-enhanced versions of other online utilizations: chat, games, passive entertainment, exercise, education, work. As such, the negative impacts on well-being attributed to 2D digital media are also attributable to (S)VR, including addiction, other mental ailments, misinformation, polarization, surveillance, and harassment or worse. Especially where vulnerable populations are concerned, it's crucial to determine how such ills might be exacerbated by HMD realism, which can produce psychological reactions, from euphoria to terror and phantom pain. Moreover, real injuries stem from VR use or overuse, such as nausea, headaches, falls or collisions, and neck and eye strain. Some have unknown long-term implications, especially for children (Pavlick 2018).

This hasn't been examined intensively, for research-ethics reasons and because VR remains an obscure phenomenon. Unsurprisingly, researchers have found that people engage via their avatars in provocation and prejudice, even (virtual) violence, just as they do elsewhere online and offline. But whether VR abuse is worse than on other digital platforms, or whether human rights might extend to avatars, remain understudied and debated (Franks 2017). It's clearer that VR can have psychological and physical benefits. Since the late 1990s, VR has proved effective in pain reduction treatments and exposure therapy for PTSD, phobias, and anxiety. Recent experiments suggest wide-ranging remedial applications, from treating psychoses, addictions, and autism, to increasing empathy (Emmelkamp and Meyerbröker 2021).

Such deployments take place in controlled, professional environments, not the private/public free-for-all of social media, with which mass-consumption (S)VR has merged. And what about the metaverse? If VR can render psychologically real the pleasures, aggravations, and horrors of virtuality, with consequences we don't yet fathom, what will it mean for barriers to blur between VR and the real world? Whether your imaginings here run more utopic or dystopian, also consider the hype-cycle history of VR, and the possibility that *metaverse* joins the graveyard of industry buzzwords proving hollow. Thus far, it remains largely indistinguishable from headset-connected VR.

## *Virtuality and Selfhood*

However weird the metaverse proves, it's already that way where VR concerns users' inmost sense of self. 'Virtual selfhood' scholarship has long focused on *avatars*, on-screen representations of users, created or selected by them. While photorealistic avatars are being worked on, presently in mass-consumption VR they're cartoony resemblances of users, other people, or inhuman creatures. In the case of (S)VR, they engage in voice-to-voice communication with other avatars, whose real-life identity may be known or not.

Research on avatars and identity reports positive psychological impacts, often involving the *proteus effect*: intense identification with avatars altering a user's subsequent attitudes, behaviour, and thus identity. Guo Freeman and Divine Maloney (2020) found that avatar-based self-experimentation built confidence in youth and those with various anxieties. Minority-population users explained how exploring gender, sexuality, and race via avatars helped them affirm their orientations and culture. The authors note others' findings that bias might be reduced through users adopting avatars of different ethnicity.

Yet, some subjects described "confusions and even fear" (Freeman and Maloney 2020, 23) arising from prolonged avatar usage, involving uncertainty about how to differentiate "VR self from the physical self" (Freeman and Maloney 2020, 24). Postmodernists have long warned that the destabilization of identity caused by contemporary changes, not least new media technologies, might not be an emancipatory metamorphosis, or at least that it also involves alienation, contestation, and reactive 'identity politics.' VR is no egalitarian paradise. Its spaces are much likelier to be native English, heterosexual-male, and white or "alien-hued," than BIPOC and/or Queer. As with social media in general, the anonymity many platforms enable frees too many to express their worst selves. Freeman and Maloney (2020) report some minority-population users adopting white or nonhuman avatars not as ontological adventure, but to avoid discrimination. For more privileged folks, there's the question of when such digital cosplay constitutes cultural appropriation (Nakamura 2020).

Some profound questions arising from studies of virtual selfhood are becoming less speculative. Computer-controlled avatars of departed loved ones are being animated by an assemblage of technologies, from VR to holograms, deepfakes, and AI (Matei 2017). How might these phantasms alter our experience of grieving? What if the metaverse coalesces not only virtual and physical worlds, but this one and the afterlife? The metaverse intensifies every question about virtual selfhood. Would liberation or estrangement predominate as we're able to alter our appearance, or that of others, with increasing ease? Doubtless, this depends greatly on the control we maintain over our digital identities, which brings us to our next subject.

### *Virtuality and Privacy*

Concerns over digital privacy, from surveillance to cybercrime, increasingly apply to VR/AR; these technologies exacerbate some such issues while introducing a host of their own. We're focusing here on threats to privacy, and efforts to protect it; however, tough trade-offs are involved, chief amongst them ensuring anonymity versus accountability for behaviours deemed unacceptable on a platform (Hamilton 2021).

AR especially puts *others'* privacy at stake, often being based on gathering information about things or people viewed through its lenses. Unobtrusive gear is being designed for mass-public usage, the most high-profile being Meta's tie-up with Ray Bans to produce Stories 'smart sunglasses,' released September 2021. Its AR functionality is nominal; the only digital overlay happens on a wearer's Bluetooth-paired smartphone. However, privacy advocates have raised alarms about the glasses' embedded video camera. A small white LED turns on while recording, but critics point out the light is easily covered, and that the industry-standard red colour would be much more noticeable, as would an accompanying noise. They also bring up Facebook's dubious record with stewardship of user data (Leufer 2021).

With VR, privacy concerns centre on the user's own identity. Current apparatuses extract immense amounts of biometric data – measurements and calculations of a person's physical characteristics – through the motion detectors of hand or body trackers, with eye tracking and facial-expression capture in development. Biometrics are increasingly able to determine a subject's unique identity, gender, age, ethnicity, personality, emotional states, cognitive capacity including inebriation or mental illness, level of fatigue, and various aspects of health (Selinger 2021).

Meta knows it faces suspicion about its metaverse motives, especially those involving privacy. At the conference announcing Facebook's new name, CEO Zuckerberg declared, "Privacy and safety need to be built into the metaverse from day one" (Hashim 2021). However, rhetorically analysing Facebook's Oculus successive privacy statements, Egliston and Carter (2021) illuminate its use of verbal ambiguity to appear "responsive and responsible in light of questions of data privacy" while still "position[ing] itself for maximal data extraction" (2).

Facebook/Meta has always been at core a company that sells targeted-ad space. With increasing corporate scepticism about the effectiveness of targeted advertising (Egliston and Carter 2021), the granular physical data gathered by equipment like Oculus kits constitute a 'Holy Grail' for advertisers (Selinger 2021). Facebook communications *seem* to state they anonymize Oculus user data that doesn't need connection with an account for basic functionalities, and prior to sharing it with other parties (Egliston and Carter 2021). However, studies have found that skilled analysts can easily identify VR users based on their 'movement signatures' (Bode 2020).

It remains to be seen how much Meta will respect privacy, whether from public pressure, competition, or compulsion. Facebook's privacy-related policies have shifted in response to government regulation in large markets, such as Europe's General Data Protection Regulation (GDPR). These policies have pushed Facebook into making changes applicable everywhere, involving matters such as user control over personal information. However, it's also been contesting such directives in court, and critics complain that levied fines are too miniscule to dissuade future infringements (Lomas 2021).

Broadly speaking, North American privacy regimes are laxer than Europe's. In the US and Canada, they comprise a complicated web of nationwide and state/provincial laws, and there are calls in both countries for more uniform regulation. In 2020, the Canadian government announced intentions for a new federal law, the Consumer Privacy Protection Act (CPPA), which would greatly enhance privacy protections, as well as financial penalties for violations, (Epiq n.d.). However, Canada's August 2021 snap election halted passage of the bill, C-11.

Instead of regulation to fend off the metaverse's negative potentials, many pin their hopes on platform competition and otherwise ensuring decentralization. Rather than a metaverse monopolized between a few tech-sector giants, this idea holds it must be based upon at least as 'open' a network as the Internet, with its universal protocols and data portability (Gent 2021). Some privacy proponents push for an even more decentralized, 'community-governed' metaverse. This vision transfers to it decade-long aspirations for a 'Web3.0' built upon blockchain: a record of digital activity making interactions both more transparent, removing need for a third-party, and more secure, safe from outside scrutiny. The most well-known blockchains are cryptocurrencies, with their peer-to-peer interactions being financial, and their conception of privacy focused on identity as monetizable private property. However, advocates argue such transactions could form the foundation of a broadly freer, including more privacy-protective, Internet/metaverse. It is debated whether this libertarian vision can strike the right balance between individual freedom including privacy, against counterweighing concerns about anonymous abuse (Smith and Burrows 2021).

## Conclusion

VR technologies impact identity in three key senses – psychological well-being, our sense of self, and digital privacy – and the metaverse would intensify those issues. In all three cases, we, as authors, have maintained neutrality as to who's correct – virtual reality critics versus the celebrants, the uneasy versus the optimistic, or sceptics certain the metaverse is just another of VR's hyped-up heydays. Our circumspection derives from the fact that VR remains understudied, and the metaverse a matter of prediction, not description. Also, we, co-authors, don't see eye to eye on everything we've been discussing. Finally, this book is a teaching tool, and we agree that as instructors, our job is to provide guidance on *how* to think, not tell you *what* to think. Nevertheless, we will conclude with a couple certainties. Whether you find VR, and its increasing encroachment into real life, exciting, hopeful, worrisome, or boring, will be largely predicated on your predispositions regarding media in general. And if your involvements with existing entertainment and social media are less than healthy, in whatever way, your inevitable exposures to this brave new Internet will likely be another reason to improve your media savviness overall.

## Key Words

**AR**: 'Augmented Reality' – digital information layered onto the real world as seen through a viewfinder, the most famous example being Pokémon Go.
**Metaverse**: The Metaverse can be referred to as the emergent blendings of virtual and physical reality, based on advances in technologies such as VR, AR, high-speed Internet, computer-graphics processing, AI, holograms, deepfakes, biometrics, and 'The Internet of Things' – a worldwide web connecting everything including you.
**Virtual Reality**: Virtual reality is an artificial environment, similar to or different from a participant's actual environments, created through technology and art.
**VR**: Computerized 'virtual reality,' typically based on 'head-mounted displays' (HMDs) or projections onto the wall-screens of a chamber/room, sometimes including body-tracking auxiliaries.

## Critical Thinking Questions

1. Pondering each of the identity aspects we've addressed – well-being, selfhood, and privacy – in relation to VR, consider whether the negative or positive findings and possibilities outweigh one another.
2. Commentary on virtual reality technology often highlights its 'hype cycle' history. Do you think this is what's happening today, or is VR/AR finally the 'next big thing'?
3. How would you define the *metaverse* to your parents or other older relatives? To some of your best friends? To your younger sibling or child?

## References

Bode, Karl. 2020. "It Took Just 5 Minutes of Movement Data to Identify 'Anonymous' VR Users." *Techdirt*, November 9, 2020. https://www.techdirt.com/articles/20201103/08555545638/it-took-just-5-minutes-movement-data-to-identify-anonymous-vr-users.shtml

Egliston, Ben, and Marcus Carter. 2021. "Examining Visions of Surveillance in Oculus' Data and Privacy Policies, 2014–2020." *Media International Australia* (Advanced online publication): 1–15. https://doi.org/10.1177/1329878X211041670

Emmelkamp, Paul M. G., and Katharina Meyerbröker. 2021. "Virtual Reality Therapy in Mental Health." *Annual Review of Clinical Psychology* 17 (May): 495–519. https://doi.org/10.1146/annurev-clinpsy-081219-115923

Epiq Angle. n.d. "Coming Soon: Canada's New Privacy Law – What You Need to Know." Accessed April 20, 2022. https://www.epiqglobal.com/en-ca/thinking/blog/canadas-new-privacy-law

Franks, Mary Anne. 2017. "The Desert of the Unreal: Inequality in Virtual and Augmented Reality." *UC Davis Law Review* 51 (University of Miami Legal Studies Research Paper No. 17–24): 499–538. https://papers.ssrn.com/sol3/papers.cfm?abstract_id=3014529

Freeman, Guo, and Divine Maloney. 2020. "Body, Avatar, and Me: The Presentation and Perception of Self in Social Virtual Reality." *Proceedings of the Association for Computing Machinery on Human-Computer Interaction* 4 (Issue CSCW3/December, Article 239): 1–27. https://doi.org/10.1145/3432938

Gent, Edd. 2021. "Why the Metaverse Needs to be Open." *IEEE Spectrum*, August 18, 2021. https://spectrum.ieee.org/open-metaverse

Hamilton, Ian. 2021. "How Will Privacy, Free Speech and Safety Coexist in VR/AR?" *UploadVR*, October 22, 2021. https://uploadvr.com/ellysse-dick-privacy-policy/

Hashim, Abeerah. 2021. "Will 'Meta' Resolve Data and Privacy Issues with 'Facebook'?" *PrivacySavvy*, November 3, 2021. https://privacysavvy.com/security/social/will-meta-resolve-facebook-data-privacy-issues/

Leufer, Daniel. 2021. "Why You Shouldn't Buy Facebook Ray-Ban Smart Glasses." *Access Now*, September 29, 2021. https://www.accessnow.org/facebook-ray-ban-stories-smart-glasses-privacy-review/

Lomas, Natasha. 2021. "Ireland's Draft GDPR Decision Against Facebook Branded a Joke." *TechCrunch*, October 13, 2021. https://techcrunch.com/2021/10/13/irelands-draft-gdpr-decision-against-facebook-branded-a-joke/

Matei, Adrienne. 2017. "New Technology Is Forcing Us to Confront the Ethics of Bringing People Back from the Dead." *Quartz*, January 27, 2017. https://qz.com/896207/death-technology-will-allow-grieving-people-to-bring-back-their-loved-ones-from-the-dead-digitally/

Nakamura, Lisa. 2020. "Feeling Good about Feeling Bad: Virtuous Virtual Reality and the Automation of Racial Empathy." *Journal of Visual Culture* 19, no 1: 47–64. https://doi.org/10.1177/1470412920906259

Newton, Casey. 2021. "Mark in the Metaverse: Facebook's CEO on Why the Social Network Is Becoming 'a Metaverse Company." *The Verge*, July 22, 2021. https://www.theverge.com/22588022/mark-zuckerberg-facebook-ceo-metaverse-interview

Pavlick, Jennifer. 2018. "Children and Virtual Reality: Where Do We Stand?" *Parenting For a Digital Future*, January 24, 2018. https://blogs.lse.ac.uk/parenting4digitalfuture/2018/01/24/children-and-virtual-reality/

Roettgers, Janko. 2021. "Facebook Has Sold 4 million Quest 2 Headsets in The US, Recall Docs Reveal." *Protocol*, July 29, 2021. https://www.protocol.com/bulletins/quest-2-4-million-units

Selinger, Evan. 2021. "Facebook's Next Privacy Nightmare Will be a Sight to See." *The Boston Globe*, November 13, 2021. https://www.bostonglobe.com/2021/11/12/opinion/facebooks-next-privacy-nightmare-will-be-sight-see/

Smith, Harrison, and Roger Burrows. 2021. "Software, Sovereignty and the Post-Neoliberal Politics of Exit." *Theory, Culture & Society* 38, no. 6: 143–66. https://doi.org/10.1177/0263276421999439

# 16 Our War Game

## Hacker Games as Laborious Play

*Alex Dean Cybulski*

It's 1AM and, as I watch, Morgan is using a tool called a web proxy to hack a website, using it to collect hidden data and send the site malicious commands. Having already tricked the website into giving him a low-level user account Morgan settles on a plan of attack that would let him take control of the system: sending the website instructions to change his account's password, but in the command substitutes his username for admin. Mumbling to himself "Oh f*** that was it?," Morgan logs into the administrator's account, where he's greeted by a code:

```
FLAG-chFWT739qjUK8ohWNTpZGbqvgz4QlxcH
```

Morgan copies the code into another window, a scorekeeping system, his team's rank shoots up the scoreboard to third place, he's just "captured a flag" worth hundreds of points in a simulated hacking exercise known as a capture the flag competition. In that moment he might act like a hacker, but now I know exactly why he's a well-respected information security expert, Morgan is an expert in finding the flaws in websites before a criminal can use them to steal customer data. **Capture the flag** (CTF) is a competitive game in which players mimic the discovery and exploitation of vulnerabilities in information systems. Like the playground game, CTF often involves players infiltrating spaces within the game, software or information systems, simulating the experience of hacking to retrieve data known as a "flag." Playing in a CTF competition requires the same knowledge and tools used by information security professionals and professional **hackers** alike to identify and leverage the weaknesses and flaws of information systems.

As a kind of hacker eSport, CTF competitions are a distinct example of what Sonia Fizek and Anne Dipple (2019) describe as "**laborious play**" the rigorous application of knowledge-intensive labour in a game or game-like context, often distinctly serious in the real-world application of knowledge sometimes described as "serious play" (266). As a game, CTF competitions exist to share knowledge of new security vulnerabilities, state-of-the-art techniques & tools used by hackers. However, CTF also reflects the hacker way of seeing the world, understanding the secrets

DOI: 10.4324/9781003310730-19

162  *Alex Dean Cybulski*

of technologies through their insecurities: the vulnerabilities and flaws which make hacking possible.

This chapter proves that the laborious play of CTF has a specific function, that the game's design and play reflect a kind of knowledge transfer, in which hacker practice and knowledge informs the work of information security through participation in such a competition. Specifically, this chapter will consider how CTF is used to playfully circulate knowledge and ways of understanding computer security, which in the hacker tradition occurs by breaking it. In support of this argument and observations, this paper will utilize data collected from observation of three CTF competitions and 56 semi-structured interviews with CTF designers and players about their experiences with these games and its relationship to their work/studies in information security.[1]

## Understanding the Relationship between Hacker Practice and Information Security

In one of the earliest books written about hacker culture, Sherry Turkle's book *Second Self,* the author observes a transgressive and playful element amongst the hackers she studied. These hackers were often fascinated with the security of early computers, particularly in undermining such functions, as Turkle noted "their pleasure is in 'beating' the lock," describing a game-like approach to security, and she understood hackers as people who related "to the machine as a puzzle" (1984, 213). By 1984, Turkle notes that hackers had already developed a reputation for trespassing into computer networks previously understood to be secure: "the pattern of hack the system, leave a trace, get a little famous and be recognized by the big guys has become part of the hacker myth" (215). This assertion seems to be confirmed, with evidence as early as the 1980s to indicate hackers were quietly hired to work as computer security consultants (Baird et al. 1987, 18). Hackers were successful in these endeavors because they could identify the vulnerabilities in the code or configuration of information systems, flaws in the design of technologies which would often allow them to bypass their security, getting access to confidential information or, to make changes to systems they shouldn't have been able to do.[2]

However, hiring hackers and their methods for assessing computer security was controversial, frowned upon by mainstream computer security experts who saw hacker methods and practices around this more offensive style of testing systems by attacking them as inferior and disrespectful to more formal, defensive methods of security work (Spafford 1992, 45). Hackers were (and occasionally still are) stigmatized by some sectors of the computing industry and beyond, who believe them to be morally compromised, having earned a reputation for unauthorized computer breaches, often simply to prove that such vulnerabilities exist

(Spafford 1992; Tanczer 2020). Hacking a system to prove its **vulnerability** reflects Chris Kelty's (2008) observation about the deliberative (argumentative) form of hacker culture: "that hackers not only argue about technology, they also argue through it" (44). Stigmatized throughout much of the 1980s and 1990s, hackers and their practices were pushed into semi-secretive communities often described using one of two synonymous terms: the "digital underground" or "computer underground." Gordon R. Meyer has described the computer underground as the "social network" through which hackers openly collected and shared information and/or software about the vulnerabilities in computer systems over electronic bulletin board systems (BBS), zines and hacked phone systems (1989, 5–6), later over websites and forums. In the past 20 years, the identity of hackers and their practices have undergone something of a rehabilitation. The security related practices of hackers are increasingly recognized by government policy and governing bodies as necessary to securing vital information systems against malicious (criminal) hackers (Lipner 2015, 29) and hackers are understood as important workers within the information security industry, who have waged a careful campaign to rehabilitate their identity as professionals by working with the media and through the public documentation of software vulnerabilities, a tactic known as "full disclosure" (Gozern and Coleman 2022). It is in this context that we can begin to understand the role that hacker games like CTF might play in the culture and knowledge work of the information security industry.

## Capture the Flag and the Circulation of Hacker Knowledge and Practice

The playful, open and deliberative qualities of hacker culture are likely contributing cultural factors to the creation of capture the flag. CTFs are a kind of global "eSport" (a form of organized videogame competition) in the hacker community, the website CTFtime.org one of the largest hubs for the game lists hundreds of competitions annually in North America, Europe and Asia. In a CTF competition, hosted online or at a local information security conference, players usually solve a variety of problems designed by the competition's creators often referred to as "challenges" over a time-limited period, such as 48–72 hours. Typically, challenges represent interesting and/or contemporary problems/vulnerabilities in information security that players must solve to retrieve data known as a "flag" which they submit to a digital scorekeeping system for points. Players must solve challenges using a similar approach to how those systems might be hacked in the real-world, using identical methods and tools.

As an example: at one CTF, I observed a challenge where players had to break into a fake company's email portal using a list of 150 paired usernames/passwords. There were three catches: (1) only one of the pairs would work, (2) attempting to log into 150 accounts is tedious and time-consuming and (3) the website would require users to authenticate using a randomly generated CSRF (Cross-Site Request Forgery) token each time they accessed the page, a security control designed to prevent a malicious hacker from attempting to consecutively log in to multiple accounts. To solve the challenge players would have to use the software Burp Suite, a freely-available program known as a web proxy, designed to test website security. Using Burp Suite the players automate the login process, testing all 150 usernames and passwords, creating a special script which would download and authenticate with a new CSRF token during each login attempt, thus bypassing the control. Eventually, one of the attempts would yield a successful username and password combination and players would gain access to the account of a fictitious employee named "Jeff" whose inbox would lead to flags which can be scored for points and/or information that could be used to pivot into accessing his company's computer system remotely to hack other systems and discover more flags.

This challenge and its solution are a demonstration that the security procedures used by some websites are not fully secure. Players confirm the insecurity of this technology by undermining the security of a website protected by CSRF tokens using commonly available software by simulating what is known as a "password spraying" attack. The challenge operates at two levels: first, these kinds of challenges are designed to help players understand the potential limitations and vulnerabilities common to these technologies. One CTF designer I spoke to referred to this process as the "knowledge transfer" involved in the design and play of a CTF challenge in which hacker knowledge of security flaws informs the work of information security professionals: that by thinking and working like a hacker, players can learn to defeat the malicious, criminal hackers that might attack the systems they protect. When developing a similar site involving usernames and passwords, a professional might implement a more reliable protection, instead of CSRF tokens or add additional security checks. The secondary function of this challenge is the way it sustains hacker practice and its deliberative properties: the deconstruction of a technology demonstrates the truth of hacker practice, its ability to produce useful knowledge about technologies from hidden flaws in their code or implementation.

The knowledge transfer and the ideas about computer security communicated in CTF challenges indicate their educational nature; that through this form of play, a distinct way of understanding certain technologies arises. However, as recent research by Daniel Votipka et al. (2021) indicates, many CTFs and similar hacker exercises do not follow best practices for teaching new skills. By design, CTFs are deliberately designed to avoid providing players with clear guidance. Learning in a CTF tends

*Hacker Games as Laborious Play* 165

to be self-directed: during the process of solving a challenge, players are generally not given clues or tools to solve the problem, instead they must determine the solution from contextual details in the systems/software to be hacked. This analytic process is referred to as "reconnaissance," the discovery details which might correlate to a vulnerability, which when properly exploited will yield a flag. As a result, CTFs involve players spending a great deal of their play time using search engines to find information relevant to a challenge, utilizing the vast sources of knowledge and software stored in blogs, code repositories and in videos which are shared freely online by hackers, security academics and professionals.

The reconnaissance process within CTF play is well understood by CTF designers and players, who often create challenges to funnel players towards specific knowledge and ways of understanding insecure technologies. For example, one designer I interviewed, Jean, made a challenge using the GraphQL database query language created by Facebook which is increasingly popular for use in mobile applications. As Jean noted, GraphQL was a "new web technology" whose "documentation is really not that good. There's not really good content about GraphQL security, I think. So, [the challenge] was really about learning the technology, how it works, how a query works, and work from there basically and then get to like the SQL injection that is more widely documented." In this quote Jean is explaining that he expects players to discover what kind of database they are accessing, read the documentation for the language and begin to piece together how it could be attacked. In that passage Jean refers to SQL (structured query language) "injections," a common and historic security problem in which a malicious user can send instructions to a vulnerable database running a query language through things like fillable forms on websites, often to steal the confidential information of other users like their passwords or other sensitive information. Jean was inspired to create this challenge having discovered the same vulnerabilities in GraphQL during his work as an application security engineer, realizing that due to its newness "developers will jump into it without really grasping all of the aspects of it." In this way, Jean's challenge is designed as an intervention, it explains that just because a technology is new does not mean it is secure.

Jean's approach to designing a challenge describes the way in which expert hackers use CTF to communicate ideas about computer security and new security problems they are thinking about. This approach was a common sentiment shared amongst many information security professionals involved in CTF that I spoke to. Another hacker, Conroy specializes in "browser exploitation," in creating web sites and web applications that can be used to steal data or run malicious code on a user's computer through their web browser. Working with a few other CTF designers, he explained: "we have started putting browser exploits in CTFs. And I feel like that's quite an impact on the community where people would actually get into this field that wasn't very approachable before." Conroy's comments here describe the way his CTF challenge drew attention to a computer security issue he thinks is important by training players in how to think about the problem. He also described how his approach had a knock-on effect: "and now you had CTF style write-ups where people would explain their approaches to these things." What's interesting about Conroy's quote here is his mention of a "write-up," this term refers to documentation created by CTF players to describe the knowledge, tools and procedures they used to solve a challenge in a competition, often shared through a blog or text hosted in a GitHub repository, the hacker equivalent of a videogame FAQ or walkthrough. Write-ups serve multiple purposes: they provide informal mentorship often teaching other hackers how they solved a problem, or might solve similar problems and as Conroy notes these documents can address shortcomings and gaps in security knowledge. Instead of giving a conference talk or writing a blog post, or journal article about a vulnerability or a new form of exploitation, CTF designers leverage the expressive capabilities of games to transfer that knowledge to their peers, giving them an experience of undermining the technology for themselves, but they also rely on their peers to do the same. This form of knowledge transfer is powerful, what we might describe as the "discursive" element of CTF play: by providing hands-on experience the designers are doing more than explaining the problem abstractly, they are proving exactly how such a vulnerability can lead to a security incident like a data breach. Documenting security vulnerabilities in CTF challenges and write-ups is emblematic of a practice known as "full disclosure" in the hacker community where a researcher discovers a security problem and documents it for their peers. Hackers do this a kind of technology activism, to draw attention to it in hopes that it will be fixed by companies responsible for the technology or by those implementing the technology in their own applications (Goerzen and Coleman 2022, 7). In creating CTF challenges documenting security problems with new technologies or emergent fields of hacking, both Jean and Conroy are working to document potential security problem by creating novel puzzle-like challenges to help other hackers understand these issues.

## Conclusion: Circulating the Hacker Worldview

At another CTF I met Claudio, a boisterous, suntanned European hacker who talks like a surfer. We are getting set to start his interview about CTF when he tells me "I like to talk with people! I'm talking about CTF! There's nothing like classified here, so it's like I'm totally chill!" Claudio's appearance and disposition fly in the face of how our culture imagines hackers as sullen, pale introverts. What he said to me also challenges our understanding of hackers as being secretive or clandestine, like CTF,

Claudio's comment reflects the fact that hackers not just share knowledge about computer security problems openly, but they also mentor other aspiring hackers to learn the tools and procedures necessary to become a hacker. Accordingly, CTF is a key tool in the circulation of knowledge in the hacker community and by extension, the information security industry. What's more, in exploiting security problems in the way a hacker might, CTF players learn to see the world like a hacker through its flaws and vulnerabilities.

## Resources

Interested in hacking (responsibly)? Beginner friendly CTFs are available at:

https://www.pictoctf.org
https://pwn.college

## Key Words

**Capture the Flag**: Capture the flag is a competitive game in which players mimic the discovery and exploitation of vulnerabilities in information systems. Like the playground game, capture the flag often involves players infiltrating spaces within the game, software or information systems, simulating the experience of hacking to retrieve data known as a "flag" which is scored for points.

**Hackers**: In the context of computer security, hackers use their expertise with technologies to produce contingent (unexpected) behavior in information systems by identifying and exploiting flaws in their design and function. This form of hacking is often utilized to undermine the security of an information system, usually by compromising the confidentiality of information it stores, or by hijacking its operations to subvert their integrity.

**Laborious Play**: A form of intense play, wherein players utilize and manage knowledge in a way which resembles forms of work. Laborious play can range from work-like activities like capture the flag where players use knowledge perform distinctly-work like tasks, to managing large amounts of knowledge required to play a game at an intense level, like a boss encounter in a massively-multiplayer online game World of Warcraft or designing the best combination of equipment in an online shooter like Destiny.

**Vulnerability**: A vulnerability, or security vulnerability is a bug or flaw in a technology which may be utilized by a hacker to cause a technology to perform an unintended or undocumented function. Often this unintended or undocumented function will allow hacker to bypass the security of that technology. When a hacker utilizes a vulnerability to make a technology perform an unanticipated function, usually to undermine its security, they are said to be "exploiting" that vulnerability.

## Critical Thinking Questions

1  How is capture the flag different from more traditional gamified learning exercises? What other industries use serious play to train its professionals?
2  There is tremendous excitement about the gamification of education, but what are the limitations of gamified learning?
3  How does the relationship between hackers and the information security industry challenge the popular conception of hackers as criminals and/or anarchists?

## Notes

1 All data presented here are provided under a pseudonym to protect the identity of research participants.
2 This is sometimes referred to as making a technology perform unintended or undocumented functionality.

## References

Baird, Bruce J., Lindsay L. Baird, and Ronald P. Ranauro. 1987. "The Moral Cracker?" *Computers & Security* 6, no. 6: 471–8.
Fizek, Sonia, and Anne Dippel. 2019. "Laborious Playgrounds: Citizen Science Games as New Modes of Work/Play in the Digital Age." In *The Playful Citizen: Civic Engagement in a Mediatized Culture*, edited by René Glas, 255–74. Amsterdam: Amsterdam University Press.
Goerzen, Matt, and Gabriella Coleman. 2022. "Wearing Many Hats: The Rise of the Professional Security Hacker." *Data & Society*. https://datasociety.net/library/wearing-many-hats-the-rise-of-the-professional-security-hacker/
Kelty, Christopher. 2008. *Two Bits: The Cultural Significance of Free Software*. Durham, NC: Duke University Press.
Lipner, Steven B. 2015. "The Birth and Death of the Orange Book." *IEEE Annals of the History of Computing* 37, no. 2: 19–31.
Meyer, Gordon. 1989. "The Social Organization of the Computer Underground." Master's Thesis, Northern Illinois University.
Spafford, Eugene H. 1992. "Are Computer Hacker Break-Ins Ethical?" *Journal of Systems Software* 17, no. 1: 41–7.
Tanczer, Leonie Maria. 2020. "50 Shades of Hacking: How IT and Cybersecurity Industry Actors Perceive Good, Bad, and Former Hackers." *Contemporary Security Policy* 41, no. 1: 108–28.
Turkle, Sherry. 1984. *The Second Self: Computers and the Human Spirit*, Twentieth Anniversary Edition. Cambridge, MA: MIT Press.
Votipka, Daniel, Eric Zhang, and Michelle L. Mazurek. 2021. "HackEd: A Pedagogical Analysis of Online Vulnerability Discovery Exercises." In *2021 IEEE(SP)*, 1268–85. San Francisco, CA: IEEE.

# 17 Listening to and Playing Along with the Soundscapes of Videogame Environments

*Kate Galloway*

What we hear and how we listen to the world around us virtually in games, as well as in our actual daily lives, is influenced by our activity at hand, actions, and our relation to our environment. A busy commuter will attend to a city's **soundscape**, the sound or combination of sounds and their relationship to each other in an environment (Schafer 1977), differently than the leisurely shopper. In games we listen in similar ways. Unlike aesthetic listening where we listen to a song or playlist on Spotify recommended to us by Spotify's algorithm that analysed our listening history and that of similar users to generate suitable recommendations or listen to the expansive orchestral scoring of Hans Zimmer as aerial shots of global desert regions pan across our computer screens as we watch *Planet Earth II* (2016), listening in **game sound** is much more like everyday listening, in that it is action-oriented. When we listen in games, it is similar to how we listen for and respond to different forms of acoustic communication where the sounds we hear inform how we relate to our situation and respond to our environment. When we hear a foghorn we understand that our location is experiencing foggy weather conditions and we don't even have to look out the window, or we often hear the siren of an ambulance and the direction this sound of alert is coming from long before we see its flashing lights as the vehicle speeds towards us. A driver pulling out of an on-street parking spot into the busy road listens and responds to this siren differently than a pedestrian walking on the sidewalk or a couple sitting by the street-side window of a café. Listening to sound and music in our virtual and actual world is information we can use to identify an object as it approaches – like the blue turtle shell in the *Mario Kart* series, gauging its direction and speed and informing the listener's decisions on how to act and respond in this context (the blue turtle shell is coming, it's too late unless you can quickly fall into second place). Diegetic (sound and music that originates from within the on-screen narrative) and extradiegetic (originates from outside the on-screen narrative) music and sound in games is oriented towards actions, responses, locations, and the conditions and rules of play.

Players listen to a range of sounds and musics, often simultaneously, that comprise the game sound of a game. When the player listens in

DOI: 10.4324/9781003310730-20

games, they are not only listening to the extradiegetic soundtrack that plays in the background of a level, location, or region of a game. The game sound also includes voice acting, sound effects, environmental sound, diegetic music originating from within the narrative, and the sounds of the playback system itself (e.g., the start-up sound of a PlayStation console). However, some of the most iconic level music is experienced in underwater levels where there is a clear correlation between the mechanics of character movement and the soundtrack. The first piece of music that Koji Kondo composed for *Super Mario Bros.* (Nintendo 1985) was the waltz that plays in the underwater levels (see Figure 17.1).

While the waltz does not contain musical features that sound obviously water-like, the triple-meter base line accompaniment and melody that moves in an upward motion (as though Mario is swimming or floating up to the surface) gives a sense of floating, weightlessness, smoothness, and feeling of slightly protracted forward momentum as though the character and the melody is fighting the water's resistance. As music theorist Sean Atkinson notes, "Stanley Kubrick's choice of the *Blue Danube Waltz* in *2001: A Space Odyssey* (1968) to accompany the first scenes of weightlessness was likely a factor for Kondo as well" as it was well-known instance of associating the dance type of the waltz "with images and experiences related to weightlessness (whether through space or in water) over the last 50 years, giving the waltz a new topical relationship within popular

*Figure 17.1* Mario swimming to the Waltz Theme in Super Mario Bros.

culture" (Atkinson 2019, 1). Musical topics are found throughout film and videogame music. For instance, the use of church bells, the organ, wordless chanting, or a specific chat like the Dies Irae are examples of medievalisms. As van Elferen observes,

> organs, in the cinema or in other contexts, always evoke not only sacred music, but also places such as churches and cathedrals, near crypts and graveyards; and the organist has mastery over the mighty sound that echoes these allusions. The organ thus serves as a meta-cinematic comment that is distinctly Gothic in taste. For this reason, it has acquired a firm place within the generic design of horror films.
> (van Elferen 2019, 11, see also van Elferen 2021)

These are musical references that directly or indirectly reference the medieval as an idea (e.g., the bardcore cover song craze or the male monk-like chanting of *Halo*'s main theme) or a historical time period (the use of the Notre Dame church bell in *Assassins Creed*) (Cook 2017, 2019, 2020).

The underwater level waltz in *Super Mario Bros* is more than just a musical trope that establishes location; it is also a representation of Mario's movements in water made audible. Moving in water is different than moving in air and the player can both hear that in the level music, as well as hear (and feel it) in Mario's movement. In the underwater levels, Mario swims up to the surface only to slowly float down again. He is no longer fast and agile. Mario moves at a slower place, his forward momentum stunted by the water. The character of Mario's movement is mimicked in slower pace and held notes of the lilting legato melody of the underwater waltz. In contrast, Mario's movement in World 1-1 of *Super Mario Bros.* is light, vertical, and bouncy, which is heard in the level music that features crisp electronic timbres, a staccato melodic line that clearly moves vertically up and down mimicking Mario's jumping motion, and a crisp energetic base line.

In the social simulation role-playing game (RPG) *Stardew Valley* (ConcernedApe 2016) diegetic and **extradiegetic music and sound** orients the player to their location on and off their farm, the activity at hand (e.g., are they collecting shells on the beach, fishing off the dock, or shopping at Joja Mart), the time of day, the season, and whether it is a holiday, event, or just a regular day in Pelican Town. By listening to their avatar's soundscape, the player comes to understand how the physical, social *and* sonic environment of *Stardew Valley* operates (Galloway 2019). For player, this means listening to both the diegetic and extradiegetic sounds of the game environment, because the player has aural access to sonic information (e.g. the extradiegetic music) that is inaudible to their avatar. As I play my farm in *Stardew Valley* I listen to individual features of the sonic environment of Pelican Town, my farm, and neighbouring forests and seaside and how they relate to each other and my avatar. These sonic environments contain an array of sonic activity that shape gameplay, including the calls of different bird species, the train that passes periodically through the countryside, to the crashing of ocean waves against the shoreline, to the cycling hum of the refrigeration system set to high in Joja Mart. Sound and music play important roles in worldbuilding. As my avatar fishes off the ocean pier in the late evening, their baited hook bobs up and down at the surface of the water with a rhythmic pulse, and the waves crash against the wooden pier and roll onto a nearby sandy beach. The piercing cries of seagulls ring in my ears and my avatar's as I manipulate the controls and attempt to reel my avatar's biggest catch of the day. Each of these sound events situates the player in a specific location, often drawing from aural cues the player is familiar with because they experience similar sounds in their actual life outside of gameplay. The supermarket chain Joja Mart, for example, has a lo-fi soundscape saturated with ambient keynote sounds including the hum of neon lights, and a regular beep that pulses and punctuates the loud mechanical drone of multiple electric powered generators and rows of refrigeration units just like those in my local grocery store in Troy, New York.

There are also other moments of listening in games during gameplay where the player is required to listen to the environmental soundscape for guidance as to how to proceed in the narrative, what to watch out for, or where they are currently located and what direction they should go next. The environmental soundscape can serve as both a narrative device and a gameplay mechanic. One example is the wind in both *Never Alone* (E-Line Media/Upper One Games 2014) and *The Ghost of Tsushima* (Sucker Punch Productions 2020). The narrative of *Never Alone* is focused on a young Inupiat girl Nuna and her arctic fox companion, who solves puzzles and travel together in search of the Blizzard Man, who is chipping away at a huge ice walls, generating relentless and unpredictable blowing icy winds and snow that threatens their communities. The Blizzard Man is an anthropomorphic representation of the growing instability of the Circumpolar North's climate resulting from global climate change. The blizzard at the centre of the narrative also plays a role in the gameplay mechanics. Strong gusts of icy wind blow across the screen at apparently random intervals, requiring the player to hold a button to brace against the ground. Players try to gauge when a gust is about to blow by listening for the wind. At times, the characters might be halfway through a jump, only for the blizzard to suddenly blow them backward to their deaths. Towards the end of the game, however, players need to adapt to these same forces, precisely timing their movements so the blizzard can boost jump length.

In *The Ghost of Tsushima* Jin Sakai, a samurai tasked with a quest to protect Tsushima Island during the first Mongol invasion of Japan. The forests of Tsushima are perpetually animated and enlivened by the wind. The ever-present wind is simultaneously a central gameplay mechanic and sensory experience that establishes how the player experiences the gameworld. The wind is a visible and audible navigation aid that guides the player where they want and need to go while also interacting with the different weather patterns that shape gameplay and the affective conditions of the island of Tsushima as a gameworld. When you swipe up on your controller's touchpad, the wind along with the leaves, pollen, and other debris and particles of the physical environment will blow toward the player's destination. The wind in In *The Ghost of Tsushima* is a keynote sound, to draw on the term used in acoustic ecology to identify sounds that are an ever-present part of our daily soundscapes, but the listener might only notice their presence by listening with intention to their soundscape or by its sudden absence (Schafer 1977). For example, the hum and clank of the old heating system in my campus office is a constant presence from late October through April so I grow used to it, forgetting it is there until the heating system is suddenly turned off and its absence reverberates. Even in photo mode, the wind continues to blow, activating the landscape's foliage, while the character pauses to be affected by their multisensory environment.

The physical geography of a gameworld is also rendered audible in games when individual regions with shared and contrasting flora and fauna are scored to contrasting soundtracks that overlap as characters travel across invisible borders. Regional soundtracks are a geospatial device, communicating to the player where they have been and where they are now (van Elferen 2011). These contrasting tracks also have shared musical features, just like adjacent, but drastically different ecological regions share a select few species of flora and fauna. The indie exploration title *A Short Hike* (Adamryu 2019) is an example of such an approach to regional ecological game sound. *A Short Hike* is set on the fictional island recreation and conservation area Hawk Peak Provincial Park, you play as Claire, a young anthropomorphic bird. In *A Short Hike*, Claire takes a break from her daily urban life and visits her Aunt May who lives and works there as park ranger (see Figure 17.2). At first, Claire is waiting for an important call instead of exploring the protected nature the park offers its visitors, but she can't receive cellphone service. She finds out from Aunt May that the only place to receive adequate cellphone service is the summit of Hawk Peak and she embarks on her hike with that destination as her goal. Along the way, she meets a variety of other anthropomorphic animal visitors and inhabitants of the park, participates in activities, and collects items that will assist her. These regional environments are defined by their terrain (close to the shoreline) as well as their altitude (by lookout point) and the soundtrack changes based on Claire's location.

*A Short Hike* is not the only game that incorporates location-based audio cues and sound design. For Tim Summers, the location-based audio cues of *The Legend of Zelda: Ocarina of Time* (Nintendo 1998) is a landmark example of the function of listening for place is a necessary gameplay mechanic, that also connects players to The Kingdom of Hyrule in *Ocarina of Time* and across future games in the series as these location cues are replayed and remixed (Summers 2021, 78–178). Other indie and

*Figure 17.2* Claire speaks with Aunt May at the Campfire while listening to the soundscape of birds, gusts of wind, and the crackle of the flames.

casual games such as *Stardew Valley* and *Animal Crossing: New Horizons* (Nintendo 2020) similarly feature location-based soundtrack changes (Galloway 2019; Grimshaw 2007; Hambleton 2020; O'Hara 2020). The main difference in sound design is that while *Stardew Valley* and *Animal Crossing: New Horizons'* soundtracks and environmental soundscapes change in response to the time of day, event, or season, giving the player a sense of the passage of time, such temporal-sonic shifts are not present in *A Short Hike*. It is always fall in Hawk Peak and the player only learns how short their hike has actually been by looking at their actual clock or observing changes in their actual environment from where they are playing. The player continues hiking as Claire and exploring new tasks and items in the world because there are no sonic and visual indicators of elapsed time on the hike. The player can be distracted at Shirley's Point talking to the Artist Racoon, who is in search of painting the perfect landscape or taking in the scenery from Lookout Point. The player can explore Hawk Peak as long as they want without disruption, unlike games like *Super Mario Bros.* where an adaptive **dynamic audio** cue punctuates the level soundtrack to signal to the player that they are running out of time to complete the level. There is no time limit on gameplay How long Claire takes to reach the summit of Hawk Peak is the player's choice.

## Conclusion

This chapter offered a range of perspectives on the function of game sound in gameworld soundscape design and innovative approaches to composing, listening to, connecting with, and playing digital sonic environments in games. I outline some of the genre conventions of soundscape design of game sound as it pertains to worldbuilding, how sonic environments shape players' perceptions and engagement, and the ways players listen to sonic environments and sense the gameworlds they are immersed in through gameplay. Listening with intention to game sound highlights the varied ways dynamic and interactive videogame soundscapes actively contribute to worldbuilding, respond to players' movement, location, and mode of sensing place, and communicate to players that their activity and navigation composes the virtual soundscape just as they are collaborative composers of their actual soundscape of their lives outside of gameplay.

## Key Words

**Diegetic and Extradiegetic Music/Sound**: Diegetic music/sound refers to sound and music where the source is visible in the narrative or whose source is implied to be present by the action on screen or game environment (e.g., we hear the sound of trickling water as Link approaches a river in *Legend of Zelda: Ocarina of Time* even though we cannot see the river yet). Extradiegetic music/sound is music or sound where the source is neither visible nor implied to be present in the action, environment, or game narrative (e.g., background level music).

**Dynamic Audio**: Game sound that responds to and interacts with the player and player character (PC) is dynamic audio. There are two key forms of dynamic audio experienced in games: interactive audio and adaptive audio. Interactive audio is sound and music that responds of a character's movement and actions (e.g., the swimming sounds made by Mario when he swims in the water or the hollow plonk as Mario jumps on top of a Goomba). Adaptive audience is sound and music that communicates to player that the conditions of gameplay have changed, and they must adjust their gameplay in order to achieve success or that failure is imminent (e.g., the crunchy sound effect and higher-pitched oscillating melodic line of alarm in *Dr. Mario* (Nintendo 1990) that signals Game Over when your pill jar is overfilled).

**Game Sound**: Game sound includes the different types of sound and music experienced while playing a game, from the moment a game console is turned on until the final credits are finished. These types of sound and music include the soundtrack, music performed by characters in the game, voice acting (including the scrolling text sounds of dialogue and instruction boxes), sound effects, and environmental sounds.

**Soundscape**: A soundscape is an environment of sound that is perceived by an individual or a society. A soundscape is comprised of sounds made by nonhuman living things, nonliving things and environmental phenomenal, humans, and human-made technologies in the actual and virtual world, including augmented reality. It is the sonic counterpart to the landscape.

**Critical Thinking Questions**

1 Using an example from a Mickey Mouse cartoon and a world level from *Super Mario Bros.* (Nintendo 1985) examine the relationships between soundtrack and the movement of the characters and objects on screen, and critically reflect on how videogames are similar to and different from films.
2 Choose a level, region, or location from a favourite videogame and a location in your actual life that you know really well (e.g., your favourite coffee shop, the forest near your family home that you played in as a child) and compare and contrast these sonic environments by identifying all of the sounds that you hear, identifying their sources where possible, and using descriptive language to detail them while also taking note of the relationship of your player character's (PC) body and your actual body to these sonic environments. What does this sonic information communicate to you about place and how you and your PC understand, sense, and relate to it?
3 How do you listen to a gameworld environment similarly or differently than your everyday environment? To answer this question, take these two listening walks. Take the first fifteen-minute walk through your neighbourhood and make a list (a soundscape inventory) of the sounds you encounter, including those made by your own body. Take a second walk, but this time take that walk in a videogame of your own choice and make a second list of the sounds you encounter within the gameworld.

**References**

Adamryu. 2019. *A Short Hike*. Adamryu/Whippoorwill Limited. PC/Mac/Linux/Playstation 4/Xbox One/Nintendo Switch.
Atkinson, Sean. 2019. "Soaring Through the Sky: Topics and Tropes in Video Game Music." *Music Theory Online* 25, no. 2. https://mtosmt.org/issues/mto.19.25.2/mto.19.25.2.atkinson.html
ConcernedApe. 2016. *Stardew Valley*. Chucklefish/Fangamer/ConcernedApe/505 Games. PC/Mac/Android/Linux//Nintendo Switch/PlayStation 4/Xbox Cloud Gaming.
Cook, Karen M. 2017. "Beyond the Grave: The 'Dies Irae' in Video Game Music." *Sounding Out!* December 18. https://soundstudiesblog.com/2017/12/18/beyond-the-grave-the-dies-irae-in-video-game-music/
Cook, Karen M. 2020. "Gaming the Medievalist World in Harry Potter." In *The Oxford Handbook of Music and Medievalism*, edited by Kirsten Yri and Stephen C. Meyer, 750–63. Oxford: Oxford University Press.

*Listening to the Soundscapes of Videogame Environments* 177

Cook, Karen M. 2019. "Medievalism and Emotions in Video Game Music." *Postmedieval* 10, no. 4: 482–97.

E-Line Media/Upper One Games. 2014. *Never Alone*. E-Line Media. PC/Mac/Playstation.

Galloway, Kate. 2019. "Soundwalking and the Aurality of Stardew Valley: An Ethnography of Listening to and Interacting with Environmental Game Audio." In *Music in the Role-Playing Game*, edited by William Gibbons and Steven Reale, 159–78. New York: Routledge.

Grimshaw, Mark. 2007. "The Acoustic Ecology of the First-Person Shooter." PhD diss., University of Waikato.

Hambleton, Elizabeth. 2020. "Gray Areas: Analyzing Navigable Narratives in the Not-So-Uncanny Valley between Soundwalks, Video Games, and Literary Computer Games." *Journal of Sound and Music in Games* 1, no. 1: 20–43.

Nintendo. 2020. *Animal Crossing: New Horizons*. Nintendo. Switch.

Nintendo. 1998. *The Legend of Zelda: Ocarina of Time*. Nintendo. Nintendo 64.

Nintendo. 1985. *Super Mario Bros.* Nintendo. Nintendo Entertainment System (NES).

O'Hara, William. 2020. "Mapping Sound: Play, Performance, and Analysis in *Proteus*." *Journal of Sound and Music in Games* 1, no 3: 35–67.

Schafer, R. Murray. 1977. *The Tuning of the World*. Toronto: McClelland & Steward.

Sucker Punch Productions. 2020. *The Ghost of Tsushima*. Sony Interactive Entertainment. Playstation 4/5.

Summers, Tim. 2021. *The Legend of Zelda: Ocarina of Time: A Game Music Companion*. Bristol: Intellect Ltd.

van Elferen, Isabella. 2011. "¡Un Forastero! Issues of Virtuality and Diegesis in Videogame Music." *Music and the Moving Image* 4, no. 2: 30–9.

van Elferen, Isabella. 2012. "The Gothic Bach." *Understanding Bach* 7: 9–20.

van Elferen, Isabella. 2021. *Gothic Music: The Sounds of the Uncanny*. Cardiff: University of Whales Press.

# Section III
# Reimagining Traditional Media

# 18 Netflix as the New Television Screen

## A Queer Investigation into Streaming, Algorithms, and *Schitt$ Creek*

*Lauren McLean*

Netflix leads the world in streaming entertainment. In fact, Netflix investors state there are currently over 167 million paid Netflix memberships. Many viewers seek out streaming services like Netflix for their watching needs, which is resulting in cable TV being less competitive in the entertainment industry (Patchunka 2019, 227). This shift to streaming platforms has changed the way viewers engage with televised material. Whether binge-watching episode after episode or scrolling through various ad-free and sometimes recommended categories, streaming services have reshaped viewing practices. Specifically, Netflix and other streaming services have transformed viewing practices by their use of algorithms to manage audience engagement and promote particular programs. As Sarah Arnold (2016) notes, "Not only does it distribute content, but Netflix has also entered the field of production" (50). This paper introduces some of the changes Netflix has made to traditional television practices by releasing entire seasons at once, promoting binge-watching, and using algorithms to understand and impact viewers.

Using *Schitt$ Creek* as a case study, I examine the way algorithmic culture engages with streaming television while investigating the progressive aspects (and lack thereof) of selected episodes in the television series. Drawing on Blake Hallinan and Ted Striphas, David Beer, Noah Tsika, and Bridget Kies, I examine the logical components of algorithms connected to serial television on Netflix. I argue the relationship between algorithmic culture and television is complex and difficult to categorize into a singularly progressive or traditional definition; however, despite *Schitt$ Creek's* praise for diversity and inclusion, I find the series lacks a true queer potential. The research questions I address are: How do algorithms hold power in shaping culture? How might streaming platforms and viewers reinforce or deny traditional aspects of Network television? What does the shift to Netflix mean? How does queerness function on a streaming platform like Netflix? Ultimately, these different forms of power held amongst viewers and platforms cannot be ignored as they continue to impact multiple areas of culture.

DOI: 10.4324/9781003310730-22

## Contextualizing *Schitt$ Creek*, Netflix, and Algorithmic Design

A white, upper-class family (who lost all their money in a tax scandal), move to their last remaining asset, a motel in Schitt's Creek, where they gain more than they ever had through their relationships as they work to rebuild their family name. From the onset, this premise does not seem all that different from many other sitcoms (for example, *Broke* or *Two Broke Girls*), and yet, *Schitt$ Creek* manages to **queer** the traditionally **heteronormative** (the persuasive idea that heterosexuality is a given and the normal expression of sexuality) sitcom. However, how progressive can this sitcom be when it remains tied to the traditional conventions of the genre? And, in what ways may the shift to a streaming service algorithmically influence the series' reception? Sitcoms, otherwise known as situation comedies, are a format of television that follow a regular cast of characters in the same realistic location (like a motel) through a succession of comedic episodes. Since the genre's introduction in the 1940s, the sitcom has faced extreme popularity. The public perception and acceptance of *Schitt$ Creek* as a sitcom is significant as genre conventions compose programs in a way that are "both comfortably familiar and innovatively unfamiliar" (Butler 13). *Schitt$ Creek* may draw such a large audience, in part, due to the familiar sitcom format they implement; however, their notoriety results from queering, rather than adhering to warn out conventions of the genre. After appearing on Netflix, *Schitt$ Creek* gained significant popularity during their fifth and sixth (final) seasons. In fact, S*chitt$ Creek* set a record with nine Emmy wins awarded for its final season. This may, to some extent, be due to the ways algorithmically driven streaming platforms have changed television. For instance, with binge-watching, rewatching and releasing an entire series at once. These examples reflect the significant shift to a new media landscape, sometimes referred to as TVIII, that Netflix has popularized (Jenner 2016, 258).

The relationship between serial television and algorithmic design is not easy to see. This unclear connection is purposeful as algorithms alone continue to function through a shield of invisibility or a "kind of known unknown" (Hallinan and Striphas 2016, 118). While algorithmic design may allow for more information to be gathered which can, in turn, inform platform practices and content design, algorithmic design is not necessarily positive. With datafication, Internet television has increased and created more concrete forms of measurement which continue to be used to monitor and surveil users (Arnold 2016, 50). This shift with audience measurement and datafication creates a potential for platforms to "predic[t] and gover[n]...audience behaviour" (Arnold 2016, 50). This leads us to wonder if algorithms are as inherently positive as they may seem from the offset. Do we need algorithms? Yes. But, are algorithms actually serving us well or are they only benefitting a particular group of privileged identities? I'd argue the latter.

David Beer's article, "Algorithms: Shaping Tastes and Manipulating the Circulations of Popular Culture," discusses an interesting idea regarding how popular culture is the code and algorithms make up/culture relies on the algorithms (as a form of a social process) to function. Building off this analysis on the important relationship between algorithms and culture, Blake Hallinan and Ted Striphas in "Recommended for You: The Netflix Prize and the Production of Algorithmic Culture," analyze the Netflix prize to demonstrate the power of algorithms as they act as judges or referees of culture. Shifting the conversation to Noah Tsika's article, "CompuQueer: Protocological Constraints, Algorithmic Streamlining, and the Search for Queer Methods Online," Tsika discusses queer methods when considering technology and algorithms. Tsika also analyzes the paradox of having a queer methodology with data and algorithms that seem to go against the stance of queerness. Furthering the conversation on queerness, in "First Comes Love, Then Comes Marriage: (Homo) Normalizing Romance on American Television," Bridget Kies looks at queerness in television, noting how TV represents dominant ideologies in culture and thus reflects culture. All four of these theorists see a cultural connection to their focus area. Although Beer, Hallinan and Striphas, and Tsika may focus on algorithmic culture while Kies analyzes television, both television and algorithms/algorithmic logics are rooted in culture because they are culture. As a result, the remainder of this paper will analyze the progressive and not progressive aspects of *Schitt$ Creek* as a popularized cultural work found on the algorithmically driven streaming platform Netflix.

## *Schitt$ Creek*: A Case Study of Queerness on Netflix

Television has changed with the introduction of online streaming platforms that are algorithmically framed and informed. For example, binge viewing (Hallinan and Striphas 2016, 129)—or as we typically call it—binge watching, has not only impacted the way we engage with television episodes but the way in which they are written. Hallinan and Striphas (2016) note that these changes to viewing practices "ha[ve] affected both the structure and content of these shows, allowing scriptwriters to side-step recaps, cliff-hangers, and similar narrative devices intended to keep viewers glued between commercial breaks and from one week to the next" (129). Netflix is able to use algorithms in order to promote selected content while also using the data to inform its practices. In fact, Beer (2013) argues that there is an "implicit claim in the Netflix competition... that the influence of algorithms on cultural taste is measurable" and that the "competition reveals how central the accuracy of the recommendation system is to such organisations" like Netflix (64). In other words, algorithmic culture is an important part of Netflix as the data is not neutral, but rather based on logics that maintain influence. These changes are interesting when considering *Schitt$ Creek* which originally aired on cable television for the first three seasons before being picked up on Netflix. With this in mind, this paper analyzes two episodes from *Schitt$ Creek*—the first episode being from season one and the second episode being from season six. One thing to note is that from the beginning, when *Schitt$ Creek* aired on cable television, a new episode was released weekly on CBC, while season six was also released on CBC, many viewers waited for its early and all at once release on Netflix.

On March 10, 2015, the "Honeymoon" episode aired as part of season one of *Schitt$ Creek*. In this episode, David and Stevie wake up in bed together and later have a conversation using wine as an analogy for their sexuality. In an unexpected turn of events, big city Johnny (David's dad) struggles to grasp David's sexuality and queerness which small town Roland (the mayor) takes no issue with and is quick to understand. This framing ultimately plays into the stereotypes that major cities like New York, where the Roses are from, are more progressive than small towns supposedly in the middle of nowhere. Arguably, this episode is progressive as it engages with sexuality in a way that expands the heterosexual/gay binary that is often the default view of sexuality or queer sexuality in mainstream depictions of the **2SLGBTQIA+** community. For instance, there is one particular scene in this episode in which Roland evokes radical acceptance. Johnny shares with Roland news on David's sexuality to which Roland responds with quick acceptance and notes that it is something others cannot control. More specifically, when Johnny shares with Roland that David is a "pansexual," Roland initially thinks that has to do with a "cookware fetish" (*Schitt$ Creek* "Honeymoon" 2015). However, when Johnny explains, "No, he loves everyone, men, women, women who become men, men who become women. I'm his father and I always wanted his life to be easy. But you know, just pick one gender, and maybe, maybe everything would've been less...confusing," Roland replies, "Well... you know, Johnny, when it comes to matters of the heart, we can't tell our kids who to love" (*Schitt$ Creek* "Honeymoon" 2015). Shortly after, the scene transitions to another subplot. This is arguably a moment of television that initially aired on a cable network and can now be found on streaming services that may be viewed as progressive as it creates a dialogue that acknowledges pansexuality and explains pansexuality, without putting that responsibility on to what could be a token queer person. Instead, two male identifying people educate one another. Kies (2016) argues, "The progress made by opening romance up to gay couples on the one hand coincides with the subsuming of alternative sexualities and identities into the normative trajectory on the other" (10, 11). *Schitt$ Creek* uses this episode to not only open up the possibility of romance for David, but to explore alternative sexualities and identities that are typically not even acknowledged in this sort of popularized sitcom content.

On the other hand, the 2SLGBTQIA+ community continues to be dominantly represented by white middle/upper class able-bodied men. And the depiction of David is not all that different. In fact, Ronnie is noticeably absent from the "Honeymoon" episode, despite her potential to offer a unique perspective as a queer woman of color. This framing and lack of visibility aligns with the reality that "While white lesbians have not been as visible on television as white gay men, they have certainly been seen more frequently than racial minorities of any non-heterosexual identity and more than those who identify as queer or trans. A lesbian in a committed relationship is more easily likened to a white heterosexual than a queer person of color" (Kies 2016, 10). These representations (or lack thereof) are not isolated to this one episode of *Schitt$ Creek* or television representation in general. Likewise, algorithms to continue to acknowledge certain privileged identities while re-categorizing identities deemed deviant into their determined categorizations/groupings to suit the platforms/Netflix's algorithmic needs. For example, Netflix does not name privileged identities within their genres, rather, content that appears to differ from the norm find itself listed under the heading of *Critically Acclaimed LGBTQ TV Shows,* for example. As Noah Tsika (2016) argues, "While various algorithmically determined approaches to making queerness more visible and interpretable online might convincingly be described—and certainly describe themselves—as queer methods, their results often favor the subjectivities of white, gay, normatively bodied cis men" (113). Expanding on Kies and Tsika, I argue *Schitt$ Creek* maybe increasing queer visibility, but it is not queering the sitcom.

During the sixth season of *Schitt$ Creek*, the episode "Happy Ending" (2020) shows the Rose family coming together with the town to put on David and Patrick's wedding. This episode offers unique and funny content while also becoming homonormative with symbolic gestures. For instance, David wears a skirt to accompany his suit jacket and has his sister walk him down the aisle where he meets his soon to be husband, Patrick, and the officiant (his mother, Moira) dressed as the pope. The classic trope of pulling together is prevalent as everyone in the town comes together and offers to help as a symbol of support for the wedding and marriage after rain risks ruining the wedding. Kies (2016) notes, "By favoring marriage and parenthood as ultimate life goals, and by depicting white, middle- and upper-class men, gay romance has succeeded in winning over audiences" (1). Arguably, gay romance has not only won over audiences who watch *Schitt$ Creek,* but there is a premise that the romance between Patrick and David has won over the town. In an earlier episode, "The Hike," Patrick proposes to David with an elaborate set of engagement ring*s* (plural). Kies (2016) finds engagement rings often demand more attention than wedding bands in heterosexual romance novels and television (9). This fact certainly seems to be true in "Happy Ending" as Patrick and David both follow the traditional components of a wedding ceremony and exchange a singular ring to one another on their fourth finger. This ring exchange acts as a symbolic gesture framed by the camera to allow audience members to feel as though they are attending the ceremony. It also makes David and Patrick more *digestible* as they follow this normative practice. Can this episode of *Schitt$ Creek* be regarded as progressive? In the following excerpt from Kies, I have replaced the character names to those from *Schitt$ Creek*:

> Series like [*Schitt$ Creek*] present gay couples to a wide audience, but do so by making the couples as normative and nonthreatening as possible. Gay couples on these series look and behave like many of their straight counterparts on other television series. [David and Patrick] are all white and middle- to upper-class. One partner is more masculine and one more effeminate, so that the pair further mirrors the traditional gender roles within a heterosexual couple. The couples' desire to remain monogamous, marry (legally or symbolically), and have children reinforces their normativity. Through their romantic storylines, these gay characters seem like 'regular people' and act 'like a couple should'.
>
> (Kies 2016, 9)

In a way, it is uncanny how accurate this description is despite the fact that Kies was talking about *Glee* and *The New Normal*. To follow-up on the question I posed earlier, it does not seem as though a show can be fully progressive if it is still following the same representations and tropes as other televisual content that ended five years prior to the airing of "Happy Ending." Overall, I argue that this episode has progressive aspects as it, in some ways, tries to introduce queerness into heteronormative traditions. For instance, on their wedding day, David receives a "happy ending" during a massage that Patrick arranged. This scene is met with humor and hints at the flexibility of gay culture when Patrick realizes what happens. However, this flexibility is short lived and regarded as nothing but a weird story to be shared in the future as Patrick's outrage is quickly squashed as the wedding and wedding plans must go on. Upon further analysis, the gay relationship between David and Patrick is often not as queer as it may seem.

With this in mind, I am left to wonder if the shift from the engagement episode that happened in the prior season (season five), to the final episode "Happy Ending" in season six was, in part, due to the series growth, anticipation, and popularity resulting from Netflix. Could *Schitt$ Creek* have adapted to heightened characteristics of the TVIII era based on its ultimate televisual platform? If we know that viewing practices influence the content of a series based on data collection from digital streaming platforms like Netflix (Hallinan and Striphas 2016, 129), then it is safe to assume that this influence may impact the approach of a series in order to keep audiences engaged. Season six of *Schitt$ Creek* was created with the intention of ultimately being released all at once on Netflix which, I contend, had an influence on the queer representation within the show. As Tsika (2016) argues, "the income potential of white gay men continue[s] to shape corporate constructions of queerness (especially on-line), it is easy to assume that queer content that doesn't 'fit' established paradigms will increasingly be confined to the 'slow-download' category, as will the users who are not identifiable with stable or salable expressions of queerness" (126). If *Schitt$ Creek* did not follow homonormative ideals, would the algorithms had promoted it in the same way? If Ronnie ever became more than a background character, would audiences and the algorithmic logics have been able to digest this content? I'd like to hope so, but as Beer (2013) reminds us, "algorithms [are] deeply embedded in social processes" (73) and homophobia and racism are still very prevalent.

## Conclusion

Codes make up our lives—television codes, social codes, algorithmic codes. As codes continue to become further entrenched in our everyday lives, it is important to begin understanding these codes and their impact. Televisual representation helps audience members make sense of themselves and others. However, there continues to be coded messages within the televisual content and within the platform the content is found on before an audience member ever engages with that content. Based on my two episode analysis of *Schitt$ Creek*, I argue that queer representations and queer potentials remain complex. Despite this complexity, it is important to remember the television content cannot be analyzed out of context as streaming platforms like Netflix continue to influence how television content is written, structured, and promoted (Hallinan and Striphas 2016, 129). While some queer representation is better than no queer representation, it is also important to consider who continues to be represented and who continues to be left out or made invisible. Identities are complex, yet white, gay, middle/upper class men have continued to dominate televisual content (Kies 2016, 10) and the televisual content promoted by algorithms on platforms like Netflix. Queer people of color deserve representation and without this representation, the 2SLGBTIA+ community continues to be reduced to certain privileged identity categories. Algorithms, algorithmic culture, and television hold significant influence which must be taken seriously (Beer 2013, 96). There remains a persistent "fantasy of queer inclusion online" (Tsika 2016, 126), both within televisual content and online streaming platforms. All I have left to say is that progress has been made, but there is, without a doubt, more progress to be made. After all, what will Netflix promote next in the "Critically Acclaimed LGBTQ TV Shows" category?

## Key Words

**2SLGBTQIA+:** 2SLGBTQIA+ is an abbreviation that stands for Two-Spirit, Lesbian, Gay, Bisexual, Trans, Queer, Questioning, intersex, asexual, and beyond. This abbreviation is not fixed, but rather fluid as it is often used in different ways by individuals within the 2SLGBTQIA+ community. Queer is sometimes used as an umbrella term to represent any non-heterosexual or non-cisgender identity. It is important to note that queer is a complex term that resists a singular definition so while it may be utilized as an umbrella term for some, it can also refer to someone's sexuality, gender, or actions. It is important to know the meanings of each letter to ensure inclusivity of these identities.

**Algorithmic Culture**: Algorithmic culture is a form of culture. Algorithmic culture is not cultural because it deals with cultural aspects (ex. identities), but because the algorithms, codes, and data are cultural as they impact and are impacted by culture. Algorithms influence how we understand and interact with various aspects of culture but are also shaped themselves by cultural practices and ideologies. While algorithms, codes, and data may seem neutral and merely technological, they are anything but. Algorithmic culture is a part of culture and often deeply entrenched in discriminatory practices that continue to marginalize equity seeking (deserving) groups.

**Heteronormativity**: The persuasive idea that heterosexuality is a given and the "normal" expression of sexuality is referred to as heteronormativity. Gender is also part of heteronormativity as this ideology presumes and enforces the gender binary (man/woman) and enforces roles attached to those identities in a persistent and preservative way, while excluding those who do not "fit" this conceptualization. An example of this would be how in many popular sitcoms, like *Friends*, people in relationships are often cisgender and straight.

**Queer**: Queer has a multitude of meanings and a complex history. There is no singular definition of queer and that is intentional. In fact, defining the term queer is quite challenging. While defining what queer is not is easy (for instance, heteronormative or straight culture), defining what queer is, is much harder. Queer, as noted above, is used as an umbrella term to refer to any non-cisgender and non-heterosexual identity. Queer can be an adjective to refer to sexuality or gender. However, queer was once a derogatory term/slur that was reclaimed as a term of empowerment by the queer community. More recently, queer can also be used as a verb that encompasses resistance, defiance, and action (typically against more traditional, heteronormative ideologies, and constructions).

**TVIII**: A concept introduced by Roberta Pearson and referenced by Mareika Jenner. TVIII is an era of television that spans from the present back to the mid-1990s. This era accounts for the technological advances and digital platforms associated with television. In other words, platforms like Netflix in this era have shifted away from the television set and towards online streaming.

## Critical Thinking Questions

1 Why is Netflix significant when it comes to queer media? In what ways can Netflix improve its 2SLGBTQIA+ representation?
2 How does streaming television impact viewing practices? Consider the ways streaming may influence televisual content.
3 Can you provide an example of how streaming services have impacted your viewing practices? Reflect on the content you watch in your answer.

## References

Arnold, Sarah. 2016. "Netflix and the Myth of Choice/Participation/Autonomy." In *The Netflix Effect: Technology and Entertainment in the 21st Century*, edited by Kevin McDonald and Daniel Smith-Rowsey, 49–62. London: Bloomsbury Academic.

Beer, David. 2013. "Algorithms: Shaping Tastes and Manipulating the Circulations of Popular Culture." *Popular Culture and New Media: The Politics of Circulation*. London: Palgrave Macmillan.

Hallinan, Blake, and Ted Striphas. 2016. "Recommended for you: The Netflix Prize and the Production of Algorithmic Culture." *New Media & Society* 18, no. 1: 117–37.

Jenner, Mareike. 2016. "Is This TVIV? On Netflix, TVIII and Binge-Watching." *New Media & Society* 18, no. 2: 257–73.

Kies, Bridget. 2016. "First Comes Love, Then Comes Marriage: (Homo)Normalizing Romance on American Television." *Journal of Popular Romance Studies* 5, no. 2: 1–13.

Patchunka, Casey. 2019. "Netflix Killed the Cable TV Star: Cable TV is Definitionally Disadvantaged for Use of Artificial Intelligence." *Federal Communications Law Journal* 71, no. 2: 275–98.

*Schitt$ Creek*. 2015. Season 1, episode 10, "Honeymoon." Created by Daniel Levy and Eugene Levy. Aired March 10, 2015 on Canadian Broadcasting Corporation (CBC).

*Schitt$ Creek*. 2020. Season 6, episode 14, *"Happy Ending." Created by Daniel* Levy and Eugene Levy. Aired April 7, 2020 on Canadian Broadcasting Corporation (CBC).

Tsika, Noah. 2016. "CompuQueer: Protocological Constraints, Algorithmic Streamlining, and the Search for Queer Methods Online." *WSQ: Women's Studies Quarterly* 44, no. 3/4: 111–30.

# 19 The Missing *Live* Ingredient

## The Search for Ephemerality in the Screening and Streaming of Theatre

*Amanda Di Ponio*

At the close of Michael D. Friedman's (2016) article in *Shakespeare Quarterly*, "The Shakespeare Cinemacast: *Coriolanus*," Friedman predicts that with "the continuing advancement and proliferation of digital technology in the twenty-first century, audiences outside major theatrical centers are likely to expect more frequent and convenient access to landmark Shakespeare productions through various media" (480). The term cinemacast was first used by The Metropolitan Opera in screening its Live in HD (2006–) series of live to screen performances of opera at the Metropolitan Opera House at the Lincoln Center in New York City. Friedman anticipates that these performances will be typified as popular and commonplace, in what he terms an ideally seamless blend of high and popular culture. The expansive consumption potential of this scenario may have tremendous significance on how we consume art.

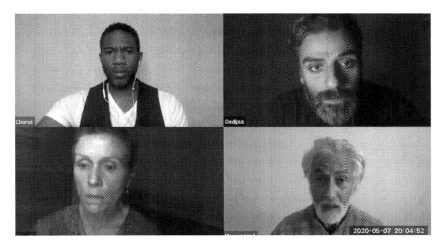

*Figure 19.1* Public Advocate Jumaane Williams (Chorus), Oscar Isaac (Oedipus), Frances McDormand (Jocasta), David Strathairn (Creon) in *The Oedipus Project* May 7, 2020. Screenshot courtesy of Theater of War Productions.

DOI: 10.4324/9781003310730-23

In the last decade, technological innovations have allowed for increased collective consumption of live theatre performances, not just Shakespeare. This is largely attributed to the increased availability and access to "**livecast**" recordings of on-stage productions. While these recordings are not particularly new – the BBC has televised live captures since the 1930s – their proliferation, and the means of their distribution and consumption, is. Shakespeare's Globe Theatre, for example, through its Globe Player platform established in 2014, was the first theatre to offer its own on-demand viewing platform, allowing patrons to purchase, stream, and/or download recordings of live theatre, thus, potentially and ideally, reaching a larger, global audience. While Globe Player content is only licensed for individual use and cannot be viewed in any classroom or educational context, patrons are offered institutional access to most of the catalogue conveniently through costly institutional library subscriptions in partnership with Bloomsbury Publishing via dramaonline.com. The importance of these recordings as teaching and research tools, and their accessibility, allows for meaningful analyses of theatrical performances of dramatic texts.

The desired result of viewing and/or downloading recordings of an **ephemeral** event, such as a live theatre performance, does not replicate the event in subsequent viewings, for its very existence was intended to be fleeting and unique, lasting only short time. Shakespeare's Globe Theatre makes no claim that renting, owning, or streaming a recording of its commercial and cultural products replaces the physically present audience experience. On the other hand, the commissioners of Digital Theatre, partnered with the Royal Shakespeare Company, The Old Vic, The Royal Opera House, and Shakespeare's Globe, to name but a few, boldly claim that recordings of ephemeral events bring "the live experience to your screen by instantly streaming the best theatre productions from around the world anytime, anywhere," captured "authentically," with all "the drama and emotion of each production" (Digital Theatre 2009, About Us). The recorded content of this esteemed group is released weekly for limited six-week runs and the Digital Theatre+ website offers supplementary educational resources. But these marketing statements are misleading: is it possible to bring the experience of live theatre to the screen? If so, whose authentic experience is captured? The viewer is watching a recording of a live event, but the performance is not *live*; it is something *other*.

## Ephemerality and Ritual

The Dada and Surrealist movements of the early twentieth century, led by Hugo Ball and André Breton, respectively, placed emphasis on the artistic act, and not the *product*. The artifact developed from the creative act was merely the by-product of the real art – i.e. the act itself. Dada was a temporary medium, meaning the action, rather than the lasting object, was most important. In performance, therefore, the source material may remain the same before, during, and after the event, but the utterance of that text inevitably varies from one performance to another. In order to preserve the transience of the event, recordings of any kind were discouraged. This way, the performance not only maintained, but demanded ephemerality as part of its very essence.

To quote theatre practitioner and theorist, Antonin Artaud (1938), in his essay "No More Masterpieces," the theatre is the only place where repetition – of utterance, of gesture, the constituents of performance – is not possible:

> What has been said is not still to be said; that an expression does not have the same value twice, does not live two lives; that all words, once spoken are dead and function only at the moment when they are uttered, that a form, once it has served, cannot be used again and asks only to be replaced by another, and that the theater is the only place in the world where a gesture, once made, can never be made the same way twice.
> 
> (Artaud 1938, 75)

In this way, every live performance is unique and cannot be recreated. The recording of a live performed event is, therefore, only the by-product of the act itself. Audience members viewing a recording of a live event are not witnessing the event itself, but what is derived from it. The audience is aware that they are not participating in the live event, and so something is lacking experientially from what otherwise is offered ephemerally.

While we can easily identify the theatre for entertainment purposes, performance theorist, Richard Schechner (2006), discusses the importance of efficacy – to produce the performance's intended effect(s), for all participants, whatever the goal: to entertain, to instruct, or to affirm the values shared by community – which aligns the theatre with ritual as detailed in his **Efficacy-Entertainment Continuum**:

## The Efficacy-Entertainment Continuum

| EFFICACY ←——→ ENTERTAINMENT | |
|---|---|
| *Ritual* | *Theatre* |
| results | fun |
| link to an absent Other | Only for those here |
| symbolic time | emphasis now |
| performer possessed, in trance | performer knows what s/he's doing |
| audience participates | audience watches |
| audience believes | audience appreciates |
| criticism discouraged | criticism flourishes |
| collective creativity | individual creativity |

(130)

As Schechner (2006) insists, this is a continuum and not a binary. If we fail to recognize the ritual of live commercial performance, from "rehearsals, backstage life before, during, and after the show, the function of the roles in the lives of each performer, the money invested by the backers, the arrival of the audience, how they paid for their tickets" – to this list, I add the dissemination of the recordings of these cultural products – and the use value of the performance, we fail to see beyond the point of view of theatre as entertainment alone, and fail to acknowledge that it is also "ritual, economics, and a microcosm of social structure" (130–1). In order for the screening and streaming of live recordings to connect to audiences, a ritual for viewing must first be established.

## The National Theatre Live

The National Theatre (NT) Live, an initiative of the Royal National Theatre Great Britain in London, provides an example of what this *other* experience might be, acknowledging both the ephemerality associated with live performance and the ritual which accompanies its viewing and participation. The advancement of satellite technology has progressively aided the broadcast of live stage events directly to cinemas, something The Metropolitan Opera has been doing successfully for over a decade. Since 2009, funded by the National Endowment for Science, Technology and the Arts (NESTA) and the Arts Council England, NT Live has broadcast over forty staged dramatic productions of classical, early modern, modern, and contemporary drama to audiences worldwide via the cinema. In an attempt to reach broader and new audiences, NT Live boasts a wide-spectrum inclusionary approach to disseminate its products via "state-of-the-art filming techniques, tailored to every play," capturing "every flicker of emotion," providing "the best seats in the house," where patrons are "part of something much bigger … This is theater for everyone" (National Theatre Live 2009, About Us).

While NT Live acknowledges the efficacy of ritual in these inclusionary statements, there are some inherent problems regarding both its proposed reach and the "liveness" of its products. Its suggestion is that *everyone* consumes live theatre, or would, if given the opportunity, and broadcasting live to cinemas is a way to reach everyone, or rather, those audience members inclined to attend an in-person event, when situated in a geographically suitable location, and with the financial means to do so. Further, depending on when and how a viewer has access to these products, the "liveness" of these performances adjusts:

> Via satellite we broadcast the live performance from the theatre we are in to cinemas across the UK, as well as many European cinemas. Our cinema partners in North America capture the live broadcast feed via satellite and screen the titles on the same day, at a customer friendly evening time in their local time zone. The live footage from

the broadcast is then packaged and shared, unedited, with cinemas for repeat encore screenings in international territories not able to screen it live.
(National Theatre, About the National Theatre Live)

In that iteration, geographical limitations can further alter the live experience.

Further still, what the audience sees on screen is very much dependent on the viewpoint of the director working within the medium of film. Director of the 2014 *Coriolanus* cinema broadcast of the Josie Rourke directed production starring Tom Hiddleston, Tim van Someren, asserts he is mindful of his need to "give the broadcast audience some extra experience which makes up for them being removed from the actual live event. They don't feel the visceral thrill of being at the event in person"; thus, he provides "a viewpoint that gives a new, enhanced perspective" (cited in Friedman 2016, 474–5). The desired result is a superior view of close-up and multi-focal shots which only a cinema audience could ever be privy to. NT Live claims command over techniques to offer "the best seat in the house," but, as Friedman (2016) corrects, it "would be more accurate to say that they provide the best seat in the house *at any given moment*," and one that no single spectator could possibly see (461). The cinema viewer observes an iteration of the live performance, and not the live performance itself.

Given the above rudimentary limitations, can NT Live still claim to make theatre for everyone? As argued, these broadcasts are something *other* than live, a representation of the event, and not the event itself. While the live reproductions may be made with everyone in mind, they are still only commonly seen by relatively few, and the audience is removed from the liveness of the event. According to Peggy Phelan (1993) in *Unmarked: The Politics of Performance*, "Performance's only life is in the present. Performance cannot be saved, recorded, documented, or otherwise participate in the circulation of representations: once it does so it becomes something other than performance" (146). Put another way, live theatre is unique because of its ephemerality. The attempt may nobly be secured in the advancement of greater consumption of theatre, but NT Live offers select viewers encore performances of the same live performance, an impossible scenario for Phelan. While I agree that the sense of occasion associated with cinematic release is analogous here, and thus aligned with ritual, the NT Live broadcasts are not marketed as cinematic releases, and they are not quite *live* events either. I would further offer that they are not necessarily secondary to the theatre performance, or disingenuous, or even artificial, as some critics have claimed, but they are something else, as observed by Stephen Purcell (2014) in "The Impact of New Forms of Public Performance" (214–15). If "in the world of Web 2.0, 'liveness' might be defined by interactivity, responsiveness and an apparent multiplicity of choices," as Purcell (2014) suggests, then these events need dissemination in other, accessible ways (222).

## COVID-19 and the Shift to Online Accessibility

The COVID-19 pandemic facilitated the increasing placement of recorded performances made available on steaming platforms. Prior to the pandemic, NT Live resisted any dissemination of its cultural products, either for rent or purchase, via Internet streaming or DVD release, despite those media being viable and receptive means of consumption by its intended audience of everyone. The motivation behind NT Live's initial reluctance to release recordings of live broadcasts was to savor the fleeting moment, according to Head of Digital Media for the NT at the time, David Sabel (2011), in "Digital Broadcast of Theatre: Learning from the Pilot Season NT Live" (9). They did so to maintain the integrity and ephemerality of the live event for those viewing in person.

However, in the summer of 2020, NT, and Canada's own Stratford Festival, both sought to make a steady *stream* of content available while patrons were confined to their homes and performance venues remained closed. Every Thursday, both providers released recordings of live theatre productions, available for a one-week limited release, accompanied by viewing parties to replace the ritual of opening night after parties. NT Live put aside its reluctance to release recordings of its live stage captures online, and broadcast 16 plays over 16 weeks from April 2 until July 23, 2020 via its YouTube channel.

The Stratford Festival was equally quick to shift to the online environment. Once its 2020 season was officially cancelled, the Festival redirected its resources to launching Stratfest@Home in October 2020, an online streaming service with a remarkably varied selection of content featuring recordings of previous productions, akin to those released online during that same sixteen-week period, along with exclusive web-only original shorts, music collaborations, writing and performance workshops, educational and coaching content, and behind-the-scenes documentary featurettes, some of which are available for free viewing. For the introductory fee of $10/month, patrons can and continue to watch recorded live performance in addition to exclusive digital content released weekly. This is yet another instance how the pandemic proves that necessity conceives invention and innovation in dire times.

A constant since the COVID-19 pandemic began is the perpetual flux experienced as priorities are frequently re-evaluated. Indeed, in December 2020, weeks after the Stratfest@Home platform launched, NT Live released its own at-home viewing service, National Theatre at Home (2020). For the price of $17.50/month or $175 annually, at home subscribers have access to recordings previously not made available to the public in any format other than live cinema broadcast, with two collections totaling forty plays in addition to web-only content and featurettes.[1] However, NT Live recommenced cinema broadcasts in January 2022; the live, ephemeral, ritualized event is clearly the priority.

## Other Live – and Online – Performance

The COVID-19 pandemic also facilitated new kinds of live performance as global and local, public/subsidized/donor-funded, for-profit, and not-for-profit theatre companies had to decide how best to reach audiences. Some shifted their dramatic projects online via peer-to-peer software platforms, such as Zoom, Microsoft Teams, and Bongo, traditionally used for teleconferencing. This began discernibly with The Theater of War's *The Oedipus Project*, a performed reading of Sophocles' *Oedipus Rex*, translated, directed, and adapted by Bryan Doerries, on May 7, 2020 (see Figure 19.1). In a June 2020 interview for *The Brooklyn Rail*, Doerries attests that the event, similar to other Theater of War projects, is devoted to half performance and half community dialogue, and that the online space was "successful at creating the conditions for people to come together across really disparate geographic and temporal boundaries and to create that sense of community" (Ghaheri and Kane 2020).

Economics have also influenced what is being played in this environment. While *The Oedipus Project* worked to maintain its ephemerality as subsequent performances featured new perspectives from the changing casts, creatives, and audiences, and only select highlights from the production are available for viewing on the Theater of War's website, other large, commercial performance art conglomerates, such as The Broadway League, were able to take advantage of content already stored in the archives. Through the BroadwayHD streaming service, established in 2015, the Broadway League's catalogue of more than two hundred Broadway and Off-Broadway shows was made available on-demand. Similarly, other large-scale platforms such as Netflix, Amazon Prime, HBO Max, Apple TV+, and Disney+ featured recordings of live stage events, and other stage-to-screen adaptations, with the latter releasing the highly anticipated, and specifically filmed and adapted for release to screen, production of the musical *Hamilton* The COVID-19 pandemic prompted the *Hamilton* film's release, one year ahead of schedule. The film was welcomed by a receptive audience, comprised of not exactly everyone, but to subscribers of the Disney+ streaming service.

Smaller for-profit theatre companies took to alternative spaces and unconventional means to keep theatre accessible, some of which are featured in Michael Paulson's July 2020 *New York Times* article, "Beyond Broadway, the Show Does Go On." One Denver, Colorado company, Buntport Theater, performed its original play, *Grasshoppers*, in a parking lot to theatregoers sitting in cars in order to reach its audience live and in real time. While "performing in outdoor spaces was much preferred," the company also made the transition to performing original works of digital theatre, "to a screen," livestreamed via Zoom, in addition to releasing edited content via their website, in order to keep supporters entertained, but always from the perspective that "none of them felt like a successful replacement for live in person events."[2] Not being able to fully immerse the audience in either space was, and is, as challenging as not being able to tailor performances to audience responses and reactions, so too was the susceptibility of audiences and performers to Zoom fatigue. Even though Buntport found the outdoor (preferred) and online experiences fun and challenging, and like Doerries, Buntport acknowledges the accessibility of that online work and would not necessarily rule out its use in the future, it does not equate to their 20 years of indoor theatre work: "If anything positive came from the pandemic shut down and its restrictions, it's the renewed feeling that as a theater company, we want to keep making theater, in person, and connected to a live audience."

The demand for a return to ephemerality is heard closer to home as well. In the summer of 2021, the Stratford Festival transformed into an outdoor festival, featuring six plays and five cabarets from the cancelled 2020 season. Initial ticket sales allowed for approximately one hundred patrons to secure socially distanced seats for the limited runs ranging from one-to-two months in duration, and the lifting of some COVID-19 restrictions in Ontario in late July 2021 allowed for an increase of twice that number. Patrons added their names to wait lists, hoping to secure tickets.[3] Audiences are speaking.

In Toronto, Mirvish's first indoor live theatre event since March 2020 opened at The Princess of Wales Theatre on August 4, 2021. The anticipated NT production of *Blindness*, a socially distanced sound narrative adaptation of José Saramago's novel by playwright Simon Stephens, featured the audience, and not actors, onstage. Patron demand for tickets was so great that the show's run was extended from September 24, 2021 to October 24, 2021. These are crisis-inspired innovations, and the return to the live event goal is clear with theatres across the globe attempting a safe return to indoor theatre spaces.[4]

## Conclusion

Ephemerality is the irreproducible, essential component of theatre that makes the live, alive. As David Sabel (2011) reflects of the NT Live cinema broadcasts, these were considered "an alternative experience" as the "unique experience of being in the actual theatre" cannot be replaced; while it is markedly "not the same as being in the theatre," it is different in its own right (8, 9). If the original goal was to increase the opportunity to see a NT production, NT Live has certainly been able to maintain its relevancy by increasing viewership through broadcasting, but the lost component of live viewing creates an audience member of a wholly different participatory spectrum. NT Live does not necessarily achieve its goal of making theatre for everyone, but it has successfully expanded viewership in part by marketing the experience of live broadcast via the cinema and, more accessibly, via its digital platform, National Theatre at Home. But the lacking emotive elements of physical presence, of seeing, of sensing, of being part of the live audience-and-performer dynamic in shared existence delivers a theatre experience entirely other than what can only be live.

The reopening of theatre spaces must be done alongside a careful balance between ephemerality – maintaining the integrity of the unique live theatre experience – and accessibility – remote and repeat access – in order to successfully see the online space as an asset, especially if extending the theatre's reach is the sincere goal.

## Key Words

**Efficacy-Entertainment Continuum**: The Efficacy-Entertainment continuum established by performance theorist Richard Schechner (2006) in his text *Performance Theory*, wherein he asserts that what we call "ritual" or "performance" is largely dependent on context and function, i.e. for whom and for what purpose performance happens (130).

**Ephemeral**: Something that is ephemeral is lasting for a short time; a fleeing moment which cannot be recreated.

**Livecast**: In *Live to Your Local Cinema: The Remarkable Rise of Livecasting*, Martin Barker (2013) considers the social value of what he terms "livecasting" in his chapter "The Cultural Status of Livecasts." He asks what future name will be used to refer to these types of events, in part because they are not exactly live, and also because the term livecast is too generic and neither captures the significance of the event, nor includes the various modes/media by which to view or interact with the cultural product. Friedman (2016) prefers "cinemacasts," one of many terms to which these events have been referred, including "event cinema," "livecast," "cinema relay," "outside broadcast," "simulcast," "streamed transmission," "cinema livecast," "beamed live performance," "live cinema," "digital broadcast cinema," and "alternative content" (457). Most recently, in "Blurring the Lines: Adaptation, Transmediality, and Screened Performance," Bernadette Cochrane (2020) uses "live relay" as a preferred term given the delayed reception of these cultural products (341).

## Critical Thinking Questions

1 Consider the online experiences you consume: how are they marketed towards you? Are you being sold a "live" performance, like *The Oedipus Project*, or a recording of a live event previously staged,

## The Missing Live Ingredient 199

like the online screenings available on platforms like National Theatre at Home and Stratfest@Home? How likely are you to choose to consume theatre performances in these spaces?

2  Consider memberships to the streaming services you hold: do you watch recordings of live events, such as theatre, concerts, or stand-up comedy? Do you feel that you are a participating member of the audience in viewing these events, or a passive observer? Do you view these recordings as a viable replacement for live performance as you've come to understand or experience it?

3  What do you think of "theatre for everyone," the idea posited by NT Live: is this realistic? What barriers – social, cultural, economic – can you identify as barring the theatre's reach?

## Notes

1  The original content offered by National Theatre at Home is not as varied as that available on the Stratfest@Home platform.
2  Buntport Theater, email message to author, November 9, 2021. All quotations from Buntport Theater Company are extracted from this source.
3  Astonishingly, I secured a ticket to *The Rez Sisters*' second performance on July 24, 2021, joining approximately 102 theatregoers in the live outdoor event.
4  In fact, while drafting this chapter, I received an invitation from The Grand Theatre in London, Ontario to complete a survey, supported by the Ontario Arts Council, in order to gauge patrons' comfort levels in returning to indoor performance spaces.

## References

Artaud, Antonin. (1938) 1958. "No More Masterpieces." In *The Theatre and Its Double*," translated by Mary Caroline Richards, 74–83. New York: Grove Press.

Barker, Martin. 2013. *Live to Your Local Cinema: The Remarkable Rise of Livecasting*. Basingstoke: Palgrave Macmillan.

Buntport Theater. 2016. Accessed November 1, 2021. https://buntport.com/

Cochrane, Bernadette. 2020. "Blurring the Lines: Adaptation, Transmediality, and Screened Performance." In *The Routledge Companion to Adaptation*, edited by Dennis Cutchin, Katja Krebs, and Eckart Voigts, 340–8. London: Routledge

*Coriolanus*. 2014. Stage direction by Josie Rourke, screen direction by Tim van Someren, Donmar Warehouse, London, December 17, 2013-February 13, 2014 (London: National Theatre Live, 30 January 2014), cinemacast.

Digital Theatre. 2009. Big Clever Learning Limited, London. www.digitaltheatre.com

Friedman, Michael D. 2016. "The Shakespeare Cinemacast: *Coriolanus*." *Shakespeare Quarterly* 67, no. 4: 457–80.

Ghaheri, Shadi, and Lucas Kane. 2020. "Jumaane Williams and Bryan Doerries with Lucas Kane and Shadi Ghaheri: Public Advocate Jumaane Williams and

Theater Director Bryan Doerries Reflect on *The Oedipus Project* and the Arts in the Current COVID-19 Climate." *The Brooklyn Rail*, June 2020. https://brooklynrail.org/2020/06/theater/Jumaane-Williams-and-Bryan-Doerries-with-Lucas-Kane-and-Shadi-Ghaheri

Globe Player. 2014. The Shakespeare Globe Trust, London. Accessed November 1, 2021. https://www.player.shakespearesglobe.com

National Theatre. "National Theatre Live." Accessed November 1, 2021. https://www.nationaltheatre.org.uk/about-the-national-theatre/national-theatre-live

National Theatre at Home. 2020. Accessed November 1, 2021. https://www.ntathome.com/

National Theatre Live. 2009. "About Us." Accessed November 1, 2021. https://www.ntlive.com/about-us/

Paulson, Michael. 2020. "Beyond Broadway, the Show Does Go On." *The New York Times*. New York, New York, July 4.

Phelan, Peggy. 1993. *Unmarked: The Politics of Performance*. London: Routledge.

Purcell, Stephen. 2014. "The Impact of New Forms of Public Performance." In *Shakespeare and the Digital World: Redefining Scholarship and Practice*, edited by Christie Carson and Peter Kirwan, 212–25. Cambridge: Cambridge University Press.

Sabel, David. 2011. "Reflections from the National Theatre." In *NT Live: Digital Broadcast of Theatre: Learning from the Pilot Season*. NESTA (National Endowment for Science, Technology and the Arts). Accessed November 1, 2021. https://www.media.nesta.org.uk/documents/nt_live.pdf

Schechner, Richard. (1988) 2006. *Performance Theory*. London: Routledge.

Stratfest@Home. 2020. https://www.stratfordfestival.ca/AtHome

"The Oedipus Project." *Theater of War*. Accessed November 1, 2021. https://theaterofwar.com/projects/the-oedipus-project

# 20 From Videotape Exchange Networks to On-Demand Streaming Platforms

## The Circulation of Independent Canadian Film and Video in the Digital Era

*Mariane Bourcheix-Laporte*

In the aftermath of the COVID-19 pandemic digital technologies are, more than ever, part of almost every aspect of our lives. Our routine engagements with audiovisual content on the Internet testify to how access to cultural goods and services is now entwined with digital technologies. Effectively, the Internet has become a primary channel for the **circulation** – the distribution and exhibition – of moving images, from high-value professional media to low-resolution user-generated content. In the era of participatory digital culture (Sterne et al. 2016), many readers will identify as both consumers and producers of digital content, via an array of online platforms, social media channels, and interactive apps. In an already-digitized media environment, it may be difficult to imagine the workings of distribution networks for **analogue media** – non-digital technologies that encode data on a physical support. But, as will be explained below, pre-digital distribution structures like **mail-based videotape exchange networks** – community-driven systems that enabled film and video makers to share their work with peers by swapping film reels and magnetic tapes encoded with audiovisual content – are not so far removed from the media distribution multiverse that we know today (Canada Media Fund 2019). Arguably, early videotape exchange networks represent analogue versions of the peer-to-peer (P2P) audiovisual distribution that emerged with the Internet and that manifests today in myriad of commercial and non-commercial **on-demand** and **livestreaming** digital broadcasting initiatives (Crisp 2015).

Building on the ideas outlined above, this chapter discusses the adoption of digital circulation practices by the Canadian independent media arts community. **Independent media arts** refer to time-based or interactive works – e.g., films, videos, sound art, multi-media performances, virtual and augmented reality works – created primarily for purposes of artistic expression and with the creator having complete artistic control (IMAA n.d.). This chapter positions digital modes of media circulation in continuity with the grassroots videotape exchange networks that were

DOI: 10.4324/9781003310730-24

developed by community-thirsty media artists and activists in the late 1960s and 1970s. After discussing this significant moment in media art history, the chapter explores how the Canadian independent media arts network has historically operated, and continues to operate, in parallel to commercial media production and distribution networks. An outline of how this ethos manifests in various online distribution and exhibition models is provided and paired with a discussion of key policy issues related to digital audiovisual circulation.

## The Early Canadian Independent Media Arts Sector and Videotape Exchange Networks

> Video had a magnetic importance. We all know the importance of seeing ourselves. In 1971, A Space started its video programme with Lisa Steele and Tom Sherman. In 1972, Video Inn opened its doors in Vancouver. In 1973, the Canada Council started video funding. In 1974, Art Metropole began video distribution. And then suddenly everyone everywhere in Canada was making video and this was a Canadian thing.
> 
> (Bronson 1983, 35)

In the quote above, General Idea member A.A. Bronson describes the euphoric beginnings of the Canadian independent media arts network. The artist refers to the community of practice that arose out of developments in image-making technologies in the late 1960s and early 1970s – notably the advent of portable video systems like the Portapak, which gave artists access to video as a new creative medium (Hencz 2020.). Video's immediacy and television-like characteristics fostered socially engaged, experimental, and critical arts practices across Canada and internationally (Baert 1987). Financial support from the Canada Council for the Arts further enabled the development of video and film collectives across the country, which soon formed a constellation of cooperative spaces where media arts communities could pool their technical resources and expertise (Murphy 2006). These artist-run centres – spaces run by and for artists – have historically played an important role in democratizing access to media production equipment and supporting the work of alternative media producers and grassroots activists, including feminist, 2SLGBTQIA+, Indigenous, and racialized communities (see, for example, Bociurkiw 2016).

Members of early film and video cooperatives soon realized the need to develop structures to circulate the works being produced through their emergent organizations. Some centres acquired significant collections of media works produced by artists, activists, and community groups and developed mail-exchange networks within Canadian and international

*From Videotape Exchange Networks to On-Demand Streaming Platforms* 203

*Figure 20.1* Front cover of the 6th International Video Exchange Directory published by the Satellite Video Exchange Society in 1979. Photo by Nomi Kaplan. Courtesy of VIVO Media Arts Centre.

media arts communities. For example, between 1971 and 1981, the Satellite Video Exchange Society in Vancouver (now known as VIVO Media Arts Centre) produced eight editions of the *Video Exchange Directory/ Bottin Video International*, a print publication that shared the contact information and tape exchange preferences of alternative media producers from around the world (Figure 20.1). To be included in the directory, individuals mailed in a postcard with their contact information and interests. Members of this analogue P2P exchange network were encouraged to contact each other and share copies of their work (see VIVO Media Arts Centre n.d. for more information). Across Canada, artist-run centres also operated media libraries and distributed film and video works in various formats – from Super 8 film to Betacam tape – to local and international networks alike (Baert 1987). In a pre-Internet age, this type of grassroots exchange network, akin to user-driven modes of digital distribution, helped to foster the development of the Canadian independent media arts sector and connect it to the global alternative media community.

## Notes on the Circulation of Independent Media Arts

Ramon Lobato (2012) defines distribution as: "the movement of media through space and time" (2). This is a broad definition, but it usefully emphasizes the circulation of media, without tying it to a specific technology or medium. Focusing on the movement involved in the act of distribution, we can establish continuity in the constantly evolving technological landscape that enables the reproduction and transmission of audiovisual materials. In this way, while they are separated by great technological gaps, the workings of mail-in tape exchange networks can be connected to the mechanisms that enable artists to self-distribute their work via user-generated platforms (e.g., YouTube, Vimeo, social media). There are several differences between these media circulation systems, but it is striking that in essence, both enable producers to connect with a community of peers and help their works reach a public. In both cases, there is an effort to make one's work "discoverable," i.e., able to reach and be viewed by an audience. Discoverability has become a key issue in the digital attention economy (McKelvey and Hunt 2019) but the quest for eyeballs has been central to the politics of media circulation both pre- and post-Internet.

Because of their inherent reproducibility, mediums such as film and video – analogue or digital – problematize the question of rarity as an economic necessity of distribution. The moving image is ontologically tied to the idea of reproduction and circulates through the copy. This logic opposes that of the unique work of art and prioritises the multiple over the singular. In the history of film and video, this has manifested through practices opposing the sanctity of the authentic work of art and the authority of the television broadcast. The distribution of moving images thus consists in a negotiation between reproduction and rarity, and between access and control (Hilderbrand 2012). Technological developments in the history of moving images have exacerbated the tensions at the heart of the circulation of film and video, with means of reproducing and sharing copies of media becoming increasingly accessible and simple. Whether in analogue or digital form, distribution should be understood as a mechanism that grants or denies access to media. Moreover, the channels through which moving images circulate are embedded in social, economic, and political structures (see Balsom 2017; Crisp 2015; Crisp and Menotti 2015). Accordingly, any intervention in the circulation modes of film and video can therefore adopt a political character. As Erika Balsom (2017) suggests, "distribution can be a site of advocacy and a way of remedying a lack of visibility" (8). The various distribution networks that the independent Canadian film and video community has fostered over the last 50 years align with this vision of the circulation of moving images as a political act.

These practices can be characterized as "informal," according to Lobato's (2012) concept of different distribution modalities. He writes: "formality refers to the degree to which industries are regulated, measured, and governed by state and corporate institutions. Informal distributors are those which operate outside this sphere" (4). It can be argued that independent media art centres, from their inception, have consciously operated in a space of informality and have developed alternative communities and publics for media artworks in this space. Coming out of the artist-run centre movement, which developed "parallel" art galleries to commercial and mainstream museum institutions, these structures have supported artists and activists working in the margins of mainstream media. Lucas Hilderbrand (2012) notes: "our written histories of video art's first decade suggest a proliferation of collectively produced video projects that strove to decentralize the media industry by giving voice to an idealistic notion of the people, rather than the privileged few with access to the airwaves" (12). From the get-go, alternative film and video circulation has sought to create a counter-space to that of formal (or institutionalized) distribution. Michael Goldberg (2000), a founding member of the Satellite Video Exchange Society, explains: "that's why we decided our core service would be a non-commercial video library, where the public could choose from a wide variety of themes and genres largely ignored by the mass media" (37). This ethos remains in the makeup of today's independent media arts network, which is dedicated to supporting the production and circulation of non-commercial media arts.

## The Canadian Independent Media Arts Sector Today and Online Circulation Practices

Today, Canada boasts hundreds of media arts centres, festivals, and collectives that support the production, exhibition, and distribution of media artworks in mediums ranging from analogue film and digital video, to sound art and new media, to augmented and virtual reality (AR and VR). The Canadian independent media arts community is vibrant and diversified, with a variety of organizational models – from DIY initiatives to international showcases – that share a commitment to supporting various forms of experimental and non-commercial production, centred on artists' creative visions. Several organizations within the network also have the mandate to support Indigenous and equity-seeking communities, including 2SLGBTQIA+ communities, women, racialized people, and persons who are unable to hear and disabled. The digital distribution and exhibition activities of the Canadian independent media arts community are continuous with prior and ongoing offline endeavours. Accordingly, these practices reimagine media distribution models driven by the platform economy and transpose the counter-political spirit of alternative media online. They use media circulation as a political tool, as suggested by Balsom quoted above. In this sense, digital editions of festivals such as the St. John's International Women's Film festival, Reel Asian International Film Festival, Rendezvous with Madness Festival, or the Vancouver Queer Arts Festival, to name a few, carve out spaces for the voices of media creators whose works sit in the margins of the mainstream. Similarly, subscription or transactional video-on-demand (SVOD and TVOD) platforms such as VUCAVU, Vithèque, or tënk, provide specialized-content alternatives to commercial VOD distribution, with content ranging from historical Canadian experimental video to contemporary media-performance, and from multi-channel installation to socially engaged documentary film. Finally, various digitally transmitted curated programs, available on-demand or livestreamed, expand the activities of media arts exhibitors into the online sphere – i.e., online exhibitions, screenings, performances, talks, AR apps, and VR experiences. Much like Video Exchange Directories discussed above, these endeavours create new ways for media artists to share their work, reach an expanded audience, and sustain a community of practice.

The COVID-19 pandemic has exacerbated the turn to digital modes of presentation and distribution in the independent media arts community, but the digitization of these practices was well underway before the global sanitary crisis forced cultural spaces to reinvent themselves through online activities. For example, VUCAVU.com was launched in 2016 as an online distribution platform for film, video, and experimental media. VUCAVU now operates as a bilingual pay-per-view distribution platform and **online presentation** space for freely accessible curated media programs. By partnering with media arts exhibitors such as galleries and festivals, VUCAVU activates its digital platform as a space for visibility through different modes of media circulation. Grouping a large spectrum of works made available through a variety of organizational sources, the platform also serves as a connective mechanism across media genres and generations of artists. In a similar fashion, several media arts centres have used digitization and online exhibition possibilities as tools to reactivate and recirculate their archival analogue collections. For instance, through the Digital Museums Canada initiative, VIVO Media Arts Centre developed an online exhibition with digitized footage of Vancouver's *Celebration '90 Gay Games III & Cultural Festival*, a milestone event in the history of Canadian 2SLGBTQIA+ communities (VIVO Media Arts Centre 2019). This type of initiative enables viewers from across Canada and internationally to have access to significant historical material maintained by a local community-driven archive.

The examples above point to how online environments offer innovative exhibition models through on-demand (asynchronous), livestreamed (synchronous), or hybrid presentation modes. Pleasure Dome's *Digital Magazine* series presents curated on-demand playlists of audiovisual works accompanied by critical writing. These programs are available for a limited time, and are often accompanied by livestreamed artists' talks. Through its *Cinematheque at Home* program, the Winnipeg Film Group also offers on-demand content for a limited time, mimicking the temporal aspect of the in-theatre experience. To the contrary, several distributors provide a continuous offer of titles available for rental but with a limited viewing window after content activation (e.g., VUCAVU, Spira, F3M). For their part, festivals have adopted different models of online presentation. Some, like Images Festival, have presented entirely livestreamed digital editions to replicate the in-person festival experience. Others, like imagineNATIVE, program a mix of on-demand and livestreamed content, which is made accessible through an online festival platform.

## Conclusion: The Policy Challenges of Online Media Circulation

The mass adoption of online circulation practices by the independent media arts community due to the COVID-19 pandemic revealed several gaps in existing policies and best-practices for online presentation. Notably, the independent media arts community has only recently adopted standards for the remuneration of artists for online presentation activities (see the IMAA Fee Schedule for 2022). Similarly, the use of various online presentation platforms and tools brings up questions about content accessibility, data security, technological compatibility, and protection of intellectual property rights (see resources developed through IMAA 2022 *Online Media Arts Presentation Standards*). While they may be accustomed to dealing with these questions for in-person presentation environments, media arts presenters have had to rethink their operations for online spaces. For example, technologies that restrict access to content based on users' Internet Protocol (IP) addresses (i.e., geo-blocking), that put digital "locks" on content through the use of digital rights management tools, and that limit the number of views through audience caping methods bring up different ethical questions. Do presenters have an obligation to geo-block political content that may be ill-perceived in certain countries, potentially leading to harm for the artist? Are presenters liable for copyright infringement if works presented on their platforms are pirated? Are the artists' best interests served if there are limitations put on content accessibility? Are distributors exposing artists to risks of censorship and copyright infringement when relying on a third-party online presentation platform? Given that digital technologies and online platforms are in constant evolution, the development of best practices for the sector is an important challenge. Much like in its burgeoning years, the independent media arts community faces an exciting time. Media arts presenters across the country have embraced the possibilities of online circulation practices and it will be interesting to witness how the legacy of early videotape exchange networks continues to develop and innovate in the digital era.

## Key Words

**Circulation or Distribution of Media**: Circulation is the process through which media finds its way from the creator to the viewer. This process encompasses distribution, which Ramon Lobato (2012) defines as "the movement of media through space and time" (2), and, in an arts context, presentation. Presentation, also referred to as exhibition, is the process through which artworks are programmed and showcased for public viewing.

**Independent Media Arts**: Time-based or interactive media works – e.g., films, videos, sound art, multi-media performances, virtual and augmented reality works. – created primarily for purposes of artistic expression and with the creator having complete artistic control (IMAA n.d.).

**Livestreamed Presentation (Synchronous Presentation Mode)**: "Livestreamed programs and events are presented at a determined date and time via a presenter's website, digital platform, or social media channels. This presentation mode is like a broadcast in the sense that once the livestream has started, viewers who tune in part way through will have missed the beginning" (IMAA 2021, Definitions and Types of Fees).

**Mail-based Videotape Exchange Networks**: Community-driven exchange networks that enabled film and video makers to share their work with peers by swapping film reels and magnetic tapes encoded with audiovisual content by mail.

**On-demand Presentation (Asynchronous Presentation Mode)**: "On-demand programs and contents are accessible at the viewer's convenience via the presenter's website, digital platform, or social media channels. On-demand programs may be freely accessible to anyone with an Internet connection" (IMAA 2021, Definitions and Types of Fees).

**Online Presentation**: "Online programs and events are presented via websites, digital platforms, or social media channels. Viewers access these programs and events remotely through a device connected to the Internet (e.g., personal computer, phone, tablet). Online presentation can be livestreamed (synchronous presentation mode) or on-demand (asynchronous presentation mode)" (IMAA 2021, Definitions and Types of Fees).

## Critical Thinking Questions

1. While they are very different from a technology standpoint, analogue and digital modes of circulation used by the independent media arts community also share many similarities. How might we conceive of today's online circulation practices as being in continuity with early mail-in videotape exchange networks?

2   Online distribution and presentation practices provide new ways to exhibit and distribute media artworks and for these works to reach expanded audiences. What are some of the opportunities and challenges associated with the circulation of media artworks online?
3   How do the circulation activities of the Canadian independent media arts community differ from those of mainstream media distribution? What is the value of alternative media production and distribution?

# References

Baert, Renée. 1987. "Video in Canada: In Search of Authority." In *From Sea to Shining Sea: Artist-Initiated Activity in Canada, 1939-1987*, edited by A.A. Bronson, 170–9. Toronto: The Power Plant.

Balsom, Erika. 2017. *After Uniqueness: A History of Film and Video Art in Circulation*. Film and Culture Series. New York: Columbia University Press.

Bociurkiw, Marusya. 2016. "Big Affect: The Ephemeral Archive of Second-Wave Feminist Video Collectives in Canada." *Camera Obscura: Feminism, Culture, and Media Studies* 31, no. 3 (93): 5–33. https://doi.org/10.1215/02705346-3661991

Bronson, A. A. 1983. "The Humiliation of the Bureaucrat: Artist-Run Centres as Museums by Artists." In *Museums by Artists*, edited by A.A. Bronson and Peggy Gale, 29–37. Toronto: Art Metropole.

Canada Media Fund. 2019. *Making Sense of the Media Distribution Multiverse: Paths to Consumers, Key Concepts and Definitions*. Montreal, QC: Canada Media Fund.

Crisp, Virginia. 2015. *Film Distribution in the Digital Age: Pirates and Professionals*. London: Palgrave Macmillan. https://doi.org/10.1057/9781137406613

Crisp, Virginia, and Gabriel Menotti, eds. 2015. *Besides the Screen: Moving Images through Distribution, Promotion and Curation*. London: Palgrave Macmillan. https://doi.org/10.1057/9781137471024

Goldberg, Michael. 2000. "Before the Generation Loss: The Early Years of Video." In *Making Video "In": The Contested Ground of Alternative Video on the West Coast*, edited by Jennifer Abbott, 33–44. Video In Studios.

Hencz, Adam. 2020. "Agents Of Change: How the Sony Portapak Has Created A New Artistic Medium." Artland Magazine. December 11, 2020. https://magazine.artland.com/agents-of-change-how-the-sony-portapak-has-created-a-new-artistic-medium/

Hilderbrand, L. 2012. "Moving Images: On Video Art Markets and Distribution." In *Resolutions 3: Global Networks of Video*, edited by Ming-Yeun S. Ma and Erika Suderburg, 1–17. Minneapolis, MN: Univ of Minnesota Press.

Independent Media Arts Alliance [IMAA]. n.d. "About Us." IMAA - AAMI. Accessed December 1, 2021. https://www.imaa.ca/about-us/

Independent Media Arts Alliance [IMAA]. 2021. IMAA Fee Schedule 2022. Accessed December 1, 2021. https://docs.google.com/document/d/e/2PACX-1vQ1mWLJeMQ-0HGTN4dNVewvUTJUIfqCWe-Vdd5Z0uj9rksN79mK1JzfXwCqn6zLEyq-uYMccPItKPBT/pub?mc_cid=d915520ce7&mc_eid=256112b276

Independent Media Arts Alliance [IMAA]. 2022. "Online Media Arts Presentation Standards." imaaamiSOURCE. Accessed May 2, 2022. https://imaa.ca/source/library/online-media-arts-presentation-standards

Lobato, Ramon. 2012. *Shadow Economies of Cinema: Mapping Informal Film Distribution*. Cultural Histories of Cinema. London: Palgrave Macmillan.

McKelvey, Fenwick, and Robert Hunt. 2019. "Discoverability: Toward a Definition of Content Discovery through Platforms." *Social Media + Society* 5, no. 1. http://doi.org/10.1177/2056305118819188

Murphy, Marsh. 2006. "Film Co-Operatives." The Canadian Encyclopedia. 2006. https://www.thecanadianencyclopedia.ca/en/article/film-co-operatives

Sterne, Jonathan, Gabriella Coleman, Christine Ross, Darin Barney, and Tamar Tembeck, eds. 2016. *The Participatory Condition in the Digital Age*. Electronic Mediations 51. Minneapolis: University of Minnesota Press. https://muse.jhu.edu/book/48363/

VIVO Media Arts Centre. 2019. "Celebration '90: Gay Games III & Cultural Festival." Celebration '90: Gay Games III & Cultural Festival. Accessed December 1, 2021. https://www.communitystories.ca/v2/celebration-1990-canadas-gay-games_gay-games-du-canada/

VIVO Media Arts Centre. n.d. "International Video Exchange Directory." VIVO Media Arts Centre Archive. Accessed December 1, 2021. http://www.vivomediaarts.com/archive/international-video-exchange-directory/

# 21 Platforms and Poetry as a Popular Form of Engagement

*Tanja Grubnic*

In 2019, *The New Republic* declared "instapoet" Rupi Kaur the "writer of the decade" (Alam 2019), an announcement signifying that contemporary literary culture is in a state of flux, as current understandings of authorship, audience, publication, and literature itself stretch across digital and analogue spaces. American journalist and author Rumaan Alam maintains that Kaur, and Indian-born Canadian poet, "understands better than most of her contemporaries how future generations will read" (2019). Specifically, her "achievement as an artist is the extent to which her work embodies, formally, the technology that defines contemporary life: smartphones and the internet" (2019). Alam's praise for Kaur, however, is undercut by derisive comments about her style of poetry: her verse is sparse, deploys the rhetoric of self-help, and is led by a confessional quality that mark her poems "easy to dismiss" (2019). Such a divisive editorial piece, which simultaneously celebrates and denigrates the poet, highlights the complexity of the reluctance, and uneasiness currently felt in contemporary Euro-Western society about the convergence of digital and print poetic forms as a result of traditional literary ecosystems colliding with **social media platforms**. Nevertheless, the resurgence of poetry as a popular form of engagement productively highlights the literary sphere's convergence with the world of social media entertainment. Though certainly not an exhaustive list, this article explains how aspects of **platformization** related to **self-branding**, participatory functions, accessibility, and transnational affordances have been significant mobilizers moving and evolving poetry into the world of popular culture. Through the innovations of social media platforms, poetry has once again become a popular form of engagement.

## Social Media Poetry

One of the most recognizable forms of social media poetry is "instapoetry," which will be the primary form under consideration in this chapter. The word "instapoetry" is a neologism that combines this social-media-born genre of poetry with the instantaneity afforded by social media platforms themselves. Throughout the 2010s, besides Kaur, a growing

DOI: 10.4324/9781003310730-25

number of poets writing in English (e.g. Najwa Zebian, Tenille Campbell [Dene/Métis], Cleo Wade, Lang Leav, Nikita Gill, R.H. Sin, and others) began sharing their poetry on platforms such as Tumblr, Twitter, and most commonly Instagram, acquiring the nickname "instapoets" after the form attracted widespread popularity among online audiences. In releasing creative productions directly to Instagram, these poets have bypassed traditional publishing routes to connect with national and international audiences. Instagram is understood by its average user as a photo- and video-based social media platform. The Meta-owned site hosts over two billion active accounts globally as of December 2021 (*Statista* 2022). Poetry on Instagram is also shaped by the formal combination of visual, textual, and paratextual affordances of the platform itself. The form is typically known for its visual nature, short, epigrammatic verse, rhetorical and technical simplicity, and attachment to self-help culture, though these qualities are not necessarily prescriptive (see Figure 21.1). Though initially written and formatted for social media, instapoetry has since captured the attention of publishers and penetrated the print book market. In practice, social media poetry should be understood in the context of the convergence of digital- and print-based poetry, as traditional and new media forms diverge and intersect.

*Figure 21.1* An example of a social media poem written by Rupi Kaur.

## A Rise in Poetry Sales

There are statistics that show the extent of the impact that Instagram-based poetry has made on popular English-language poetry sales. According to BookNet Canada, in 2018, "for the second year in a row, unit sales in the poetry category increased significantly. In 2016, poetry sales increased by 79% over 2015, and between 2016 and 2017 the units sold increased by another 154%." Similar narratives have come out of the United States and the United Kingdom. In 2018, The NPD Group reported that 47% of poetry books sold in the U.S. in 2017 were written by "instapoets." While it might seem as though the digital orientation of instapoetry alone is responsible for the sudden rise of poetry sales, it is important to heed that advances in communication technologies have impacted how literature is written, published, and read for decades. Yet such significant changes in the popularity of poetry did not occur at once with the emergence of computers, the Internet, fax machines, or other technologies.

In 2003, for an editorial piece in *Newsweek Magazine*, Bruce Wexler wrote that "it is difficult to imagine a world without movies, plays, novels and music, but a world without poems doesn't have to be imagined" (2003, 18). Just over one decade later, however, poetry has seemingly resurged everywhere in the world of popular culture in digital and analogue spaces. The staggering statistics underline that social media platforms, in particular, are changing how we create, share, and read literature—as best witnessed through the resurrection of poetry as a mainstream, best-selling literary form and a popular and accessible mode of engagement. These statistics also indicate that popular audiences of poetry are changing, too, given the influx of new readerships enjoying, consuming, and buying this poetry: "[T]hrough social media, traditional models of poetry are dismantled, notions of the traditional reader challenged, and the definition of poetry itself is up for radical reconsideration" (Jani 2017). Young poets are writing prolifically and taking up space in society—both online and offline. Yet the widespread popularity of social media poetry has sparked polarizing debates not only among literary scholars, critics, and audiences concerning literary merit and high/low culture but also in relation to racism, Euro-Western gatekeeping, and issues of social class. With social media blamed for "reinventing poetry" as "short-form communication" (Watts 2018, 14), what constitutes "real" poetry has come up for debate under the auspices of platformization.

## Platformization

If it is not the advances of communications technologies alone that have catapulted poetry back into the domain of popular culture, then what is responsible? It is important to understand that it is not one thing alone that has sparked the resurgence of some poetry as a form of popular culture, but rather a complex system of interrelated changes related to the rise of platforms and platform-based forms of cultural production. To define the present situation, the proliferation of poetry on social media points to the wider trend of what Anne Helmond calls "platformization": "the rise of the platform as the dominant infrastructural and economic model of the web" (2015, 1). Platforms are typically understood as simple technological tools or social spaces that allow people "to do things online: chatting, sharing, commenting, dating, searching, buying stuff, listening to music, watching videos, hailing a cab, and so on" (Dijck et al. 2018, 10). But platforms are highly regulated, powerful systems that control, limit, and sensor users and the flow of cultural production (Cotter and Reisdorf 2020, 748; Dijck et al. 2018, 10; Gillespie 2015, 1). They are not irrelevant to the social dynamics they support, but rather, they "hide a system whose logic and logistics are about more than facilitating: they actually shape the way we live and how society is organized" (Dijck et al. 2018, 10). In this context, aiming to understand the implications of the platformization of popular poetry shows that there are numerous changes related to the presentation of the text; its participatory nature; authorly labour, self-presentation and identity; and also concerning methods of publishing and transnational forms of literary circulation, literacy, and readerly communities.

Working with Helmond's term, David Nieborg and Thomas Poell argue that platformization affects the cultural industries, too, and "can be defined as the penetration of *economic, governmental,* and *infrastructural extensions* of digital platforms into the web and app ecosystems, fundamentally affecting the operations of the cultural industries" (2018, 4276). In *Platforms and Cultural Production*, Poell, et al. point out that "while platforms regularly generate new genres and engender diverse business models, it is also clear that they constrain the *creative* process in various ways" (2022, 7). Cultural production across sectors and genres of all sorts have been impacted: podcasting, music streaming, live streaming, and social media content creation are just some of the novel creative productions that have emerged due to platformization. While these might seem like completely new types of media, they are ultimately extensions of older, traditional media such a film, television, music, and literature. Stuart Cunningham and David Craig define this sphere of digital cultural production as "**social media entertainment (SME).**" This new, globalized screen media industry is in large part fueled by content creators who develop platform-dependent careers to connect with an audience and expand their cultural and economic reach (Cunningham and Craig 2019 5). At the same time, SME operates independently, convergently, and disruptively with older media industries – like the publishing or literary awards industries, for example. Poetry, too, has been affected by this widespread platformization: the digitally enabled rise of instapoetry as a particularly popular genre of poetry supported by Instagram points to how social media platforms are changing aspects of literary production. While this list is not exhaustive, here are some of the ways in which instapoetry represents how literature is being "platformized" and why it has contributed to the resurgence of poetry as a mainstream form of engagement.

## Self-Branding

Communications scholar Alice Marwick points out that self-branding is one of the key elements to succeeding commercially on social media: "[t]he idea of turning yourself into a brand is now presented as an essential Web 2.0 strategy, and is firmly instilled in modern business culture" (2013, 164). And through social media, the process of self-branding has become accessible to many without the help of the larger media powers. In their work on the "selfie" as a composite visual and verbal text, Toni Eagar and Stephen Dann argue, for instance, that "the self has become commodified for all through technology. Individuals who were excluded from human branding performance because of the traditional media's control of access to production can now create a mediated human-brand image" (2016, 1836). With the advances of social media, "the internet allows noncelebrities to build and display an image of themselves to a mass audience without the power ascribed by fame" (Eagar and Dann 2016, 1837). Through this conscious process of self-branding, which "requires creating a persona, producing content, and strategically appealing to online fans by being 'authentic'" (Marwick 2013, 114), instapoets are able to manufacture their own microcelebrity personas to gain the attention of fans. Coincidingly, Lili Pâquet argues that "Instagram poets can amass followers on their sites by branding themselves in certain ways, using not only poetry but also selfies" that construct a certain public persona (2019, 297). In their capacity as microcelebrities, instapoets foster intimate relationships with their readers that increase engagement by turning their lives into a brand that is congruent with the values their poetry purports to represent (see Figure 21.2). The poet's online persona becomes enmeshed with their poetry, and also functions as a way to self-publicize their writing.

## Participatory Functions

Instagram offers interactive features like commenting, tagging, direct messaging, and sharing that enable instantaneous virtual communication among users from different locations (Kumar et al. 2021; Ty 2018), turning the reading of poetry into a participatory, community-oriented activity. As literary scholars Bronwyn Williams and Amy A. Zenger write, "[d]igital technologies allow individuals to sample and remix popular culture content, write back to popular culture producers, and connect with fellow fans from around the corner and around the world" (2012, 2). As a space of participatory culture, social media poetry engages readers in a way that is more intimate and immediate than what the traditional model of publishing allows. Participatory culture is a term coined

216  Tanja Grubnic

*Figure 21.2* An example of instapoet Yyrsa Daley-Ward's Instagram feed, featuring personal photographs, book publicity, and personal reflections that create a uniform self-brand that becomes associated with the poetry itself.

by Henry Jenkins to describe most commonly online cultures where fans interact with each other as well as with creative productions and the users who made them. This new participatory matrix essentially creates digital poetry fandoms positioned around texts uploaded to Instagram. Readers can leave comments, tag others, engage directly with the author and other readers, and so forth, that foster growing fandom communities of readers and consumers. Rahma Sugihartati suggests that "people who are part of the online fandoms do not just understand the popular cultural texts they are font of and consume; they also interpret, and produce meaning and new cultural texts as a form of expression" (2020, 307). Such participatory functions allow for reading and cultural communities to flourish into popular spaces of interaction and consumption around poetry as a pleasure activity.

## *Accessibility*

The logic of the social networking site necessitates that social media poetry fits within its cultural constrains in order to be uploaded to the platform, receive visibility, and attract an audience. As a visual form, textual and literary considerations are often governed by aesthetic principles: material conditions fundamentally require that poems on Instagram are uploaded as a picture file that fits within standardized photographic dimensions, such as 1:1 among other traditional photographic aspect ratios. Such size restrictions necessitate that length be adjusted for the poem to fit on the platform's interface. The logistical basis is that instapoets have a short time to pique their readers' curiosity: instapoems compete with other images in both the user-curated and algorithmically-sorted explore feeds that feature influencers and other creators, gourmet meals, photo shoots, fashion, selfies, memes, exotic travels, and more. For this reason, James Mackay writes, social media poets are often described in derisive terms that undercut their work's emphasis on "emotional honesty and direct statement over figurative language, complex symbolism, or even metaphor: confessionalism shorn of craft" (2020, 240). While it is true that this line of poetry can be intentionally unambiguous in order to attract readers by evoking an immediate emotional response, this is in itself a particular type of aesthetic constraint suited to the medium, and not necessarily deserving of such harsh criticism. On Instagram, for example, poems are usually written in short free verse and simple language in order to simultaneously emphasize the beautiful appearance of the poem as a piece of visual media alongside its sentimental textual message, blending both the lexical and the textual. Based on this criteria, this form of poetry deviates from conventional understandings of poetry as a "high art" form containing the formal elements of structure, rhythm, meter, imagery, and so forth. As literary scholar Aarthi Vadde observes, social media poets "operate outside the professional literary circles that dictate prestige" (2017, 38). As the logic of the platform influences the poetry to be more accessible, its popularity has increased among the masses – average users who turn to social media for entertainment.

## *Transnational Dimensions*

An important aspect of social media is that it allows literary productions to travel across the platform to users in disparate locations with an ease and ubiquity that is much easier and cheaper than what the traditional model of publishing allows. Eleanor Ty points out, for instance, that social media "has enabled instantaneous sharing of information and images, and communication between people in different geographical locations" (2018, 213). A poem produced in one country can be shared and read in other countries around the world that have access to that particular platform within minutes. These transnational dimensions have allowed poems to reach audiences much more quickly, not to mention attracting audiences from many different locations. Authors interact with readers in countless geographical locations, and fandoms are made up of readers across regional, national, and even linguistic lines that support transnational networks of readers and innovative modes of literacy that collapse under the category of the nation-state. Rather, "[t]he global expansion of the Internet through networked devices is enabling emerging cultures of production that are revealing new webs and patterns of cultural affinity based on language, culture, and region" (Kumar et al. 2021, 171). The international parameters of virtual spaces, at the level of the platform, conceptualize cultural production within and between a network of many interconnected national borders – which is fundamentally changing how texts circulate in the digital sphere, undermining "notions of national identity and culture as the primary organizing category for cultural circulation" (2021, 171). The transnational dimensions of these participatory texts forge large communities of international readers in online spaces that trouble national frameworks of literature, and allow creative productions to spread and multiply across countries to create mass cultural networks of readers.

## Conclusion

As the platform model becomes more fully integrated into the digital literary sphere, it is clear that the innovations of social media have helped turn poetry into a form of popular engagement. Platform affordances have supported the revival of some poetry, like social media poetry, into a popular cultural phenomenon. What constitutes "real" poetry is up for debate, however, as the rising popularity of poetry has re-ignited beliefs that poetry is an elite form of literature – a category to which social media poetsshould not belong, some critics argue, for their craft is too commercial, too popular, to be aligned with traditional poetry. Arguably, social media poets are one of the most diverse groups of poets. Future research that intersects with gender and sexuality studies, race studies, or globalization studies, for example, should be discussed to analyze how these digital spaces challenge or exacerbate systemic inequalities that mirror the realities of social life beyond the digital platform. Just as other industries have been affected by platformization – news, fashion, and music industries, for example – poetry, too, is being affected and must be examined through a critical, platform-centric framework.

## Key Words

**Social Media Platforms**: Social media platforms are apps and programs that enable social and public interaction, and the sharing of ideas, information, and creative productions. As platforms, they function as digital structures that support applications, businesses, and a wide range of corresponding ecosystems.

**Self-Branding**: The act of marketing oneself as a brand is self-branding, usually involving the development of a distinct public persona that communicates their lifestyle, values, and authentic personality traits.

**Platformization**: Platformization is the influence of platforms in reshaping and re-directing various aspects of virtually all cultural industries not only in form, content, or appearance, but in the realm of distribution, production, and reception, too (Helmond 2015; Poell et al. 2022).

**Social Media Entertainment (SME)**: a new globalized screen media industry comprising a digital ecology of content creators, platforms, interactive cultural productions, engaged audiences, and more. (Cunningham and Craig 2019). SME often intersects with older, more established industries, like the publishing industry and other literary ecosystems (Holm 2022).

## Critical Thinking Questions

1 What other aspects of social media do you think are responsible for re-igniting a mass cultural interest in poetry as a form of popular engagement?
2 What are some of the negative repercussions of the platformization of poetry? While this article raised some of the basic points of platformization, what do we make of labour practices, algorithms, censorship, and so forth?
3 This chapter has mainly focused on the digital aspect of social media poetry. How do we grapple with the digital and analogue dichotomies of social media poetry than goes on to become a print publishing phenomenon?

## References

Alam, Rumaan. 2019. "Rupi Kaur Is the Writer of the Decade." *The New Republic*, 2019. https://newrepublic.com/article/155930/rupi-kaur-writer-decade

BookNet Canada. 2018. "Poetry Sales Increase Again in 2017." BookNet Canada. 2018. https://www.booknetcanada.ca/press-room/2018/3/7/poetry-sales-increase-again-in-2017

Cotter, Kelly, and Bianca C. Reisdorf. 2020. "Algorithmic Knowledge Gaps: A New Dimension of Inequality." *International Journal of Communication* 14: 745–65. https://ocul-uwo.primo.exlibrisgroup.com/discovery/fulldisplay?context=PC&vid=01OCUL_UWO:UWO_DEFAULT&search_scope=MyInst_and_CI&tab=Everything&docid=cdi_gale_lrcgauss_A632409950

Daley-Ward, Yrsa [@yrsadaleyward]. Yrsa Daley-Ward's Instagram feed. Instagram, 4 May 2022, www.instagram.com/yrsadaleyward.

Dijck, Jose van, Thomas Poell, and Martijn De Waal. 2018. *The Platform Society. Public Values in a Connective World.* Kettering: Oxford University Press. https://ocul-uwo.primo.exlibrisgroup.com/permalink/01OCUL_UWO/1brq4iv/cdi_oup_oso_oso_9780190889760

Eagar, Toni, and Stephen Dann. 2016. "Classifying the Narrated #Selfie: Genre Typing Human-Branding Activity." *European Journal of Marketing* 50, no. 9/10: 1835–57. https://doi.org/10.1108/ejm-07-2015-0509

Gillespie, Tarleton. 2015. "Platforms Intervene." *Social Media + Society* 1, no. 1: 1, 2. https://doi.org/10.1177/2056305115580479

Helmond, Anne. 2015. "The Platformization of the Web: Making Web Data Platform Ready." *Social Media + Society* 1, no. 2: 205630511560308. https://doi.org/10.1177/2056305115603080

Jani, Radhika. 2017. "Your Guide to 'Instapoet' Rupi Kaur." *Dazed*, October 3, 2017. https://www.dazeddigital.com/life-culture/article/37599/1/rupi-kaur-the-instapoet-revolutionising-prose

Kaur, Ripi [@rupikaur_]. "the self: a lifelong relationship of learning to love ♥ page 167 from home body." Instagram, 9 Sep. 2021, https://www.instagram.com/p/CTnkYMeM-1c/?utm_source=ig_web_copy_link.

Kumar, Sangeet, Sriram Mohan, and Aswin Punathambekar. 2021. "Beyond the Nation: Cultural Regions in South Asia's Online Video Communities." In *Creator Culture*, edited by Stuart Cunningham and David Craig, 170–88. New York: New York University Press.

Mackay, James. 2020. "You Are Enough: Love Poems for the End of the World by Smokii Sumac (Review)." *Studies in American Indian Literatures* 32, no. 1: 239–42. https://muse.jhu.edu/article/764481

Marwick, Alice E. 2013. *Status Update: Celebrity, Publicity, and Branding in the Social Media Age*. New Haven, CT: Yale University Press.

Nieborg, David B., and Thomas Poell. 2018. "The Platformization of Cultural Production: Theorizing the Contingent Cultural Commodity." *New Media & Society* 20, no. 11: 4275–92. https://doi.org/10.1177/1461444818769694

Pâquet, Lili. 2019. "Selfie-Help: The Multimodal Appeal of Instagram Poetry." *Journal of Popular Culture* 52, no. 2: 296–314. https://doi.org/10.1111/jpcu.12780

Poell, Thomas, David B Nieborg, and Brooke Erin Duffy. 2022. *Platforms and Cultural Production*. Cambridge: Polity Press.

Statista Research Department. 2022. "Number of Monthly Active Instagram Users from January 2013 to December 2021." Statista. 2022. https://www.statista.com/statistics/253577/number-of-monthly-active-instagram-users/

Sugihartati, Rahma. 2020. "Youth Fans of Global Popular Culture: Between Prosumer and Free Digital Labourer." *Journal of Consumer Culture* 20, no. 3: 305–23. https://doi.org/10.1177/1469540517736522

Ty, Eleanor. 2018. "Teaching Literatures in the Age of Digital Media." *Canadian Review of Comparative Literature/Revue Canadienne de Littérature Comparée* 45, no. 2: 213–21. https://doi.org/10.1353/crc.2018.0020

Vadde, Aarthi. 2017. "Amateur Creativity: Contemporary Literature and the Digital Publishing Scene." *New Literary History* 48, no. 1: 27–51. https://doi.org/10.1353/nlh.2017.0001

Watts, Rebecca. 2018. "The Cult of the Noble Amateur." *PN Review* 44, no. 2: 13–7.

Wexler, Bruce. 2003. "Poetry Is Dead. Does Anybody Really Care?" *Newsweek*, 2003. https://ocul-uwo.primo.exlibrisgroup.com/permalink/01OCUL_UWO/t54l2v/cdi_proquest_miscellaneous_214274920

Williams, Bronwyn, and Amy A. Zenger. 2012. *New Media Literacies and Participatory Popular Culture across Borders*. New York: Routledge.

# 22 Lil Nas X, TikTok, and the Evolution of Music Engagement on Social Networking Sites

*Melissa Avdeeff*

The emergence of Lil Nas X in the public eye, and the record-breaking success of "Old Town Road" (2019), established a new understanding of musical outputs as both "music" and "content" in a way that distinctly reflects the current media landscape and the prevalence of memes and viral content. TikTok dance challenges secured the song's initial success, following a series of meme attempts on various other social networking site platforms (Figure 22.1). The array of remixes following the song's presence on the Billboard charts further capitalised on meme culture, keeping "Old Town Road" as number one on the US charts for 19 weeks in 2019. The connections between social media platforms, music, and audiovisual content were made quite transparent over Lil Nas X's rise to fame, but there is a longer history leading up to this moment, which this chapter explores.

The advent of TikTok marks the next stage in the evolving relationship between music, social networking sites (SNS), and participatory fan practices. From MySpace to TikTok, music has been central to SNS, embedded into a variety of mediating practices, from demonstrating one's music preferences, to self-promotion, to dance challenges, and the creation of archives.

This chapter explores the shift in participatory media practices and music fandom that has occurred with the rise of TikTok, and how music, sociability, and creativity have converged on the platform. After a brief overview of the evolution of music on SNS, this chapter outlines a distinct type of playful fandom that has developed on TikTok, where users have become **cultural intermediaries**, translating and embodying the musical content of others, encouraging remix and virality, and subsequently impacting the traditional music charts as the popularity is extended "offline." Lil Nas X and "Old Town Road" are used as a case study to demonstrate this process, as one of the first artists to capitalise on this pathway to success.

## TikTok: An Overview

TikTok originated as the Chinese app Douyin by ByteDance in 2016 and was launched as TikTok outside of China in 2017. The international launch corresponded with ByteDance purchasing the lip-synching platform Musically, an app where users could create short-form videos from 15 seconds

222  *Melissa Avdeeff*

*Figure 22.1* Lil Nas X overlaying "Old Town Road" onto a video of a dancing cowboy, posted to Twitter on 3 December 2018, as part of the song's unofficial first release.

to one minute utilising licensed music, often incorporating dance and gesture challenges (Anderson 2020). The use of sounds and music has been retained in the evolution of TikTok; music plays a central role in the platform where a large proportion of videos are based on lip synching, dance challenges, creative audiovisual editing, gestures, and/or the creation of general meme-worthy content. Videos were originally capped at 15 seconds, but as of 2022 videos can be up to three minutes in length. As of September 2021, there are approximately 1 billion monthly active users (Iqbal 2022).

TikTok also incorporates many elements from Vine, which was founded in 2012 and discontinued in 2016. In Vine, humour, play, and creative editing within a 15 second timeframe challenged users to create viral content within what was a new form of temporal restriction. The short-form videos were easily sharable off the platform, particularly to Twitter, and sparked a new scrolling culture, or method of engagement, that has become amplified with TikTok, and has been observed to maximise watch time (Kendall 2021).

As of November 2022, 41.7% of TikTok users are between the ages of 18 and 24, with the next largest category being those 25 to 34, at 31% of users. TikTok is also dominated by female users, at 54.2% (Ceci 2022). The demographic profile is interesting as it reflects wider trends of gendered labour on social networking platforms, particularly the often "invisible" labour associated with women's work that has become extended onto digital platforms like Instagram, Pinterest, and others, where success is often discredited because of the perceived lack of labour involved (Warren-Crow 2016). TikTok is also geographically oriented, with users most often being shown videos created within their country or locale of use, and tied to place-based copyright restrictions in regard to the licensing of commercially released songs for use on the app. Trends are therefore often geographically dependent.

Unlike previous platforms that tend to rely on a high degree of followers to enable viral success, TikTok popularity is much more of a black-box phenomenon, where algorithms curate highly personalised feeds, as seen on each user's "For You" page. Through user movements on (and off) the app, the TikTok algorithm quickly determines user interests, identities, and ideologies and responds by positioning users into quite specific ambient affiliations, a term coined by Michele Zappavigna to describe temporary groups that come together around topics of interest (2011).

## SNS and Music: A Brief History

It is generally accepted that we have seen a marked shift in both the production and consumption of popular music since the advent of YouTube in 2006, and the subsequent rise of the YouTube influencer model, as popularised by Justin Bieber (Avdeeff 2019). In Bieber's case, his curated illusion of authentic fan interaction and bedroom music production masked major music industry involvement until the successful shift "offline" into the traditional market systems. As this model for success developed, and evolved on other platforms, success became increasingly tied to novelty, virality, and **memetic** creation across platforms and streaming services.

YouTube, in addition, has a history of dance challenges – largely emerging either from the original music video, or by choreographies that go viral. For example, Kirsten Pullen has discussed recreations of Beyonce's "Single Ladies" video on YouTube as a production of counterpublics (2011), not unlike many productive fan practices whereby counterstorytelling is used to insert new perspectives and narratives into a media text (Kirkpatrick 2019; Thomas 2019). YouTube dance challenges really moved into the mainstream in 2018, however, with a series of highly visible challenges: Fortnite, Baby Shark, the kiki challenge, and #DoTheShiggy. Each of these moved into mainstream media, as a form of "legitimization" by demographics less involved in YouTube youth cultures (Marshall 2019).

Following the YouTube model of success, another key moment of this evolution was the SoundCloud Rap movement in the early to mid-2010s, which was marked by a focus on shareability, the production of content for the purpose of cross-platform virality, "lower" production techniques, and music that is often reduced to a singular "idea" instead of the historical verse-chorus-verse format (Rindner 2021). These short, digestible tracks are not bound by industry release schedules, "professional" production/mixing, and largely exist outside the traditional music industry gatekeepers. In many ways, it is a culmination of the bedroom producer era, and the virality of content on social media. SoundCloud rap is music that is meant to be shared, and, as such, needs to fit into those temporal conventions, thereby removing now-extraneous materials like a verse. The hook is central, it is viral, and it is engaging. And, from an economic point of view, when it enters commodity systems like Spotify, shorter pieces are actually more beneficial to artists when they are paid on a per-stream basis.

While the Spotify model of nontraditional release schedules and importance of singles within a streaming economy (Kaimann et al. 2021) is still ongoing, TikTok challenges it, combining influencer-style commodification with **cultural intermediaries**. To explain further, music/sound promotion is often outsourced to influencers through the app; fans may function as intermediaries between the artist (with or without record label support), and other users who are either a fan of the influencer, original artist, or both. The promotion of music in this process ultimately depends less on the aesthetics of the track, but on its ability to go viral; on its usability in a dance or meme challenge. What constitutes that usability, however, can be quite random, in the same way that Top-40 music consumers, and the popular music industries at large, either highly engage with, or reject, novelty. Lil Nas X's "Old Town Road," for example, partially thrived on the novelty of his new approach to the cross-genre aesthetics of hip-hop and country music.

High view counts on TikTok are often related to participation in challenges. This is not to say that viral challenges are unique to TikTok, but they have ensured the success and ongoing involvement people have with the app. This is reflective of wider popular music practices, where music has long been associated with particular social dance styles, especially since the advent of TV (Harlig 2014). The relationship between popular music and dance/movement is no less integral to the consumption of popular music than the relationship between popular music and technology in its production and circulation (Frith 1986; Jones 1992).

## Ludic Fandom in a (Post)Digital Landscape

In our contemporary (post)digital landscape (Cramer 2014), platforms, particular for youth audiences, have become backgrounded, largely invisible in the consumption of music. It almost seems inaccurate to use terms like "music fandom" or "music consumption" in our current context, as most creative outputs have come to be known under the broader category of *content*. The content that users engage with on the TikTok platform would not function without music, but it is largely distinct from traditional fan-artist relationships. Younger artists have, indeed, capitalized on this; for example, Lil Nas X's "Old Town Road," which will be further discussed, was originally released without a music video, and gained popularity on TikTok through cultural intermediaries promoting the song in viral challenges.

These consumption and engagement practices on TikTok are examples of the **ludic self** that is afforded by many social media platforms. Ludic is defined by play and playfulness, and the ludic interactions on TikTok, based in this idea of play, demonstrate what Jonathan Follett (2007) refers to as "interactive silliness." Ana Deumert also describes the idea of the ludic self and finds that in digital communication, what matters is "amusement, laughter, and creative enjoyment" (2014, 27); processes that are at the heart of TikTok.

While ludic theory emerged from game theory, there are parallels to how ludic fandom is enacted within applications like TikTok. As a platform, it affords a degree of everyday creativity whereby users are encouraged to continually post, update, and engage in creative practice. As generally recognized, this has become normalized across most social media platforms. But where this ludic fandom may differ from game theory, or perhaps extends that discussion, is how it also functions to negotiate the neoliberal landscape and underlying assumptions of competition. Johan Huizinga, in his concept of Homo Ludens, notes that although play is integral to all society, it is difficult to define, but can generally be understood as a voluntary act. Play is not focused on dominating others, but to achieve the recognition of others. For Huizinga: "winning means showing oneself superior in the outcome of a game" (1944, 50). For TikTok, superiority, or excellence, is mediated through likes, shares, and virality.

Similarly, Paul Booth has explored the idea of ludic fandom, defining it as "the deliberate focus on play and games within fans' creative works" (Booth 2017, 268). In his research on *Storium*, he situates this playfulness in the wider digital environments whereby fans are "given control over particular aspects of their media, but are constrained by digital corporate factors" (Booth 2017, 269). Parallels can be made to TikTok influencers, or intermediaries. The control over one's brand is illusory, the aesthetics prescribed not only by corporate measures, but also by overt competition.

There are interesting connections to be made between TikTok, play, and wider social pressures. It could be argued that a focus on everyday creativity, and play, in our current society could be a reaction to the rise of precarity and crisis. As we progress further into late-stage capitalism, it is no surprise that many find joy and community within creative acts, and playful fandom practices tied to music. But that play is also bound to those underlying elements of competition inherent in capitalism and neoliberal society: the search for the most likes, the most views, to start the next viral challenge, and to make it "big," to capitalize on the advertising revenue of making it as an influencer. The "challenge" memes make this competition transparent, but it is underlying and inherent within all aspects of the app.

## Lil Nas X and Music Industry Success via TikTok

As a brief example of how these practices unfold on TikTok, the remainder of this chapter discusses Lil Nas X's rise to success both within and outside of TikTok with "Old Town Road," (see Figure 22.2) widely considered to be the first commercially successful track to be produced with the intention of being a platform meme (Jackson 2019). The track first gained success on TikTok prior to dominating the industry charts (Alexander 2019; Arditi 2020).

No stranger to social media cultures, Lil Nas X built his Internet presence as a tweetdecker, or meme-creator/promoter/clickbaiter, and originally uploaded "Old Town Road" to TikTok in a cross-platform promotional attempt. He originally posted the track laid over a variety of meme videos to Reddit, in order to gain traction, with limited success. It was TikTok user nicemichael's use of the song, whereby he can be seen dancing with a quick-change effect into Western wear (Figure 22.3). Subsequent videos using this challenge are then tagged as the #YeeHaw challenge and #YeeYee juice, pushing the track into both viral and traditional systems of industry success (Cevallos 2019). This challenge became an emblem for the wider "Yee Haw Agenda," a term coined by Bri Malandro to describe the resurgence and history of cowboy aesthetics in American Black popular culture, paying tribute to the history of the Black cowboys

*Figure 22.2* Still from the official "Old Town Road" (2019) music video, showing Lil Nas X drinking "Yee Yee Juice."

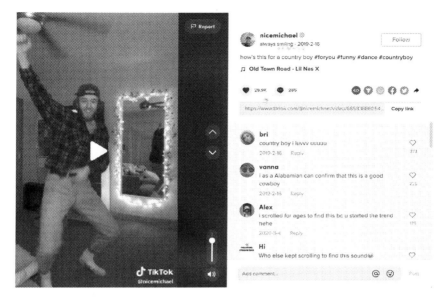

*Figure 22.3* Still from nicemichael's TikTok video using "Old Town Road" (2019), serving as the catalyst for the #YeeHaw challenge.

in the states, an often-overlooked part of late nineteenth-century American cattle rancher history (Reese 2019).

The "Old Town Road" #YeeHaw challenge, and subsequent #YeeYee juice variants, formed an imitation public around both the original track, and the related challenges. As such, TikTok users, such as nicemichael, became intermediaries between Lil Nas X and the wider TikTok publics, creating a multi-layered field of ludic fandom and/or playful engagement. Success on the TikTok platform translated into 19 weeks in the top position on the Billboard Hot 100 chart, as the platform intermediaries shifted to the backstage and the mainstream visibility of Lil Nas X, as celebrity figure, emerged.

While this rise in celebrity and industry success marked a new industry pathway, it should also be noted that success on TikTok does not always guarantee such a trajectory. Interestingly, the role of TikTok user intermediaries, and the focus on memetic challenges, has often resulted in the resurgence of older songs onto the Top-40 charts, like the 2020 resurgence of Fleetwood Mac's "Dreams" following a video by Nathan Apocado, and countless remakes, both on and off TikTok (Richards 2020). But that success is most often ephemeral and tied to the popularity of each challenge. Or, highly used songs will circulate through TikTok intermediaries, often evolving into variant challenges using covers, remixes, or mashups of the original sound/song, with no attribution to the original author. In these instances, while playful fandom may exist around the song, it remains within the space of the intermediaries, and the challenges themselves, and may not necessarily translate into cross-platform success. TikTok users often find pleasure in uncovering that they've "found the original sound," to assign authorship for the original artist, but also gain social and viral capital for themselves.

## Conclusion

Over the past decade we've experienced the evolution of music platformization through the SoundCloud rap model, the Instagram marketing model and Spotify distribution models, bringing us to the current TikTok model of not only music production, but also fandom, audience, and distribution. Ultimately, TikTok's popularity as an app and platform is tantamount to the society in which it is produced – it makes public the typically private or semi-primate moments of youth "silliness" and creativity, and supplants them into a postdigital landscape marked by precarity, ludicity, and neoliberal competition. In many ways these content producers can be considered a part of music fandom, but in many ways, they are also training grounds towards entering into the highly commoditized influencer market. Artists like Lil Nas X are able to capitalize on this, commoditizing the intermediaries for free advertising. "Old Town Road," particularly, is a testament to the DIY Internet culture, and has brought about important conversations and debates about the ongoing racialization of genres and mainstream industry charting conventions to the general public. Through this track, Lil Nas X forged a new pathway to music industry success, building on the influencer and YouTube models that came before, and combining them with new notions of virality informed by the affordances of the platform.

## Key Words

**Cultural Intermediaries**: The term cultural intermediaries has become quite contextual, and has often become used to describe "any creative of cultural occupation of institution" (Maguire and Matthews 2012, 552). As Jennifer Smith Maguire and Julian Matthews note, cultural intermediaries construct value through their engagement with goods/texts, and impact perceptions of legitimacy and worth.

**Ludic Self**: Scholars, such as Ana Deumert (2014) and Jonathan Follett (2007), note that the interactive elements of the Internet, and SNS in particular, encourage a type of playful engagement that could be referred to as our ludic self. This form of self-construction allows for people to relate to themselves and each other in a playful manner, through the process of mediation (Deumert 2014).

**Memetic**: Based on the concept of memes, or the spread of phenomena through the copying of behaviour/ideas, memetic refers to the process of such spread. In the context of this chapter, memetic is referring to the copying of behaviours/ideas/content as they exist on social media platforms.

## Critical Thinking Questions

1  The "playfulness" of Lil Nas X's "Old Town Road" extends further than the ways in which people used the song for challenges on TikTok. How might the playful nature of the song and music video engage with deeper themes of racialization in traditional genre and chart distinctions in the music industries?
2  How do TikTok intermediaries help fuel the success of songs and other audio content? If you have created your own TikTok videos based on pre-existing sounds/music, what were your motivations?

## References

Alexander, Julia. 2019. "'Old Town Road' Proves TikTok Can Launch a Hit Song." *The Verge*. April 5, 2019. https://www.theverge.com/2019/4/5/18296815/lil-nas-x-old-town-road-tiktok-artists-spotify-soundcloud-streams-revenue

Anderson, Katie Elson. 2020. "Getting Acquainted with Social Networks and Apps: It is Time to Talk about TikTok." *Library HI Tech News* 37, no. 4: 7–12.

Arditi, David. 2020. *iTake-Over: The Recording Industry in the Streaming Era*, 2nd ed. London: Lexington Books.

Avdeeff, Melissa. 2019. "Canadian Pop in the Digital Age: Pioneering Pathways to Stardom and Representation via Justin Bieber." In *The Spaces and Place of Canadian Popular Culture*, edited by Victoria Kannen and Neil Shyminsky, 273–82. Toronto: Canadian Scholars Press.

Booth, Paul. 2017. "Playing by the Rules: Storium, *Star Wars*, and Ludic Fandom." *Journal of Fandom Studies* 5, no. 3: 267–84.

Ceci, L. 2022. "Distribution of TikTok Users Worldwide as of April 2022, By Age and Gender." *Statista*. November 14, 2022. https://statista.com/statistics/1299771/tiktok-global-user-age-distribution/

Cevallos, Charles. 2019. "Media Review: Lil Nas X and Billy Ray Cyrus, *Old Town Road (Official Movie)*." *Journal of the Society for American Music* 13, no. 3: 396–400.

Cramer, Florian. 2014. "What is 'Post-Digital'?" *APRJA* 3, no. 1: 11–24.

Deumert, Ana. 2014. "The Performance of a Ludic Self on Social Network(ing) Sites." In *The Language of Social Media: Identity and Community on the Internet*, edited by Phillip Seargeant and Caroline Tagg, 23–45. London: Palgrave Macmillan.

Follett, Johnathan. 2007. "Engaging User Creativity: The Playful Experience." *UX Matters*. December 17, 2007. https://www.uxmatters.com/mt/archives/2007/12/engaging-user-creativity-the-playful-experience.php

Frith, Simon. 1986. "Art versus Technology: The Strange Case of Popular Music." *Media, Culture & Society* 8: 263–79.

Harlig, Alexandra. 2014. "Communities of Practice: Active and Affective Viewing of Early Social Dance on the Popular Screen." In *The Oxford Handbook of Dance and the Popular Screen*, edited by Melissa Blanco Borelli, 57–67. Oxford: Oxford Handbooks.

Huizinga, Johan. 1944. *Homo Ludens: A Study of the Play Element in Culture*. London: Routledge.

Iqbal, Mansoor. 2022. "Tiktok Revenue and Usage Statistics (2022)." *Business of Apps*. January 19, 2022. https://www.businessofapps.com/data/tik-tok-statistics/

Jackson, Dan. 2019. "How Lil Nas X's Controversial Country-Rap Hit 'Old Town Road' Conquered the Internet." *Thrillist*. July 30, 2019. https://www.thrillist.com/entertainment/nation/old-town-road-lil-nas-x-memes-explained

Jones, Steve. 1992. *Rock Formation: Music, Technology, and Mass Communication*. London: Sage.

Kaimann, Daniel, Ilka Tanneberg, and Joe Cox. 2021. "'I Will Survive': Online Streaming and the Chart Survival of Music Tracks." *Managerial and Decision Economics* 42, no. 1: 3–20.

Kendall, Tina. 2021. "From Bing-Watching to Bing-Scrolling: TikTok and the Rhythms of #LockdownLife." *Film Quarterly* 75, no. 1: 44–6.

Kirkpatrick, Ellen. 2019. "On [Dis]play: Outlier Resistance and the Matter of Racebending Superhero Cosplay." *Transformative Works and Cultures* 29. https://doi.org/10.3983/twc.2019.1483

Maguire, Jennifer Smith, and Julian Matthews. 2012. "Are We All Cultural Intermediaries Now? An Introduction to Cultural Intermediaries in Context." *European Journal of Cultural Studies* 15, no. 5: 551–62.

Marshall, Wayne. 2019. "Social Dance in the Age if (Anti-)Social Media: *Fortnite*, Online Video, and the Jook at a Virtual Crossroads." *Journal of Popular Music Studies* 31, no. 4: 3–15.

Pullen, Kristen. 2011. "If Ya Liked It, Then You Shoulda Made a Video Beyoncé Knowles, YouTube and the Public Sphere of Images." *Performance Research* 16, no. 2: 145–53.

Reese, Ashley. 2019. "What Everyone Is Getting Wrong About the 'Yee Haw Agenda,' According to Bri Malandro, the Woman Who Coined the Term." *Jezebel*. March 27, 2019. https://jezebel.com/what-everyone-is-getting-wrong-about-the-yee-haw-agenda-1833558033

Richards, Will. 2020. "Stevie Nicks Says Viral Fleetwood Mac TikTok Video has 'Blown My Mind.'" *NME*. October 26, 2020. https://www.nme.com/news/music/stevie-nicks-says-viral-fleetwood-mac-tiktok-video-has-blown-my-mind-2798913

Rindner, Grant. 2021. "Comfort in the Discomforting: The History of SoundCloud Rap, the Face-Tatted, Hair-Dyed Vision that Showed Hip-Hop's Future." *The Ringer*. December 16, 2021. https://www.theringer.com/2021/12/16/22838951/juice-wrld-soundcloud-rap-history-retrospective

Thomas, Ebony Elizabeth, and Amy Stornaiuolo. 2019. "Race, Storying, and Restorying: What Can We Learn from Black Fans?" *Transformative Works and Cultures* 29. https://doi.org/10.3983/twc.2019.1562

Warren-Crow, Heather. 2016. "Screaming Like A Girl: Viral Video and the Work of Reaction." *Feminist Media Studies* 16, no. 6: 1113–7.

Zappavigna, Michele. 2011. "Ambient Affiliation: A Linguistic Perspective on Twitter." *New Media & Society* 13, no. 5: 788–806.

# 23 "No Friends in the Industry"
## The Dominance of Tech Companies on Digital Music

*Kristopher R. K. Ohlendorf*

When was the last time you listened to music and how did you access that music? Most likely, you used a website or app to stream it. Accessing music wasn't always so easy.

It started in the 1990s with **record companies**, but began growing massively due to the success of compact discs (CDs), a form of physical media that stored music, like vinyl, cassette tapes or 8 tracks. At the time, CDs would cost $15–20 each and typically held an album worth of music. Even if you just wanted one song, you usually still had to buy the full album.[1] This was great for business and profits soared for the music industry. At the same time, access to digital technology grew and nearly half of all households in the US and Canada had both computers and Internet access by the year 2000 (Statistics Canada 2005). Computer users started copying CDs onto their computers as individual **.mp3** song files, an increasingly popular format for digital music. At the time, the music industry had little interest in exploring .mp3s and digital technology as a form of distribution. CDs were more successful than ever. People outside of the music industry, however, saw the potential. Over the next two decades, the way digital music was shared, sold, and accessed online changed with a series of different tech companies taking control.

Figure 23.1 shows recorded music revenue in the US by format from 1990 to 2021. Here, we can see the rise of CDs in the 1990s, which was later overtaken by digital downloads, and now music streaming.

This chapter explores three key companies – Napster, Apple, and Spotify – who at one point in time, each had a prevailing influence on the distribution and access of digital music from the 1990s to today. The evolution of these companies shows how the music industry went from being resistant to digital music distribution to now reliant on it as the leading format for music revenue. This chapter also includes a profile of Canadian artist Drake, the most streamed artist on Spotify[2], and discusses how music streaming changes the way he creates his music. It concludes by considering who now holds control of the music industry and what that could mean for the future of popular music.

DOI: 10.4324/9781003310730-27

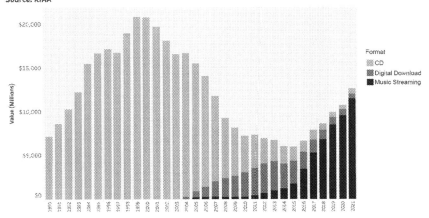

*Figure 23.1* US Recorded Music Revenues by Format, 1990–2021 Source: RIAA.

## *Thank Me Later*: The Napster Revolution

In 1999, 19-year-old "hacker" Shawn Fanning created Napster and opened the doors for mainstream **digital piracy**. Napster ran on **peer-to-peer file sharing** technology, which allowed anyone connected to Napster's network to make their computer's .mp3 files available to other users on the network to download.

Users could type a song title in Napster's search bar, receive a flock of results of other users' files of that song, and then click on one to download. Napster became the perfect way for fans to obtain music for free outside of traditional retail formats. Napster, as a company, had no clear business model. Even so, it was deemed the fastest growing company in history at the time (Menn 2003, 2). Napster never turned a profit and was kept afloat by millions of dollars in venture capital investments, which is used to finance companies with the hope they will eventually succeed. Napster's main drive was to get as many users as possible and reached 70–80 million at its peak. Napster hoped to work with the music industry to turn these users into paying customers by offering subscriptions or pay-per-download sales – methods that future companies would find successful (Knopper 2017, 140). The industry, however, had no interest in working with a company they felt encouraged piracy, nor did they have any interest in turning focus away from CDs as the main form of music distribution.

Industry heads and major label artists like Metallica and Eminem criticized Napster for freely sharing work they felt deserved compensation.

*The Dominance of Tech Companies* 233

Other artists and fans, however, saw Napster as a revolutionary tool. Napster's supporters thought money from music sales rarely made it to artists anyway due to exploitative record contracts, so cutting into the pockets of major corporations was seen as a radical act to bring power back to artists and music fans. As an example, independent British rock group Radiohead intentionally leaked their album *Kid A* on Napster ahead of retail release to generate exposure. When it was officially released, it became their first No. 1 album. Lead singer Thom Yorke stated, "[Napster] encourages enthusiasm for music in a way that the music industry has long forgotten to do...anybody sticking two fingers up at...the whole f***ing thing is wonderful as far as I'm concerned" (Farley 2000).

Napster was particularly popular on college campuses where young music fans shared this radical mindset and had access to Internet speeds faster than at home. Downloads from Napster overloaded campus Internet networks, impairing education and research, causing schools to ban the service (Knopper 2017, 133). Industry representatives kept tabs on downloading offenders and would later sue college students for millions of dollars in damages (208). Napster ushered digital music into the 21st century. The service created new possibilities for distributing music without the barrier of physical media, but their methods were deemed illegal. The music industry sued Napster for aiding copyright infringement and shut it down in 2001. This had a lasting impact on its users who became used to the idea of having access to any music they wanted, and piracy continued with services built on Napster's technology like Kazza and Limewire. It was now up to the music industry to figure out how they could get these fans back on their side as paying customers.

## *So Far Gone*: Apple's Music Stranglehold

After Napster was shut down, the music industry continued to fight piracy with no successful solutions, and CD sales declined (as seen in Figure 23.1). Steve Jobs, the founder and CEO of Apple Inc., took advantage of this desperation and pitched the iTunes Store as a digital music marketplace to all the major labels. Customers could use it to purchase individual songs for $.99 cents each, with $.67 cents of each sale going to the labels and the rest to Apple (Knopper 2017, 193). All major labels signed on to license their music and the iTunes Store launched in 2003 with a library of 200,000 songs (Chen 2010). Important to the iTunes Store's success was Apple's portable digital music player, the iPod, which released in 2001. Users could organize their music as playlists in iTunes, import the music files onto their iPods, and listen to their personalized music on-the-go. The iTunes Store grew over the next few years to become the central marketplace for music sales, surpassing physical retailers. The music industry was initially satisfied with a working solution for digital music distribution. Apple was even more pleased, due to the sales numbers of their iPods. Song files purchased on iTunes were encoded to only work on iPods, so, if someone purchased music on iTunes and wanted to listen to them on-the-go, they had to buy an iPod.

Selling iPods turned out to be a much more lucrative business than distributing music, and Apple's profits soared while the music industry continued to fall (as seen in Figure 23.1). The labels felt cheated by Apple. They could have taken their music off iTunes in protest, but since Apple now led the marketplace, that would have omitted a major customer base. Like with Napster, the music industry was influenced by the control of a tech company, except this time, not only was it legal, but they signed up for it.

## *Nothing Was the Same*: Spotify and Streaming Supremacy

Swedish entrepreneur and young millionaire Daniel Ek launched the **music streaming** service, Spotify, in 2008. Spotify improved upon peer-to-peer technology, combined with increased Internet speeds, to create a searchable database that allowed users to find music and listen to it instantly. This shifted music fans away from downloading music files and toward accessing a service that provides a library of music. Spotify operates on a freemium model, which allows users to either listen to music for free with ads or pay a monthly subscription to remove ads and access more features. Spotify's revenue comes from advertising and subscription payments, although the company has only managed to turn a profit for 6 months of its 15-year lifespan (YCharts 2021). In contrast, the value Spotify holds on the market is in the billions of dollars.

Major tech companies like Google and Apple started their own streaming services after Spotify's success. Streaming now makes up over 80% of the US music industry's revenue (Friedlander 2021) with Spotify leading the market (Mulligan 2022). Key to Spotify's success is its accumulation of user data, which the company uses to generate automated playlists and recommendations to fit the user's feelings throughout the day. This has caused another change in listening habits away from genre-based listening and toward mood-based listening and music classification (Eriksson et al. 2019, 5).

Spotify had initial difficulty convincing record companies in the US to license their music on the platform. The industry was still feeling bruised by Apple's bait-and-switch and was hesitant to embrace a new tech company that was promising music for free. Spotify was able to strike a deal. Rather than only paying the record companies royalties and fees for licensing their music, Spotify would also give them partial ownership of the company. This meant if Spotify continued to grow and succeed on the market, so would value held by major music labels. This led to the music industry's first period of revenue growth (RIAA) and a decline in music piracy (RouteNote 2020) since the arrival of Napster.

How money gets to the artists whose work is streamed on Spotify is confusing and tied to opaque deals with record companies. There is no clear pay-per-stream system. Payment unpredictably fluctuates on several factors like how many subscribers Spotify has at any given time and how many total streams are spread across the platform. Money that Spotify pays to record companies passes through their own hierarchies and individual contractual deals before getting to the artists, which is usually negligible. Many artists criticize Spotify because executives at tech and record companies are who reap in the success of streaming, not the artists whose work fills the platform. An analysis from *The New York Times* found that of the seven million artists on Spotify, only around 13,000 generated $50,000 or more in payments during 2020 (Ovide 2021). Conversely, top shareholders at Spotify hold values in the billions (Johnston 2021). This dynamic sets a strong distinction of who benefits most from music streaming.

## *Certified Lover Boy*: Drake, the World's Most Streamed Artist on Spotify

Toronto native Drake holds over 40 billion streams on Spotify[3]. The next artist on this list, Ed Sheeran, lags by over 10 billion (ChartMasters 2022a). How did Drake reach such numbers? It is argued that Drake "engineered his own popularity" by gaming the streaming system (Andrews 2019). Crucial to Drake's streaming success is his immense music output of at least one major release per year since 2015, which has changed over time to suit streaming platforms. One way he has done this is through long track lists, which ensures more song streams per album listen than those with shorter track lists. Drake's album with the most tracks, *Scorpion* (25 tracks), holds the record for most streams for an album debut in its first week on Spotify[4] (Chartmasters 2022a). Drake's songs have also gotten shorter over time. Figure 23.2 shows how the average track length on Drake's solo releases gradually shortened since the start of his career. Streaming numbers don't consider a track's length (i.e., listening to a 2-minute song and listening to a 10-minute song each count as 1 stream), so the shorter the song, the more opportunity to generate streams at a faster rate.

Drake is not the only artist trending toward shorter songs in the streaming era. Fellow hip-hop artists Kendrick Lamar, Kanye West, Nicki Minaj, and J Cole, as well as country artists Eric Church and Jason Aldean, have also had followed this trend (Kopf 2019). The number of songs under 2 minutes and 30 seconds on the Billboard Hot 100 noticeably increased during the 2010–2019 decade (Kopf 2019). This change coincides with the rise of streaming platforms as a primary method of music distribution.

Also important to Drake's streaming success is how the style of his music has come to suit the streaming listening experience. Listening to

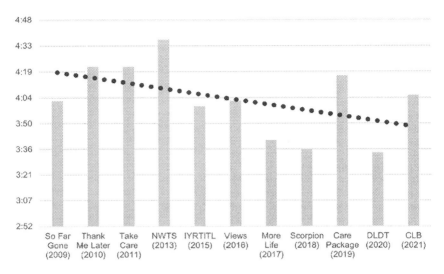

*Figure 23.2* Average Track Length on Drake's Solo Album Releases.

music via streaming is continuous and benefits from passive engagement, where users simply press play on a playlist or album and let the music stream endlessly. Drake's recent music has been described by critics as increasingly familiar (Strauss 2021) and said to "replicate softness in abundance" (Richards 2017). The replication and familiarity of Drake's music leads to a hassle-free streaming experience without interruption. The brief discussion here of Drake's success begs the following question: Is streaming not only influencing music distribution, but also the music itself?

## Conclusion

This chapter followed three key tech companies that succeeded one another for digital music distribution dominance. Napster unleashed digital piracy, Apple used music to sell their devices, and Spotify now has become intertwined with record companies as a joint effort to accrue value. The profile on Drake revealed how artists have adapted to create music that suits streaming platforms. What's next?

Something Napster and Spotify have in common is the reliance on venture capital investments. Napster had no clear business model, but Spotify has one with ad revenue and subscription payments. Even so, Spotify struggles to make a profit (Ingham 2019). They must placate to the needs of their investors – not the needs of artists and listeners – to stay afloat. If this investment were to disappear, would Spotify suffer a tumultuous fate, and pull the music industry down with it? One cursory tale is of MySpace, an early social network from the 2000s that was a popular tool for independent artists to host and share their music. In 2019, the company revealed they lost all uploaded music from before 2015 in a botched server migration. Over 52 million songs uploaded by more than 14 million artists disappeared in an instant (Kreps 2019). Fans were able to recover around 490,000 songs (Internet Archive 2019), but any of the remaining songs that weren't stored elsewhere are simply gone forever. A gap of recorded music history is lost.

The influence of digital music distribution cannot be undermined in how much it allows artists to share their music and reach listeners across the globe. Data shows that more people are listening to music now than at any point in history (McIntyre 2017). This is an interesting finding, but it leads to broader questions on who artists and fans now rely on for distributing and accessing music, and who benefits from it. It is the companies who provide this access, and their pursuit of value, that controls the foreseeable future of popular music.

## Key Words

**.mp3**: .mp3 is a file format for compressed audio files. This compression happens through removing data in the audio that is mostly unnoticeable to human ears. The smaller size of .mp3s makes it an ideal format for storing and sharing music files.

**Digital Piracy**: Digital piracy is the act of illegally obtaining downloading copyrighted files online. Media industries have fought against digital piracy since it arose in the late 1990s.

**Peer-to-Peer File Sharing**: Peer-to-peer file sharing is a technology for sharing files online. Users connected to a peer-to-peer network can make their hard drive's files available to other users on the network, and vice versa, creating a massive file sharing database. These files are catalogued and accessed through peer-to-peer software like Napster to easily search and download files.

**Record Companies**: Record companies are organizations that sign artists to contractual deals to fund the recording, promoting, touring, and selling the artist's music. Record deals are notoriously unfavourable toward artists, with the company often taking a significant amount of any money generated by the artist's work. There are a handful of record companies that control over half of the music industry in North America – Universal, Sony, and Warner.

**Music Streaming**: Music streaming is a method of near-instantaneous music listening on high-speed Internet networks. Streaming has removed the need for digital downloads and users instead pay for access to companies like Spotify, Apple, and Google to stream their vast libraries of music.

## Critical Discussion Questions

1. If you were a student in 1999, would you use Napster? Why or why not?
2. What might a successor to Spotify and music streaming look like?
3. What does the influence of tech companies on cultural works mean for artists and creators?

## Notes

1. CD Singles did exist, but they were not promoted or released as often as CD albums in the US and Canada due to lower profit margins. Even at their peak in 1997, CD Singles only accounted for 2.7% of all CD sales revenue for that year (RIAA 2022).
2. As of April 2022 (ChartMasters 2022a).
3. As of April 2022 (Chartmasters 2022a).
4. As of April 2022 (ChartMasters 2022b).

## References

Andrews, Travis. 2019. "Drake Was Spotify's Most-Streamed Artist of the Decade. What Does That Mean?" *The Washington Post*. WP Company. Accessed August 1, 2022. https://www.washingtonpost.com/arts-entertainment/2019/12/03/drake-was-spotifys-most-streamed-artist-decade-what-does-that-actually-mean/

Chartmasters. 2022a. "Most Streamed Artists on Spotify (Live Database)." *Chartmasters*. Accessed April 29, 2022. https://chartmasters.org/most-streamed-artists-ever-on-spotify/

Chartmasters. 2022b. "Spotify's Top All Time Album Debuts (Live Database)." *Chartmasters*. Accessed April 29, 2022. https://chartmasters.org/2021/09/spotifys-all-time-top-album-debuts/

Chen, Brian X. 2010. "April 28, 2003: Apple Opens iTunes Store." *Wired*. Accessed August 1, 2022. https://www.wired.com/2010/04/0428itunes-music-store-opens/

Eriksson, Maria, Rasmus Fleischer, Anna Johansson, Pelle Snickars, and Patrick Vonderau. 2019. *Spotify Teardown: Inside the Black Box of Streaming Music*. Cambridge, MA: The MIT Press.

Farley, Christopher. 2000. "Radioactive." *TIME Europe*. Accessed August 1, 2022. https://web.archive.org/web/20110311074531/http:/www.time.com/time/europe/magazine/2000/1023/radiohead.html

Friedlander, Joshua. 2021. "Mid-Year 2021 RIAA Revenue Statistics Report." *RIAA*, October. https://www.riaa.com/wp-content/uploads/2021/09/Mid-Year-2021-RIAA-Music-Revenue-Report.pdf

Ingham, Tim. 2019. "Spotify is Profitable. How Did That Happen?" *Rolling Stone*. November 12. Accessed August 1, 2022. https://www.rollingstone.com/music/music-features/spotify-profitable-how-happen-910456/

Internet Archive. 2019. "The Myspace Dragon Hoard (2008-2010)." *Internet Archive*. Accessed August 1, 2022. https://archive.org/details/myspace_dragon_hoard_2010

Johnston, Matthew. 2021. "Top Spotify Shareholders." *Investopedia*. Accessed August 1, 2022. https://www.investopedia.com/news/top-3-spotify-shareholders/

Kreps, Daniel. 2019. "Myspace Lost All Music Uploaded to Site Prior to 2015." *Rolling Stone*. Accessed August 1, 2022. https://www.rollingstone.com/music/music-news/myspace-lost-music-809455/

Knopper, Steve. 2017. *Appetite for Self-Destruction: The Spectacular Crash of the Record Industry in the Digital Age*. Steve Knopper.

Kopf, Dan. 2019. "The Economics of Streaming is Making Songs Shorter." *Quarts*. January 17. https://qz.com/1519823/is-spotify-making-songs-shorter/

McIntyre, Hugh. 2017. "Americans Are Spending More Time Listening to Music Than Ever Before." *Forbes*. Accessed August 1, 2022. https://www.forbes.com/sites/hughmcintyre/2017/11/09/americans-are-spending-more-time-listening-to-music-than-ever-before/?sh=126af8592f7f

Mulligan, Mark. 2022. "Global Music Subscriber Market Shares Q2 2021." *Midia Research*. Accessed January 18, 2022. https://www.midiaresearch.com/blog/music-subscriber-market-shares-q2-2021

Menn, Joseph. 2003. *All the Rave: The Rise and Fall of Shawn Fanning's Napster*. New York: Crown Business.

Ovide, Shira. 2021. "Streaming Saved Music. Artists Hate It." *The New York Times*. Accessed August 1, 2022. https://www.nytimes.com/2021/03/22/technology/streaming-music-economics.html

RIAA. 2022. "U.S. Sales Database" *RIAA*. Accessed April 29, 2022. https://www.riaa.com/u-s-sales-database/

Richards, Chris. 2017. "Soft, Smooth and Steady: How Xanax Turned American Music into Pill-Pop." *The Washington Post*. Accessed August 1, 2022. https://www.washingtonpost.com/lifestyle/style/soft-smooth-and-steady-how-xanax-turned-american-music-into-pill-pop/2017/04/19/535a44de-1955-11e7-bcc2-7d1a0973e7b2_story.html?itid=lk_inline_manual_9

RouteNote, Jacca. 2020. "Music Piracy Continues to Die After Services Like Spotify Saved An Industry From Illegal Download Doom." *RouteNote*. Accessed June 29, 2022. https://routenote.com/blog/music-piracy-continues-to-die-after-services-like-spotify-saved-an-industry-from-illegal-download-doom/

Strauss, Matthew. 2021. "Review – Drake – *Certified Lover Boy*." *Pitchfork*. Accessed August 1, 2022. https://pitchfork.com/reviews/albums/drake-certified-lover-boy/

Statistics Canada. 2005. "Household Penetration of Various ICTs, Canada, 1990 to 2003." *Statistics Canada*. Accessed December 5, 2021. https://www150.statcan.gc.ca/n1/pub/56f0004m/2005012/c-g/c1-eng.htm.

YCharts. 2021. "Spotify Technology Net Income (Live Database)." Accessed December 1, 2021. https://ycharts.com/companies/SPOT/net_income_ttm

# 24 Say Their Name

## How Online News Reports the Death of Transgender People and Its Intersection with Transnormativity

*Rachel Patterson*

There have been at least 600 **transgender** people who have been murdered across the world since October 2018, with 2021 being the deadliest year yet (TMM Update Trans Day of Remembrance 2021). However, there is no accurate data source showing the exact number of transgender deaths (Stotzer 2017). The misrepresentation of transgender people in the media may be a contributing factor as to why the exact number is unknown. While efforts have been made from the Associated Press to include guidelines for how to appropriately report transgender people, the public still sees the use of birth names and incorrect pronouns in the media when a transgender person is mentioned (Bates 2017). According to GLAAD. org (2022), pronouns that match a person's gender identity are important because they "serve as an extension of one's name and a person's identity. This means that the correct use and recognition of one's pronouns are linked directly to recognition of their core identity" (Schwartz 2019).

Transgender people already face stigma in society because of their transgender identity. Stigma in relation to transgender individuals can be defined as "a social process of blaming and shaming that leads to status loss and discrimination" (Poteat et al. 2013, 22). We cannot ignore that stigma and discrimination by society can be an attribute to increasing rates of transgender violence and death. The news media plays a role in how society views transgender people by either choosing to identify and present them as their current gender identity or by continuing to link them to their assigned gender (Billard 2016).

The purpose of this research is to explore how online news stories have or have not followed Associated Press guidelines when it comes to assigning gender to transgender individuals' violent deaths. This research shows that there are various connections between **transnormativity**, misogynoir, unwitting bias, and agenda setting, and that they all contribute for or against the reasoning of why a transgender person may be misrepresented in the news. This is significant for those entering the media themselves as professionals. It is important to know how these people's deaths are being reported, why they are being reported in this way, and how to potentially know how to handle reporting better in the future.

DOI: 10.4324/9781003310730-28

## Terminology

The term **transgender** is previously described by GLAAD as a "term for people whose gender identity differs from the sex they were assigned at birth" (GLAAD 2022). The term "cisgender" means a person's gender identity "aligns with" and is associated with the sex they were assigned at birth. The terms 'transsexual' or 'transvestite' are no longer an appropriate way to describe transgender individuals (Bates 2017). Transphobia is when someone has an irrational fear of, an aversion to, or displays discrimination against transgender people.

**Passing** is an important term to use when speaking of transgender people. This concept means that society treats the transgender person as the gender they identify with rather than their assigned gender at birth. This may be because of medical and non-medical forms of transitioning to their current gender identity, such as displaying an external manifestation of gender. Gender expression can be seen as "clothing, haircut, behavior, voice, and/or body characteristics" (GLAAD.org 2022).

Society identifies these cues as masculine and feminine, although what is considered masculine or feminine changes over time and varies by culture (GLAAD.org 2022). Most transgender people have a desire to pass in their desired social gender, and that in social situations, "their appearance is taken to be proof of their biological sex" (Schilt and Westbrook 2009, 446). Transgender people typically, but not always, do a combination of things to help "align their gender expression with their gender identity, rather than the sex they were assigned at birth" (GLAAD.org 2022). When a transgender person chooses to go by a name different than their birth name, whether they legally change it or not, the process of being called or referred to by the name they were given at birth is called **deadnaming** (HRC Foundation 2022a).

## Established Guidelines for Reporting Transgender People

GLAAD has a media reference guide listed on its website for how LGBTQ+[1] people should be discussed in the news (GLAAD.org 2022). The media reference guide has guidelines for two large news outlets, the New York Times and Reuters, based on the 2013 and 2015 Associated Press guidelines. The Associated Press Stylebook is a guideline that journalists are required to follow and in 2017, the stylebook included updated information about reporting on transgender people (Bates 2017).

Earlier editions of the Stylebook may have mentioned how to address transgender individuals, but in 2017, the associated press included new guidelines stating that "news sources must use a person's preferred name that they went by in public" instead of their birth name "even if they have not legally changed it" (Shepherd 2017, para. 2). Guidelines explain the difference between gender and sex, specifically stating that "gender is the person's social identity" (Bates 2017, para. 5). Therefore, even if a transgender person's name has not been legally changed and/or if their family does not use their preferred name, journalists are instructed to use a transgender individual's preferred name.

The Human Rights Campaign (HRC) serves as a resource to educate anyone, including journalists, about the issues surrounding the 2SLGBTQIA+ community. Their page, "HRC's Brief Guide to Getting Transgender Coverage Right" begins by discussing what it means to be transgender. It acknowledged that "writing about transgender people, including those making the very personal decision to transition, can be challenging for reporters unfamiliar with the LGBTQ community, and, in particular, the transgender community" (HRC Foundation 2022b). HRC explicitly stated that journalists should not get caught up on the gender a person was assigned at birth, but instead "focus on the whole and current person." HRC explained that using current names and pronouns are "crucial for a transgender person to feel wholly themselves, comfortable, and respected" and explained issues transgender individuals can face when trying to change legal identification to match their preferred name and gender (2022).

Journalists and other online writers usually face difficult workloads and an expectation to report news quickly after learning about an incident. Journalists may not have time or feel like it is necessary to do additional fact checking besides information that is given to them by the police (Lang 2017, para. 9). This information, usually including the individual's legal name and assigned gender at birth, may be incorrect because not all transgender people have changed their name or gender on government identification (Lang 2017). HRC further explains that misgendering individuals is an indication of "anti-transgender bias and discrimination too often seen from law enforcement, the media" and that "accurate reporting is imperative" to know and address the violence against transgender people. HRC explains that crimes against them often "go uninvestigated, unreported, or misreported" (HRC Foundation 2022). Misgendering transgender people is considered a type of double victimization, meaning that they are disrespected and insulted both in life and in death when they are misrepresented by the news media (GLAAD.org n.d.).

My research aims to explore if and how the concepts of "passing" and unwitting bias have in the representation of transgender individuals and what effects they may have on journalists' decision to follow Associated Press guidelines.

## How do Online News Organizations Follow Procedures and Policies around Naming and Using Pronouns and/or Identifiers for Transgender Individuals?

In order to observe how online news outlets reported instances of transgender death, I gathered and examined news stories from both small and large news agencies in the United States using something called content analysis. Content analysis is a research tool that allows researchers to identify patterns, reach conclusions, and assign meaning (Krippendorff 2004). Online news was chosen instead of searching for print or recordings of broadcast news, because that is how most people in the United States and Canada consume news (Shearer 2021).

In order to find the most relevant news stories, I conducted a Google search of each of the 15 individuals and used purposive sampling to decide which news stories about each individual that would be analyzed. To minimize potential bias, articles were chosen strictly based on dates of news articles that I determined were published at the beginning, middle, and end of the news cycle. Purposive sampling means that I selected the five articles on each person out of a larger pool of articles based on the subjective belief that they would be the most useful during analysis.

## Misrepresentation by Name and Identifiers

Most of the news articles identified the victims by using both their birth name (also known as a **deadname**) and their preferred name. In the case of Sean Hake, news station WKBN in Youngstown, Ohio, identified Hake by saying: "an officer-involved shooting resulted in the death of 23-year-old Sean Marie Hake" (Wilaj 2017). An article written on Hake by the Associated Press continued to use his birth name in quotation marks despite having published guidelines that year stating that preferred names must be used at all times instead of birth names. In some cases, the correct name was used in the headline or beginning of the story to identify a victim, but used their birth name later on. Most of the articles still used deadnames or identifiers that did not match the victim's gender identity even though they included information about why using information that confirms their gender identity was important.

Along with including the incorrect name, incorrect identifiers/pronouns were also used. Identifiers mean pronouns such as she/her and he/his, using words such as "brother," "daughter," and other words to indicate they are viewed as male or female. Some articles used correct names but incorrect pronouns. In the case of Muhlaysia Booker, CBS Dallas/Fort Worth used incorrect pronouns by saying "his desire to live his life as a transgender woman" (CBS DFW 2019). CNN repeatedly used incorrect identifiers after the death of Jordan Cofer by saying "she" and "her," and that "the family mourns the loss of their daughter" (Drash, Levenson, and Watts 2019). Both CNN articles continually labeled him as cisgender woman, and this was not later corrected even after his transgender identity was brought up by other news outlets at the end of his news coverage cycle (see "His Name is Jordan Cofer. Not Megan Betts" n.d.).

## Police Misrepresentation and Involvement

Several articles included information that was released to them by the police following the victim's death. In many instances where an article used incorrect identifiers, the articles were written based off of police statements which identified the victims based off of their ID. In the case of Sean Hake, news outlets repeatedly used his deadname and incorrect identifiers because local police refused to use his correct name and gender, which were on his ID, despite being legally recognized as a man. The Patriot-News quoted a friend of the victim who said "they reported he was a female. His name was Sean Ryan Hake. His license said male. The State of Pennsylvania recognized he was a man."

Washington Blade reported that Baltimore police recognized the harm that misgendering can cause the transgender community. Baltimore police told the Washington Blade the department has an LGBT Advisory Committee dedicated to "identifying victims correctly" by reaching out to local advocacy groups. In an article written by local outlet WBAL11, Interim Police Commissioner Kevin Davis was quoted saying "We need to do more and we need to do better to form the necessary partnership with the LGBT community."

## Structuring Reality and Unwitting Bias

The news outlets and journalists writing these stories may have internal bias that influenced which photos they chose to display in news coverage of transgender individuals (Johnson 2016). Furthermore, this can structure the reality of how transgender people are viewed (Mundy 2013, 69) and possibly even searched online. Despite the frequency that a transgender person displays physical traits or characteristics to align with their gender identity, the world still has a lot of bias around transgender individuals of all ages, races, or nationalities. News media has a part in structuring reality and determining how viewers see the issues and people in the news, as well as influencing the emotions and behavior of an audience. It can be argued that while some of the news articles included information about why misgendering is harmful and issues that the transgender community faces, their continued misgendering and misrepresentation still pushes a narrative that transgender people have a link or connection to the gender they were assigned as birth. This can make it even more difficult for people to view and respect transgender individuals as the gender they identify with. It can also heighten mental health issues such as depression and anxiety for transgender individuals when they see others like themselves being misrepresented and linked back to their assigned gender at birth in the news (Yang et al. 2015).

## Conclusion

It is absolutely crucial that journalists fact check multiple sources surrounding the death of a person who may be transgender. Oftentimes the family of a transgender individual is either not aware of the victim's transition or does not agree with it and therefore do not use the correct name and pronouns of the individual. Also, many states and/or provinces have various laws about changing legal name and gender on a driver's license or other form of ID, which is the most common way that police and emergency staff identify victims. Furthermore, there is difficulty surrounding changing these identifiers for government ID. Many transgender people face financial barriers to legally changing their name, financial barriers to medical transition, and it is important to note that there are transgender individuals who simply do not want gender reassignment surgery (HRC Foundation 2022). Going by a government ID for information, or police report that uses this information, on a person's gender is not an accurate way to fact check. Transgender individuals face the threat of violent death due to their gender identity, and journalists should consistently use guidelines for transgender people as outlined by the Associated Press in addition to doing extensive fact checking with a person's friends, family, and local advocacy groups to ensure that correct information about a person's gender identity is published.

## Key Words

**Deadname**: A deadname that a transgender person was given at birth that they no longer go by or refer to themselves as.

**Passing**: When society treats a transgender person as how they identify rather than their assigned gender at birth, it is referred to as passing. Passing is often connected to medical transitioning, body modification, or other non-medical ways of displaying traditionally masculine or feminine traits.

**Transgender**: Transgender is a term for people whose gender identity differs from the sex they were assigned at birth.

**Transnormativity**: Transnormativity describes the specific framework to which transgender people's presentations and experiences of gender are held accountable, such as grooming, clothes, voice, and mannerisms.

## Critical Thinking Questions

1 If you worked in the media, how would you "fact check" to make sure that a person's name and identifiers are correct, whether or not you suspect that person is transgender?

2  Do you think the guidelines for writing about transgender people should be updated or more detailed? Why or why not?
3  Do you think you may have any assumptions or biases about transgender people? How could you challenge them to be more inclusive and to be more understanding?

## Note

1 In this edited collection, we have chosen to use the acronym 2SLGBTQIA+, but for the purposes of the discussion of GLAAD's work, this chapter will use their acronym of LGBTQ+.

## References

Bates, Don. 2017. "AP's 2017 Stylebook Includes New Rules for Citing Gender." *Public Relations Society of America*. Accessed August 1, 2022. https://prsay.prsa.org/2017/05/23/aps-2017-stylebook-includes-new-rules-for-citing-gender/

Billard, Thomas J. 2016. "Writing in the Margins: Mainstream News Media Representations of Transgenderism." *International Journal of Communication* 10: 4193–218. https://doi.org/10.1080/21565503.2018.1532302

CBS DFW. 2019. "'That Was My Sister', Transgender Murder Victim Muhlaysia Booker Laid to Rest." Dallas Fort Worth. *CBS DFW*, May 29, 2019. https://dfw.cbslocal.com/2019/05/28/that-was-my-sister-transgender-murder-victim-laid-to-rest/

Drash, Wayne, Eric Levenson, and Amanda Watts. 2019. "The Gunman's Sister Was One of the 9 Shooting Victims in Dayton." *CNN*, August 6, 2019. https://www.cnn.com/2019/08/04/us/dayton-shooting-victims/index.html

GLAAD.ORG. n.d. "Doubly Victimized: Reporting on Transgender Victims of Crime." *GLAAD*. Accessed August 1, 2022. https://www.glaad.org/publications/transgendervictimsofcrime

GLAAD.ORG. 2022. "GLAAD Media Reference Guide – 11th Edition." *GLAAD*. Accessed August 1, 2022. https://www.glaad.org/reference/style

"His Name Is Jordan Cofer. Not Megan Betts." n.d. *Daily Kos*. Accessed August 9, 2022. https://www.dailykos.com/stories/2019/8/8/1877792/-His-Name-is-Jordan-Cofer-Not-Megan-Betts

HRC Foundation. 2022a. "Glossary of Terms." *Human Rights Campaign*. Accessed November 29, 2021. https://www.hrc.org/resources/glossary-of-terms

HRC Foundation. 2022b. "HRC's Brief Guide to Getting Transgender Coverage Right." Human Rights Campaign. Accessed January 2, 2022. https://www.hrc.org/resources/reporting-about-transgender-people-read-this

Johnson, Austin H. 2016. "Transnormativity: A New Concept and Its Validation through Documentary Film about Transgender Men." *Sociological Inquiry* 86, no. 4: 465–91.

Krippendorff, Klaus. 2004. "Measuring the Reliability of Qualitative Text Analysis Data." *Quality and Quantity* 38, no. 6: 787–800.

Lang, Nico. 2017. "A 'disgusting slap in the face': Reporters Must Stop Misgendering Trans Murder Victims. *Colombia Journalism Review*. Retrieved August 1, 2022. https://www.cjr.org/criticism/transgender-murders-news-journalism.php

Mundy, Dean E. 2013. "One Agenda, Multiple Platforms: How 21st-Century LGBT Advocacy Organizations Navigate a Shifting Media Landscape to Communicate Messages of Equality." In *Coming Out of the Closet: Exploring LGBT Issues in Strategic Communication with Theory and Research*, edited by Natalie T. J. Tindall and Richard D. Waters, 65–9. New York: Peter Lang.

Poteat, Tonia, Danielle German, and Deanna Kerrigan. 2013. "Managing Uncertainty: A Grounded Theory of Stigma in Transgender Health Care Encounters." *Social Science & Medicine* 84: 22–9. https://doi.org/10.1016/j.socscimed.2013.02.019

Schilt, Kristen, and Laurel Westbrook. 2009. "Doing Gender, Doing Heteronormativity: 'Gender Normals,' Transgender People, and the Social Maintenance of Heterosexuality." *Gender & Society* 23, no. 4: 440–64. https://doi.org/10.1177/0891243209340034

Schwartz, Athena. 2019. "6 GLAAD Campus Ambassadors Share Why Pronouns are Important to Them." *GLAAD*. Accessed November 23, 2021. https://www.glaad.org/amp/6-glaad-campus-ambassadors-share-why-pronouns-are-important-them

Scutti, Susan. 2019. "The Dayton Shooter's Family Requests Privacy as They Mourn the Loss of 2 Children and 'Process the Horror'." *CNN*, August 7, 2019. https://www.cnn.com/2019/08/07/us/betts-family-statement/index.html

Shearer, Elisa. 2021. "More Than Eight-in-Ten Americans Get News from Digital Devices." *Pew Research Center*. Accessed November 23, 2021. https://www.pewresearch.org/fact-tank/2021/01/12/more-than-eight-in-ten-americans-get-news-from-digital-devices/

Shepherd, Ken. 2017. "AP Stylebook on Transgender Coverage: Don't Say Trans Person was 'Born a Girl or Boy'." *The Washington Times*, October 10, 2017. https://www.washingtontimes.com/news/2017/oct/10/ap-stylebook-transgender-coverage-dont-say-trans-p/

Stotzer, Rebecca L. 2017. "Data Sources Hinder Our Understanding of Transgender Murders." *American Journal of Public Health* 107, no. 9: 1362, 1363. https://doi.org/10.2105/AJPH.2017.303973

Wilaj, Stephen. 2017. "23 Year Old Killed in Officer-Involved Shooting in Sharon." *WKBN.com*, January 7, 2017. https://www.wkbn.com/news/23-year-old-killed-in-officer-involved-shooting-in-sharon/

Yang, Mei-Fen, David Manning, Jacob J. van den Berg, and Don Operario. 2015. "Stigmatization and Mental Health in a Diverse Sample of Transgender Women." *LGBT Health* 2, no. 4: 306–12. https://doi.org/10.1089/lgbt.2014.0106

# 25 The 'Affinityscapes' of Young Adult Dystopian Fiction

## A Study of *The Hunger Games* Series' Participatory Culture

*Zahra Rizvi*

In 2012, *The Hunger Games* series made headlines for outselling all the *Harry Potter* books (Doll 2012). By 2014, the trilogy had sold more than 65 million copies in the US, only one of the 56 territories that it was sold in (Hall 2014. This trend is more than just a mutation from one series to another if studies focus on the contemporary popularity of **dystopian** novels—a twenty-first-century revival which came about with a merging of young adult fiction, sci-fi and fantasy genres. Bookstores increasingly made space for a new 'Young Adult Dystopian' section featuring bestsellers like *The Hunger Games* trilogy (2008–2010; 2020) by Suzanne Collins, *The Maze Runner* series (2009–2011; 2016; 2020) by James Dashner, and *Divergent* series (2011–2013; 2014; 2018) by Veronica Roth. Mark Fisher attempts to explain the change in trend,

> *The Hunger Games* was published in 2008, at the very moment that the financial crisis was pitching the world into panic and confusion. The label "Young Adult Dystopian" tells us much more than which demographic *The Hunger Games* is aimed at. The film and the novel have no doubt resonated so powerfully with its young audience because it has engaged feelings of betrayal and resentment rising in a generation asked to accept that its quality of life will be worse than that of its parents.
>
> (Fisher 2012, 27)

Growing out of the fantasy genre boom that was spearheaded by novels like the *Harry Potter* series (1997–2007) by J. K. Rowling and the *Twilight* series (2005–2008) by Stephanie Meyers, the Young Adult Dystopia genre is now a vibrant force revising these genres by projecting 'near-future dystopias' into the imagination of its readers, to emerge as an independent genre with its specific concerns, in itself. The degree of "reducing the distance" between our present world and the dystopian world to be portrayed is a conscious move on the writers' part to generate a politically charged picture, one which "once more make(s) strange what has become too conventional; the dystopian features of the present and the horrors of the future" (Murphy 1990, 25).

DOI: 10.4324/9781003310730-29

## The 'Affinityscapes' of Young Adult Dystopian Fiction 249

Suzanne Collins constructs *The Hunger Games* in Panem, a country that has risen out of the destruction of a futuristic Civil War that destroyed North America. The population is brutally segregated into compartments: the Capitol, surrounded by 13 districts. Each of these districts have particular functions in the production process with resources carefully and geographically partitioned in such a way that while raw materials are present in the districts, their survival is utterly at the mercy of the Capitol. To discourage the Districts from rebelling, the Capitol hosts a survival reality TV show where two children from each district compete with each other in a dangerous arena to fight until death. The protagonist, Katniss Everdeen, is one such participant (or 'tribute' in the parlance of the series).

One of the most popular discourses about *The Hunger Games* series is its depiction of violence and whether it is appropriate for children of a specific age.[1] This debate became one of the major arguments surrounding what it means to be a 'young adult', what can be the ages which can successfully cordon off the 'young adult' category and what is the nature of this audience that would emerge from such a categorization. Behind this debate, lies the tradition of articulating the 'Child', a tradition that is upheld by the 'adult who knows better'. Lee Edelman presents his thoughts on this signification in his book *No Future: Queer Theory and the Death Drive*, a signification which bonds the signifier of the Child and the signified of the future and, on the other hand, according to him, figures queerness as "the place of the social order's death drive" (2004, 3). Young adult dystopias and their near-future representations populated by 'killer children' puts the 'Child' on a new plane that departs significantly from such a signification process while criticizing this very process for its reproduction of dystopian values. Riley McGuire, extrapolating on Edelman's works, comments on this phenomenon as, "children represent more than a nebulous conception of forward-reaching temporality; instead, they are the embodiment of *a* specific future..." and talks about how dystopian heroines like Katniss disrupt this futurism of the Child by being both queer[2] and embodying death in the series (McGuire 2015, 65).

The series is also visually, especially if one takes into account the movie adaptations that came up, about violence. More specifically, the series depicts state violence, public executions, prisoner torture, hospital bombings, biowarfare, and more. In the context of the Games, it must be noted, this violence is also carried out and inflicted by children upon each other as they are controlled by adults for a compulsory futurism.

## What Does It Mean to Be a Young Adult Reading Dystopian Fiction like *The Hunger Games*?

The three-finger salute, a gesture from *The Hunger Games* that signifies rebellion and solidarity, became popular in the 2014 Thailand protests against the militarist coup and following government. The call for democracy in Thailand drove young protestors to show the salute as a silent act of rebellion and subsequently became banned in public in the country, with the saluting protestors getting arrested. "Five students in T-shirts bearing the slogan "We don't want the coup" flashed the sign during a speech by Prime Minister Prayuth Chan-ocha, who led the coup and later became head of the military government" and news of the protests spread online, especially through the various channels of *The Hunger Games* fandom (Mydans 2014). The salute, a sign appropriated from the dystopian world of a piece of young adult fiction became a popular symbol in the youth protests and gave the youth a way to articulate their position vis-à-vis the political climate and amplify their condition to the rest of the world. One of the detained students, Natchacha Kongudom, told reporters, "The three-finger sign is a sign to show that I am calling for my basic right to live my life" (Mydans 2014). The influence of the series was noted on both sides with *The Hunger Games: Mockingjay, Part 1* movie getting cancelled in theatres in both Thailand and China, in what many believed to be a crackdown on the "overtly political narrative" of the fiction (Tharoor 2014).

Young adult dystopias continue to resurface in stories of protests all over the world. Emma Gonzalez, the co-founder of the #NeverAgain movement, protesting against the gun laws after the Parkland massacre, has been compared to Katniss and other heroines from YA Dystopian fiction, sparking off heated discussions articulating youth movements and protests both online and offline.

Online, social media provides a rich space for young adult dystopias and their readers to present arguments using symbols and signs from fiction which is reworked and localized, depending on the specificities of usage and participation. Twitter is just one of the spaces where *The Hunger Games*'s readers, though it is better to use the term 'fanbase' or even 'fandom' from now on, seeing the cross-platform media manifestations of the series, are finding new ways to articulate themselves. Fans are playing and creating role-playing, virtual reality or augmented reality games, writing *THG*-inspired stories or 'fanfictions', creating fanart, creating videos and short films, composing music and formulating online communities. In short, they are creating **'affinityscapes'**, a mediatized worldview born through articulation, made of linkages between spaces and spatial formations based on affinity, that is, "physical, virtual or blended spaces where people interact around a common interest or activity" (Gee qtd. in Curwood 2013, 417). While sci-fi has a long **subculture** of conventions, role-play, clubs and zines, YA dystopian fiction fanbase seeks to articulate itself, an articulation which is a re-reading of the Child, towards a formulation of the youth which uses texts detailing the horrors of the future to define itself against the horrors of the present. "We found that, particularly with younger ages, preteens and young teens were using the language of *The Hunger Games*—everything from protecting the family to having to enter an arena—to describe their experiences in everyday life," says Allison Novak, in a 2013 study by Rachel M. Magee et al. at Drexel University, "#TwitterPlay: A Case Study of Fan Roleplaying Online." Working on other teen-fandom-heavy movies like *The Dark Knight* too, Novak continued to find that, "Sometimes their uses seem kind of silly, or they're just being dramatic, which fits in with what we already know about teenagers, but at the same time, it's doing something healthy: It's giving them a vocabulary to articulate things that are stressful" (Magee et al. 2013). In online affinityscapes, role-playing becomes a crucial method of articulating the inarticulate and the unarticulate. Experiences of teens struggling in a world which is facing not only economic inequality and political corruption but also the very real consequences of climate change, find voice in role-playing characters online. One such project is #MyHungerGames started by *The Harry Potter Alliance* which encouraged people to voice their real-life problems using *The Hunger Games* as a metaphor while seeking to "bridge the gap between the Hunger Games: Mockingjay, Part 1 marketing and the series' resonance with human stories" (*CBCBooks.org* 2014). Here are some of the stories that people told online, via Twitter and Tumblr.

> Small biz owner dad couldn't afford health care. Dad died at 49 w/problems that could have been helped by regular dr visits #MyHungerGames.
>
> November 17, 2014

> #MyHungerGames Memories of my mom breaking down in tears because she spilled the mac&cheese and didn't know what she would feed us now.
>
> November 17, 2014

> Me in FinAid office, freshman year, crying: "My dad won't help me out with $." FinAid worker: "Then why are you in college?" #MyHungerGames
>
> November 17, 2014

> #MyHungerGames is that I've never felt able to discuss my childhood homelessness with any of my closest friends.
>
> November 17, 2014. (*CBCBooks.org* 2014)

Andrew Slack, the co-founder of *The Harry Potter Alliance*, talks of how the hashtag and the Alliance is a way to articulate the otherwise inarticulate, to bring to attention the problems that have rendered invisible many. "In America, the first rule of classism is don't talk about classism. With #MyHungerGames, we are breaking that rule. Sharing our personal stories around classism is just the beginning" (*CBCBooks.org* 2014). Articulation here is not mere voicing of concerns but also the creation of specific affinityscapes online, providing access to these spaces, helping voices reach across distances and forging connections and community. This community with its connections and networks produces affinity, empathy, and learning.

Alanna Bennett, a popular culture writer on *TheMarySue.com*, writes about how YA dystopian fiction, specifically *The Hunger Games* helps people articulate struggles which are common but not usually advertised or shared,

> American culture carries a taboo around discussing the realities of money, possibly because it's a very slippery slope from there to class. In a country that believes in its own foundational myths about equality, and in the possibility – no, guarantee – of transcending class barriers through hard work and sheer grit, and where a statistically impossible proportion of the population identifies as middle class, we don't like to talk about class as a barrier. And yet.
>
> For many of us, *The Hunger Games* is personal, not only because we love the writing or the heroine, but because we live under Capitol-like policies ourselves.
>
> (Bennett 2014)

It is crucial to notice how this process of articulation stemming from identification with *The Hunger Games* and its characters has sparked off empathy and action towards real-life situations. Expressions of accounts of poverty, homelessness, childhood hunger, worker abuse, and comparisons with despair and horrors of the present from Syria to Gaza to Ferguson, Missouri, help keep the conversation going and youth activism flourishing. Young adults are now more than ever aware of the media they consume. They use this media as a tool for articulating their own needs and desires but are critically and vocally aware of how the culture industry is using this media. The outcry against *The Hunger Games* becoming "an allegory of its own making" and using hashtag rhetoric to underline the gap between the story and its glamorous marketing is an excellent instance of youth restoring culture to politics by rearticulating cultural products like dystopias, dystopian literature, and movies (Keller 2013).

Gayani DeSilva, child and adolescent psychiatrist at St. Joseph Hospital who also works with teens in the prison systems of California and New Mexico, comments that engaging with YA dystopian literature like *The Hunger Games* is related more to affinity and empathy against the violence in the media rather than the violence itself—"The teenage years are a time to question social mores… and develop and commit to their individual set of morals and values…Teens actively look for a better way to do things. Coupled with a broad belief in their invincibility, they truly believe they can change their world" (qtd. in Maloney 2014). The violence in YA dystopian fiction, then, is an articulation against the futurism of the Child, "a reaction against the 'juvenilization' of the young in a culture that still seeks to enclose the young within a restrictive cultural category that offers few ways for them to demonstrate their growing maturity or express their autonomy" (Mintz qtd. in Maloney 2014).

## Conclusion

Participation in affinityscapes open meaning-making and skill-sharing on a communal level which helps not just create this kind of space but also talk about it critically and transform it. In a case study of online affinity spaces, Curwood presents the case of thirteen-year-old Jack who is a fan of *The Hunger Games*, having read the first book when he was ten years of age. Jack became a member of *Mockingjay.net* which housed discussion panels, podcasts and news blogs to discuss *The Hunger Games* and create fan-theories and analyses with other fans while waiting for the second and third books to be released. From June 2010 to January 2011, Jack posted more than 1,800 times on the site, taking part in discussions with like-minded people, talking about not just *The Hunger Games* but also about his own life and opinions on religion, politics, and 9/11. In 2011, Jack joined *Panem October*, an alternate reality game and social network, using social media like Twitter, YouTube, and Facebook, where fans could form teams, scan QR codes and play the interactive game. To help other fans with tutorials for *Panem October* games, Jack created *Panemonium* writing blogs and hosting podcasts. Soon, *Panemonium* became the official support site for *Panem October*. "We can see Jack move from legitimate peripheral participation (Lave and Wenger 1991) to full participation as he acquires the discourses and ways of being in the affinity space"; as he creates character index, learning from another user strategies of specialized discourse like adding quotes to character descriptions and scenes to add to the "credibility of the index" (Curwood 2013, 422). Jack becomes motivated via articulating affinity spaces to be a programmer, tutor, game designer, and website creator. Others become writers, role-players, actors, artists, critics and so on, through creating **paratexts** which are based on the act of articulation, that is, active participatory expression, in online spaces. Articulation as a tool in pedagogy, thus, has immense value as it helps create affinityscapes as "for adolescents who struggle with decoding and encoding, perhaps we need to rethink the relationship between motivation, text selection, and comprehension, and consider the role science fiction novels...can play" (Curwood 2013, 419).

Online affinityscapes work on a contribution economy that depends on articulation, that is, an economy of producing, sharing, and receiving not just information but also knowledge, experiences, skills, and insights, giving rise to a collective intelligence. There is a multilogic rearticulation of the futurism of the Child into a network of futurisms rooted in active analyses of the present, produced and shared by young adults when they turn reading into affinityscaping practices.

## Key Words

**Affinityscape**: An affinityscape is a space which allows for the engagement of liking, empathy, understanding, and care, formed due to and on the basis of shared interests, characteristics, or opinion.

**Paratext**: Text and material about a text is referred to as a paratext. Usually (but not necessarily limited to) provided by authors, editors, printers, and publishers.

**Subculture**: A subculture is a group within a culture which shows characteristics that are at variance to the larger culture to some degree or the other.

**Dystopian**: Of or relating to dystopia, the 'bad place', which is often represented as the opposite of utopia, the 'good place.'

## Critical Thinking Questions

1   What do you think it means to read and interact with young adult dystopian fiction in the current day and age?
2   What are some of the affinityscapes that you believe are cropping up with the advancement and popularization of interactive media?
3   How does cross-platform media rework and localize young adult dystopian fiction?

## Notes

1 See, for example, "Should I Let My Ten-Year-Old Read The Hunger Games?" (*MorningSideCenter.org*), "Should parents let their children feed on 'The Hunger Games'?" (*Today.com*), "Should Children see Hunger Games?" (*PsychologyToday.com*) and "Is Hunger Games Appropriate for Kids?" (*HelpingMomsConnect.com*)
2 For more on queer children and 'lifedeath.' See McGuire's reading of Edelman.

## References

"#MyHungerGames Exposes Realities of Income Inequality By Hacking The Hunger Games Narrative." 2014. *CBCbooks.org*, Nov 25, 2014. www.cbcbooks.org/2014/11/25/myhungergames-exposes-the-realities-of-income-inequality-by-hacking-the-hunger-games-narrative

Bennett, Alanna. 2014 "#MyHungerGames: My Story of Poverty, and Why the Hashtag Is So Important." *TheMarySue.com*, Nov 21. www.themarysue.com/my-hunger-games

Curwood, Jen Scott. 2013. "'The Hunger Games': Literature, Literacy, and Online Affinity Spaces." *Language Arts* 90, no. 6: 417–27.
Doll, Jen. 2012. "'The Hunger Games' Breaks the Potter Book Barrier on Amazon." *TheAtlantic.com*, August 17. www.theatlantic.com/entertainment/archive/2012/08/hunger-games-breaks-potter-book-barrier-amazon/324573
Edelman, Lee. 2004. *No Future: Queer Theory and the Death Drive*. London: Duke University Press.
Fisher, Mark. 2012. "Precarious Dystopias: *The Hunger Games, In Time,* and *Never Let Me Go*." *Film Quarterly* 65, no. 4: 27–33.
Hall, Gina. 2014. "'Hunger Games-Mockingjay Part 1' Set for World Premiere in London." *TheWrap.com*, October 16. www.thewrap.com/hunger-games-mockingjay-part-1-set-for-world-premiere-in-london
Keller, James. 2013. "Meta-Cinema and Meta-Marketing: Gary Ross's "The Hunger Games", an Allegory of Its Own Making." *Studies in Popular Culture* 35, no. 2: 23–42.
Magee, Rachel M., Melinda Sebastian, Alison Novak, Christopher M. Mascaro, Alan Black, and Sean P. Goggins. 2013. "#TwitterPlay: A Case Study of Fan Roleplaying Online." *CSCW 2013 - Proceedings of the 2013 ACM Conference on Computer Supported Cooperative Work Companion*. New York: Association for Computing Machinery.
Maloney, Devon. 2014. "The Violence in *The Hunger Games-Mockingjay* is Actually Good for Teens." *Wired.com*, Nov 25. www.wired.com/2014/11/mockingjay-violence-teens
McGuire, Riley. 2015. "Queer Children, Queer Futures: Navigating 'lifedeath' in *The Hunger Games*." *Mosaic: An Interdisciplinary Critical Journal* 48, no. 2, a special proceedings issue: A MATTER OF LIFEDEATH I: 63–76.
Murphy, Patrick D. 1990. "Reducing the Dystopian Distance: Pseudo-Documentary Framing in Near-Future Fiction." *Science Fiction Studies* 17, no. 1: 25–40.
Mydans, Seth. 2014. "Thai Protesters Are Detained After Using 'Hunger Games' Salute." *The New York Times*, Nov 20. www.nytimes.com/2014/11/21/world/asia/thailand-protesters-hunger-games-salute.html
Tharoor, Ishaan. 2014. "Why are China and Thailand scared of the 'Hunger Games'?" *The Washington Post*, Nov 20. www.washingtonpost.com/news/worldviews/wp/2014/11/20/why-are-china-and-thailand-scared-of-the-hunger-games

# 26 Reboot and Rebirth

Artificial Intelligence and Spiritual Existence in *The Good Place*

*Liz W. Faber*

Computer scientists John McCarthy, Marvin Minsky, Nathaniel Rochester, and Claude Shannon (2006) first defined artificial intelligence (AI) in 1955: "every aspect of learning or any other feature of intelligence can in principle be so precisely described that a machine can be made to simulate it" (12). In other words, AI is human intelligence, programmed into a machine. It is a reflection of humanity. But in order to understand how to create AI, we must first understand our own intelligence. Indeed, the study of AI is also the study of what it means to be human. And even before the term artificial intelligence was coined, science fiction writers have been pondering the nature of humanity through AI characters.

One recent example of science fiction exploring human existence through AI is the NBC sitcom *The Good Place* (2016–2020). The show is both a masterclass in philosophy and a show about human mortality. Set mostly in the afterlife, the series follows four humans—all-around dirtbag Eleanor Shellstrop (Kristen Bell), compulsively indecisive philosophy professor Chidi Anagonye (William Jackson Harper), insecure philanthropist Tahani Al-Jamil (Jameela Jamil), and himbo dancer/criminal/Florida Man Jason Mendoza (Manny Jacinto). Each episode becomes a sort of case study for a school of thought as the humans bond with one another and attempt to improve not only themselves but also all of humanity. The only main characters in the series who are not dead are immortal demon/architect Michael (Ted Danson), and an artificially intelligent being named Janet (D'Arcy Carden). While demons in the afterlife are a staple of Western afterlife imagery, Janet's existence there raises an interesting question about AI: if artificial, sentient beings can live, can they also die? Is Janet alive, in any sense of the word? The closest Janet comes to dying is when she is **rebooted**, or turned off and turned back on again, just like a regular computer. Each time an AI in *The Good Place* is rebooted, they are slightly upgraded. Another AI in the series, Derek Hofstetler—Janet's rebound/boyfriend/son (Jason Mantzoukas) is rebooted so many times that he enters another plane of consciousness. In the philosophical spirit of the series, I will read the AI reboots in *The Good Place* through the lens of Buddhist rebirth, a metaphysical cycle of life and death. After all, we must understand human existence in order to

DOI: 10.4324/9781003310730-30

design AI, and one major part of human existence is spirituality and the drive to understand what happens to us when we die.

## What Does It Mean to Be Alive?

The first question to examine is whether Janet and Derek are alive. The series is somewhat unclear about this. On the one hand, Janet describes herself as an "informational assistant," an "anthropomorphized vessel of knowledge," and repeatedly, "not a girl." Meanwhile, Derek is Janet's creation, a rebound boyfriend after her relationship with Jason in season 2. She literally materializes Derek just like she does any other non-sentient object in the afterlife. But, on the other hand, in the first season episode "The Eternal Shriek," Michael is condemned to "retirement" (i.e., demon death), and the only way to keep him from being hauled away on the train to the bad place is to prevent Janet from calling the train. To do so, Chidi and Eleanor determine that they must go out to the beach on the edge of the neighborhood and activate Janet's "kill switch," a big red button on a pedestal. Janet reveals that, each time her kill switch is pressed, she is rebooted and given an upgrade; in response, Chidi reasons that, through each reboot, "Janet has learned and grown. She's essentially living a life. We can't kill her." This line of thought presupposes that the "kill switch" literally kills Janet. But Eleanor counters by pointing out that everyone in the afterlife is dead anyway, so it doesn't matter. What's important in this exchange is the way life and death are defined. Living leads to dying, and for Janet, dying also leads to developing, learning, and living. Life requires death, and death requires life. To emphasize this point, Chidi accidentally pushes Janet's kill switch, she falls motionless onto the sand, and a giant screen appears in the sky with an image of Janet repeating, "Attention, I have been murdered."

Of course, the words "killed," "murdered," and "dead," don't necessarily mean that Janet is alive. After all, how many of us say things like, "My phone died," to mean its battery has been depleted? Still, in the realm of *The Good Place*, where everyone is simultaneously dead, un-dead, re-dead, or just plain immortal, the concept of "alive" stretches beyond the traditional sense of corporeal—bodily—existence. Janet, as a moving, thinking, and feeling being, is every bit alive as Eleanor, Chidi, Tahani, and Jason—all of whom are mostly dead or un-dead throughout the series. A more interesting question, then, is not whether Janet and Derek are alive, but rather, are they *human*?

## What Does It Mean to Be Human?

The humans in *The Good Place* also experience reboots, just like Janet. While much of the narrative in the first season revolves around the fact that Eleanor and Jason think they've been mistakenly sent to the good place, the season finale reveals to us that they've actually been in the bad place all along, and in season two we learn that Michael is a demon architect who's designed a fake good place neighborhood, complete with demon actors, to torture the four humans for eternity. Michael just reboots the whole neighborhood, wipes the humans' memories, and starts over. Yet, one of the humans—usually Eleanor—always figures out the conceit, leading Michael to reboot the neighborhood once again.

In the essay "Conceptions of the Afterlife: *The Good Place* and Religious Tradition," Michael McGowan (2021) likens the human reboots to Hindu reincarnation or rebirth. Each human has an **atman**, an essence that "transcends corporeal boundaries" (196), sort of like a soul in the Judeo-Christian religious tradition. In the Hindu tradition, the *atman* is reborn again and again until it is "liberated from its corporeal existence" (196). For McGowan, the four humans in *The Good Place* are *atman*, and each time Michael reboots them, they get closer and closer to transcending their corporeal boundaries: "some immaterial essence, a soul, really moves from one iteration of the self to the next" (197). I would add that, by the end of the series, the four humans, along with Michael and Janet, have gone to the actual good place, where they find that everyone has grown bored with eternal happiness. In response, Michael and Janet decide to create a doorway that allows each person to return their essence to the universe. In the series finale, "Whenever You're Ready," Eleanor walks through the door and dissolves into specks of light, suggesting that she has literally transcended her bodily existence and become noncorporeal, light itself.

It's important to note that there is a difference between Hindu and Buddhist conceptions of **rebirth**. While Hindu tradition sees the self as atman, for Buddhists, "there is no atman, no 'self' or 'soul' to be reborn from one body to the next" (McGowan 2021, 196). Instead, there is **anatman**, or no-self. Basically, there is no singular essence; rather, in Buddhist philosophy, humans—like everything else in the universe—are made up of all of our parts, and our parts are constantly in flux. We simultaneously are and are not, "consistently inconsistent" (196). Buddhist monk and scholar Bhikkhu Analayo (2018) explains that this flux is like "a continuously changing process of being conscious.... A staccato-like series of micromoments of being conscious, each of these micromoments passing away immediately on having come into existence" (12). You might think of this as a series of "nows." Now. Now. Now. Now. Each time you just read the word "now," you were a slightly different version of yourself, your body in a slightly different position, your mind connecting words to slightly different meanings. You can't ever go back to the person you were a few seconds ago before you started reading those "nows." You are always conscious in the present, in *this* now.

We can liken the difference between atman and anatman to digital files. Think about the last time you wrote an essay for class. You probably used MS Word, Pages, or maybe Google Docs. The file itself is like atman: you can download it, upload it, attach it to an email, put it on a flash drive and hand that to your roommate. But no matter where the file is, it is still your file. That is like the *atman,* moving from body to body but staying the same. On the other hand, the *anatman* is like the essay as you write it. Every time you hit save, your essay is a little different. Maybe there are new words, or you remembered to double-space, or you added citations. But it is always an essay in progress, always a collection of words and fonts and digital data. That is like the *anatman:* you are always like an essay in the process of being written, you are always a person in this exact moment, made up of all your parts.

In rebirth, then, a person's consciousness moves from one corporeal form into the next, with continuity, but no memory of it (Analayo 2018, 14). For Buddhists, knowledge of one's self across lifetimes is possible through meditation and mindfulness (19), rather than a continuous soul that moves from body to body. With these definitions of rebirth in mind, if the four humans in *The Good Place* may be seen as experiencing Hindu rebirth, I argue that Janet and Derek are experiencing Buddhist rebirth. When Janet is rebooted, her consciousness continues from micromoment to micromoment. The difference between Hindu and Buddhist rebirth is most clearly demonstrated in the third season episode "Janet(s)," in which Janet takes all the humans and Michael into her void. They all look exactly like her, so she has to dress them in different outfits to differentiate. Here, the humans' souls, or *atman,* can transfer from one body to another, while Janet's consciousness remains consistently inconsistent, meaning she can be anywhere and everywhere at any moment, with or without her body.

However, Janet returns to her original **tabula rasa** state. In Latin, tabula rasa means literally a clean slate, and some philosophers use this concept to describe a time in a person's life (usually birth through infancy) when they have no knowledge of themselves or the world around them. For Janet, reboot renders her in this infantile state, with no memory or idea of what is going on around her. After her first reboot in "The Eternal Shriek," the humans hold a funeral for her, where, like a new iPhone, she pops up out of her casket to say, "Hello, Architect, please enter your 4 digit pin." From here, she's like a child learning how language works. In one scene, Chidi calls on Janet to recite the English alphabet, and all she can say is, "A, B, Janet." Chidi, horrified at having murdered Janet, tells Eleanor that Janet "literally knew everything in the universe, and now she's a baby." Through several subsequent scenes, Michael asks for Eleanor's file, and Janet hands him a cactus, until his entire office is covered in cacti. Although these mistakes are played comically, they represent an important part of Buddhist rebirth: the loss and rediscovery of continuity of self. Only through learning—itself positioned as a kind of meditative practice in the series—can Janet recapture her continuity of self and grow past her previous iterations.

Janet's subsequent iterations are increasingly complex. Shortly after her first reboot, she falls in love with and marries Jason. In season 1 episode 11, "What's My Motivation," she tells Michael, "Each time I am updated, I accrue new knowledge and abilities.... I seem to have gained a new understanding of love." Michael, however, sees love as a glitch and decides to reboot her again to get rid of it. But even a reboot, followed by 800 more reboots, does not free Janet of her newfound feelings. By this point, Jason and Tahani have begun a relationship, which deeply hurts Janet. Yet, she does not seem to remember that she loves Jason each time. In fact, she agrees to be a relationship counselor for Jason and Tahani, after which she begins to glitch. First, her thumb inflates and flies off, then the entire neighborhood disappears and reappears, and finally she vomits pennies all over Michael's office. As it turns out, each time she glitched, she said something affirming about Tahani and Jason's relationship. She is programmed not to lie, but she has to lie about her feelings in order to appear to approve of Tahani and Jason's relationship. Despite the fact that she has no memory of having been married to Jason, her love for him continues from iteration to iteration. In other words, her emotional self, the feelings that she experiences from moment to moment, are the consciousness that she continuously rediscovers through each rebirth. And as with Buddhist rebirth, only through meditation is she able to access her previous experiences.

At this point, Janet begs Michael to kill her by turning her into a marble, a form of final death for Janets in *The Good Place*. But, having grown fond of their friendship, he refuses. Eleanor, however, suggests that Janet needs to find a way to get over Jason. In response, Janet creates Derek, a rebound boyfriend who lives in her "void," has a windchime for a penis, and is barely intelligible. When he first meets Eleanor and Chidi, for example, Derek says, "Goodbob, I hope we same place again, very now." Janet quickly responds, "His brain is wrong." Eventually, Janet breaks up with Derek, and a few episodes later confesses her love to Jason. Jason responds, "I think I love you too, girl." Janet quickly says, "I'm not a girl. I'm also not just a Janet anymore. I don't know what I am!" Here, Janet is once again developing and growing, and in a sense becoming even more human than ever.

The ultimate goal of rebirth for Buddhists is enlightenment: "[T]hey are nonreturners in the sense that they are beyond returning to be born in the material realm, and will take birth only in heavenly realms" (Analayo 2018, 21). Although neither Janet nor Derek returns to the universe, as the humans do by walking through the door in the good place, they both achieve a sense of enlightenment that moves them beyond their corporeal forms. In the final episode, Derek has been rebooted more than 151 million times and is now a floating head on another plane of existence. As he explains: "Derek is now both a singular point in space, and yet Derek also contains space itself. The nexus of Derek is without dimension. The moment of Derek's creation and the eventual heat death of the universe are not inexorably the same." Here, Derek is not only *not* a corporeal form in the space of the afterlife, but he has become "space itself." He is both everywhere and nowhere.

Janet, on the other hand, goes to the good place with Michael and the humans. In the last episode, Chidi tells Eleanor about the Buddhist perspective on death, in which a wave rises up and then returns to the ocean. And for the humans, that's the goal—to return their essence to the universe. It requires reboots and reboots and constantly trying to improve themselves to get there, but they make it. For Janet, though, rebooting and rebooting makes her more human, more flawed, but also more caring and capable of love. When she says goodbye to Jason before he walks through the final door, she tells him that she can experience all moments simultaneously, and so their past and present are always with her. In this sense, she has achieved her ultimate Buddhist awakening: an emotional one in which she is perpetually in the moment, both there and not there.

## Conclusion

And so, the real story of *The Good Place* is a hopeful one: the essence of humanity is goodness, and we're all capable of getting there if we help each other to face our innermost insecurities and fears to eventually become the best versions of ourselves. And this holds true for artificial life as well. Derek's best version is existence itself, while Janet's is a human (though still not a girl). And that's really what the quest for AI is supposed to be about: we can create AI when we understand human intelligence, and questions about artificial life will ultimately lead us to questions about artificial death. But maybe, as *The Good Place* teaches us, death isn't the point—the journey to your best self is. The drive to create AI has always simultaneously been the drive to understand the essence of humanity. What makes us, us? And this is the exact same drive that leads us to question our existence, to wonder about the afterlife, to ponder life and death.

## Key Words

**Anatman**: In Buddhist belief, the anatman is the "no-self," or the lack of individual permanence.
**Atman**: In Hindu belief, the atman is the essence of a person's consciousness, which passes from body to body through reincarnation.
**Rebirth**: In Hindu and Buddhist belief, a cycle of birth, life, death that continues on until a person's core essence is able to be freed from bodily existence.
**Reboot**: To reboot is to turn a computer off and back on again, e.g. restarting.

**Tabula Rasa**: Tabula rasa also known as a "clean slate," meaning the state of having no prior memory or knowledge.

## Critical Thinking Questions

1. What other examples of fictional artificial intelligence can you think of from movies, TV shows, and books? How does the representation of Janet and Derek in *The Good Place* compare to other fictional artificial intelligence?
2. If scientists had the ability to create an artificially intelligent being that could die, would it be ethical to do so? Why or why not?
3. What happens to our digital self after we die?

## References

Analayo, Bhikkhu. 2018. *Rebirth in Early Buddhism & Current Research*. Sommerville, MA: Wisdom Publications.

McCarthy, John, Marvin L. Minsky, Nathaniel Rochester, and Claude E. Shannon. 2006. "A Proposal for the Dartmouth Summer Research Project on Artificial Intelligence: August 31, 1955." *AI Magazine* 27, no. 4: 12–4.

McGowan, Michael. 2021. "Conceptions of the Afterlife: *The Good Place* and Religious Tradition." In *The Good Place and Philosophy*, edited by Kimberly S. Engels, 191–201. Hoboken, NJ: Wiley & Sons, 2021.

# Index

.mp3 231, 232, 237

2SLGBTQIA+ 8, 184–5, 188, 189, 202, 205, 206, 242, 246

affinityscapes 250–4
affordances 10, 11, 42, 43–5, 97–8, 99, 101, 102, 103, 124, 139–41, 142, 144–5, 149, 211, 212, 218, 228
Amazon Prime 12, 196
ambient rhetoric 136, 142
analogue (media) 201, 203, 204, 205, 206, 208, 211, 213, 219
anatman 258, 259, 261
anti-Government Discourse 57, 64, 65
Apple 12, 92, 196, 231, 233–4, 236, 237
apps 9, 10, 28, 89, 136, 139, 140, 142, 201, 206, 214, 221, 223, 224, 226, 228, 231; dating 21–7, 28, 118; games 82, 108–10, 114, 115; social media 31, 201
assemblage 2, 69–76, 156
atman 258–9, 261
AR *see* augmented reality
augmented reality 107, 110, 114, 152, 153–4, 156, 158, 159, 176, 201, 205, 206, 208, 250
avatar 7, 9, 11, 14, 38, 41, 44, 89, 91–2, 93, 130, 144–5, 147, 148, 149, 150, 152, 153, 154–6, 171–2

BIPOC 8, 155
BLM *see* Black Lives Matter
Black Lives Matter 49–50, 51

CTF *see* Capture the Flag
Capture the Flag 161–7, 168
cinemacast *see* livecast
circulation 124, 140, 163, 167, 183, 194, 201–2, 204–8, 209, 214, 218, 224
clicktivism 10, 48–54
cognitive dissonance theory 51, 54

communication 2, 12, 14, 15, 27, 31, 32, 35, 39, 40–1, 42, 43, 45, 46, 53, 58, 72, 89, 94, 98, 100, 118, 140, 149, 155, 157, 170, 213, 215, 217, 225
compilation scores in film 119, 124
conspiracy movements and theories 57–65, 66
COVID-19 pandemic 1, 21, 29–35, 48, 51, 57, 63, 66, 107–8, 111, 114, 137, 153, 195–7, 201, 206–7
Crenshaw, Kimberlé 6, 114, 138
critical digital pedagogy 21–2, 26, 27
cultural intermediaries 221, 224, 225, 228
culture 2, 4, 6–7, 8, 13, 14, 82, 83, 91, 97, 99, 101–2, 119, 155, 163, 166, 183, 186, 212, 213, 215, 216, 218, 221, 222, 223, 226, 228, 241, 252, 253, 254; algorithmic 181, 183, 184, 187, 188; digital 3, 7, 8, 10, 13, 48, 71, 76, 93, 124, 201; hacker 162–3; Indigenous 81, 82–3, 86, 87; popular 99, 101, 171, 183, 191, 212, 213–4, 215, 226, 252; subculture 250, 254

deadname 241, 243, 244
dehumanization 21, 26, 27
digital 1–8, 10–3, 14, 15; activism 50–1, 54; age 69, 76; body 91, 93, 95, 96; bundle 83, 85, 86, 87; community 8, 97, 124; culture 1, 3, 7–8, 10, 13, 71, 76, 93, 124; ethnography 71–2, 76; identity 21–3, 27, 28; literacy 71, 140, 142; media 2, 7, 12, 15, 79, 97, 101–2, 118–9, 123, 154, 195; music 231, 233, 236–7; pedagogy (*see* critical digital pedagogy); piracy 232–4, 237; redlining 107, 111, 114, 115; security 71; spaces 11, 26, 27, 28, 48, 76, 98, 118, 119, 218; technology 76, 111, 114, 136, 190, 201, 207, 231, 232; underground

264  *Index*

163; violence 70–6, 77; world 50–1, 139–40
Disney+ 196
D&D *see* Dungeons and Dragons
Dungeons & Dragons 97–102
dynamic audio 174, 175
dystopian 155, 248–9, 250, 252, 254

Efficacy-Entertainment Continuum 192, 198
embodiment 92–3, 95, 127, 249
ephemeral 192–8, 227
ethnography 69, 145; digital 71–2, 76
extradiegetic music and sound 169, 170–1, 175

Facebook 9, 21, 24, 38–45, 46, 50, 53, 58, 59, 62, 63, 80, 121, 153–4, 156–7, 165, 253
far-right populism 57, 61, 64, 66
feminism 10, 71, 74, 100
feminist activism 69, 71, 73, 76, 77

game 1, 7, 8, 9–11, 14, 25, 43, 63, 82, 92, 97, 99–101, 107–11, 113, 114, 127–33, 134, 137–42, 144–8, 150, 154, 161–3, 166, 167, 169–75, 225, 249–52; theory 225; videogame 3, 10–11, 15, 38, 82, 117, 126–30, 133, 134, 137–8, 144, 147–9, 153, 163, 166, 171, 175, 176
game sound 169–70, 173, 174–5
gender 4–5, 6, 14, 15, 100, 114, 130, 133, 147, 155, 156, 184, 186, 188, 218, 223, 240–5; cisgender 5, 99, 128, 188, 243; transgender 4, 5, 240–5, 246; violence 70, 72, 73, 76
ghost: ceasing to communicate 24, 27; in video games 3, 172–3
Goffman, Erving 6, 39, 49, 51
Google 33, 234, 237, 243, 259
guild 145–6, 149, 150

hacker 161–7, 168, 232
hacktivism 49, 72
heteronormative 127, 128, 133, 182, 186, 188
hyperpersonal communication 41, 46
hyper-public 23, 26, 27

impression management 6, 48–9, 51–3, 54
independent media arts 201–7, 208, 209
Instagram 9, 13, 21, 24, 30, 35, 58, 118–21, 123, 212–3, 214, 215–7, 223, 228

institutional violence 69, 77
intersectionality 6, 14, 107, 114, 115, 138
intimate publics 9, 97–102, 103

laborious play 161–2, 167
liminal 3, 14
livecast 191, 198
livestream 12, 100, 197, 201, 206–7, 208
ludic self 225, 228

mass media 12–3, 14, 205; traditional 12, 13, 15
massively multiplayer online role playing game 144–5, 147, 149, 150, 167
media logic 46, 58; social 42–3, 45, 46
memetic 223, 227, 228–9
mental health 29–35, 36, 84, 244
meta 171; Meta (company) 152, 153–4, 156–7, 212
metaverse 152–8, 159
microcelebrity 57–61, 62, 64–5, 66, 215
modding 144, 147–9, 150; modder stance 148, 150
montage 23, 26, 27, 28, 120
moral balancing 48, 51, 54
Microsoft 89, 152, 196
multimodal 129; multimodality 134
Musicking 117, 124, 196
MMORPG *see* massively multiplayer online role playing game

Netflix 12, 13, 120, 141, 181–4, 186–7, 189
networks 9, 11, 41, 42–3, 69, 74, 76, 98, 117, 120, 157, 181, 184, 201–5, 218, 232, 237, 252, 254; computer 2, 14, 162, 218, 233; exchange 201–4, 207, 208; social 15, 38–9, 42–3, 58, 69, 70, 73, 75, 77, 98, 100, 103, 163, 216, 217, 221, 223, 237, 253
new media 12, 14, 97, 101, 102, 155, 182, 205, 212
Norman, Don 98, 139, 149

on-demand 12, 191, 196, 201, 206–7, 208
online 1, 3–5, 6–10, 11, 13, 21, 22–5, 27, 28, 29, 33, 41, 43, 45, 49–54, 57–8, 62, 66, 71–2, 74, 76, 80, 83–4, 86, 87, 89–95, 96, 97–8, 102, 103, 118, 123, 131–2, 142, 144–5, 154, 163, 165, 183, 185, 187, 189, 195–6, 198–9, 201–2, 205–8, 209, 212–16, 231, 237, 241–3, 250–2; activism

Index   265

48–50, 52–3, 54; body 89, 92, 95; community 8, 9; identity 7–8, 28, 45, 46, 48, 51, 89–90, 126, 144; games 10, 146–7, 167; presentation 206–7, 208; representation 4, 38; spaces 4, 9, 11, 91, 97–8, 103, 196, 198, 207, 218, 253; streaming 10, 183, 187, 195; teaching and learning 1, 29, 31, 35, 85, 89

P2P *see* peer-to-peer
paratext 130, 134, 253, 254; paratextual 212
passing 241, 242, 245
peer-to-peer 196, 201; file sharing 237
platformization 211, 213–4, 218, 219, 228
play 1, 7, 9–11, 14, 15, 82, 98–9, 107–14, 117, 130–1, 133, 136–42, 144–9, 161–7, 169–73, 193, 196, 222, 225, 253; community 142; critical 44, 146–8, 149; gameplay 99, 100, 109–11, 113, 130–1, 144, 147, 148, 150, 171–5; laborious 161–7; player 9, 11, 97, 99–100, 102, 107–14, 115, 128–32, 139–42, 144–9, 150, 161–7, 169, 171–5, 176, 191, 233, 253
produsers 41, 46
prosumers 41, 46
public space 23, 58, 72–4, 98, 108, 110, 114

QAnon 58, 60–1, 65
queer 21, 93, 98, 100, 103, 155, 181–7, 188, 206, 249; queerness 13, 100, 181, 183–7, 249

race 4, 5–6, 14, 15, 110, 111, 114, 147, 155, 218, 244
racialization 6, 228, 229
rebirth 256, 258–60, 261
reboot 256–61
record companies 232, 234–6, 237
relationality 79–83, 85–6, 102; unconscious 87

security vulnerability 163, 165–6, 167–8
self-branding 211, 215, 218
semiotic 40, 129, 130, 133, 134
slacktivism 49–51, 53, 54
social loafing 50, 53, 54
social media 1, 9, 12, 14, 15, 21, 28, 29–30, 35, 41–5, 46, 48–50, 52, 54, 58, 61, 72, 79, 89, 98, 117, 119–21, 123, 124, 153–5, 158, 201, 204, 208, 211–8, 219, 221, 224–6, 229, 250, 253
Spotify 12, 124, 169, 224, 228, 231, 234–7
storysharing 83, 86
streaming 10, 12–3, 15, 123, 181, 189, 191, 193, 195–6, 199, 224, 234, 236, 237; livestreaming 12, 99, 193, 202; media 12; music 124, 214, 232, 234–6, 237, 238; platforms and services 9, 13, 181–2, 184, 186–7, 195, 196, 223, 235
stress 31, 34, 35, 64, 75, 84, 251; stressors 29, 32, 33
soundscape 118, 169, 171–4, 175, 176
subculture *see* culture

tabula rasa 259, 262
technological determinism 98, 102, 103
technology 1–3, 7, 10, 12–3, 14, 15, 21, 23, 26–7, 28, 33, 42, 45, 46, 50, 71, 73, 80–3, 86, 89, 93, 97, 103, 124, 138–9, 141, 142, 145, 153, 158, 159, 163–6, 167, 183, 190, 193, 204, 208, 211, 215, 224, 231, 233–4, 237
therapy 10, 32–4, 35, 154; therapist 25, 32
TikTok 9, 24, 29–35, 118–21, 123, 124, 221–8, 229
transnormativity 240, 245
Turkle, Sherry 21, 23, 25, 162
TVIII 182, 186, 188
Twitch 9, 11, 97, 99
Twitter 9, 11, 13, 24, 98, 103, 108, 111, 212, 222, 250, 251, 253

unconscious bias 110, 111, 114
universal design 107, 109–10, 115

videogame *see* game
virtual 1, 3–4, 7–9, 10, 11, 13, 15, 39, 83, 85–6, 90–3, 95, 137, 152, 155–6, 158, 169, 175, 215, 218; community 8–9; identity 3, 7–8, 13, 39, 153–4; reality (VR) 3, 63, 92, 153, 156, 158, 159, 201, 205, 208, 250; world 85–6, 92, 176
virtue signalling 49, 51, 52, 54
vulnerability *see* security vulnerability

YouTube 3, 9, 11, 12, 43, 59, 97, 195, 204, 223, 228, 253

Zoom 1, 33, 84–5, 89–91, 95, 137–41, 142, 196–7

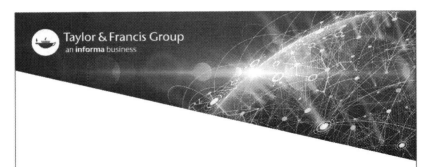

Printed in the United States
by Baker & Taylor Publisher Services